MCSE ◄ Ex 70-

Microsoft® Windows® XP Professional

Readiness Review

Kurt Dillard and
Anthony Northrup

PUBLISHED BY
Microsoft Press
A Division of Microsoft Corporation
One Microsoft Way
Redmond, Washington 98052-6399

Library of Congress Cataloging-in-Publication Data
Dillard, Kurt, 1964-
    MCSE Microsoft Windows XP Professional Readiness Review: exam 70-270 / Kurt
    Dillard, Anthony Northrup.
        p. cm.
    Includes index.
    ISBN 0-7356-1460-1
    1. Electronic data processing personnel--Certification. 2. Microsoft Windows XP. 3.
Operating systems (Computers). I. Northrup, Anthony. II. Title.

    QA76.3 .D545 2001
    005.4'4769--dc21   2001044746

Printed and bound in the United States of America.

1 2 3 4 5 6 7 8 9   QWE   6 5 4 3 2

Distributed in Canada by Penguin Books Canada Limited.

A CIP catalogue record for this book is available from the British Library.

Microsoft Press books are available through booksellers and distributors worldwide. For further information about international editions, contact your local Microsoft Corporation office or contact Microsoft Press International directly at fax (425) 936-7329. Visit our Web site at www.microsoft.com/mspress. Send comments to *mspinput@microsoft.com*.

Microsoft Press
Acquisitions Editor: Thomas Pohlmann
Project Editor: Kurt Stephan

nSight, Inc.
Project Manager: Lisa A. Wehrle
Technical Editor: Piotr Prussak
Manuscript Editor: Bernadette Murphy Bentley
Desktop Publisher: Donald Cowan
Indexer: Jack Lewis

Body Part No. X08-24429

Contents

Objective Domain 3: Implementing, Managing, Monitoring, and Troubleshooting Hardware Devices and Drivers 83

Objective Domain 4: Monitoring and Optimizing System Performance and Reliability 129

Objective Domain 7: Configuring, Managing, and Troubleshooting Security 233

Welcome to Installing, Configuring, and Administering Microsoft Windows XP Professional

Welcome to *MCSE Readiness Review—Exam 70-270: Installing, Configuring, and Administering Microsoft Windows XP Professional*. The Readiness Review series gives you a focused, timesaving way to identify the information you need to know to pass the Microsoft Certified Professional (MCP) exams. The series combines a realistic electronic assessment with a review book to help you become familiar with the types of questions that you will encounter on the MCP exam. By reviewing the objectives and sample questions, you can focus on the specific skills you need to improve before taking the exam.

This book helps you evaluate your readiness for the MCP Exam 70-270: Installing, Configuring, and Administering Microsoft Windows XP Professional. When you pass this exam, you earn core credit toward Microsoft Certified Systems Engineer (MCSE) certification. In addition, when you pass this exam you achieve Microsoft Certified Professional status.

Note You can find a complete list of MCP exams and their related Objectives on the Microsoft Certified Professional Web site at *http://www.microsoft.com/mcp*.

The Readiness Review series lets you identify any areas in which you might need additional training. To help you get the training you need to successfully pass the certification exams, Microsoft Press publishes a complete line of self-paced training kits and other study materials. For comprehensive information about the topics covered in the Installing, Configuring, and Administering Microsoft Windows XP Professional exam, see the corresponding MCSE training kit—*Microsoft Windows XP Professional*.

Before You Begin

This MCSE Readiness Review consists of two main parts: the Readiness Review electronic assessment program on the accompanying compact disc, and this Readiness Review book.

The Readiness Review Components

The electronic assessment is a practice certification test that helps you evaluate your skills. It provides instant scoring feedback, so you can determine areas in which additional study might be helpful before you take the certification exam. Although your score on the electronic assessment does not necessarily indicate what your score will be on the certification exam, it does give you the opportunity to answer questions that are similar to those on the actual certification exam.

The Readiness Review book is organized by the exam's objectives. Each chapter of the book pertains to one of the seven primary groups of objectives on the actual exam, called the *Objective Domains*. Each Objective Domain lists the tested skills you need to master to adequately answer the exam questions. Because the certification exams focus on real-world skills, the Tested Skills and Suggested Practices lists provide practices that emphasize the practical application of the exam objectives. Each Objective Domain also provides suggestions for further reading or additional resources to help you understand the objectives and increase your ability to perform the task or skills specified by the objectives.

Within each Objective Domain, you find the related objectives that are covered on the exam. Each objective provides you with the following:

- **Key terms** you must know to understand the objective. Knowing these terms can help you answer the objective's questions correctly.

- Several sample exam questions with the correct answers. The answers are accompanied by explanations of each correct and incorrect answer. (These questions match the questions on the electronic assessment.)

You use the electronic assessment to determine the exam objectives you need to study, and then use the Readiness Review book to learn more about those particular objectives and discover additional study materials to supplement your knowledge. You can also use the Readiness Review book to research the answers to specific sample test questions. Keep in mind that to pass the exam, you must understand not only the answer to the question, but also the concepts on which the correct answer is based.

MCP Exam Prerequisites

No exams or classes are required before you take the Installing, Configuring, and Administering Microsoft Windows XP Professional exam. However, in addition to the skills tested by the exam, you must have a working knowledge of the operation and support of hardware and software on Windows XP Professional computers. This knowledge must include:

- Installing and configuring Windows XP Professional

- Implementing resources such as local and shared files, folders, and printers

- Implementing, managing, and troubleshooting hardware devices and drivers

- Monitoring and optimizing system performance and reliability

- Configuring and troubleshooting the desktop environment

- Implementing, managing, and troubleshooting network protocols and services

- Configuring, managing, and troubleshooting security

Note After you have used the Readiness Review and determined that you are ready for the exam, use the Get MCP Information link provided in the home page of the electronic assessment tool for information about scheduling for the exam. You can schedule exams up to six weeks in advance, or as late as one working day before the exam date.

Know the Products

The Microsoft certification program relies on exams that measure your ability to perform a specific job function or set of tasks. Microsoft develops the exams by analyzing the tasks performed by people who are currently working in the field. Therefore, the specific knowledge, skills, and abilities relating to the job are reflected in the certification exam.

Because the certification exams are based on real-world tasks, you need to gain hands-on experience with the applicable technology to master the exam. In a sense, you might consider hands-on experience in an organizational environment to be a prerequisite for passing an MCP exam. Many of the questions relate directly to Microsoft products or technology, so use opportunities at your organization or home to practice using the relevant tools.

Using the MCSE Readiness Review

Although you can use the Readiness Review in a number of ways, you might start your studies by taking the electronic assessment as a pretest. After completing the exam, review your results for each Objective Domain and focus your studies first on the Objective Domains for which you received the lowest scores. The electronic assessment allows you to print your results, and a printed report of how you fared can be useful when reviewing the exam material in this book.

After you take the Readiness Review electronic assessment, use the Readiness Review book to learn more about the Objective Domains you find difficult and to find listings of appropriate study materials that might supplement your knowledge. By reviewing why the answers are correct or incorrect, you can determine whether you need to study the objective topics more.

You can also use the Readiness Review book to focus on the exact objectives that you need to master. Each objective in the book contains several questions that help you determine whether you understand the information related to that particular skill. The book is also designed for you to answer each question before turning the page to review the correct answer.

The best method to prepare for the MCP exam is to use the Readiness Review book in conjunction with the electronic assessment and other study material. Thoroughly studying and practicing the material combined with substantial real-world experience can help you fully prepare for the MCP exam.

Understanding the Readiness Review Conventions

Before you start using the Readiness Review, it is important you understand the terms and conventions used in the electronic assessment and book.

Question Numbering System

The Readiness Review electronic assessment and book contain reference numbers for each question. Understanding the numbering format will help you use the Readiness Review more effectively. When Microsoft creates the exams, the questions are grouped by job skills called *objectives*. These objectives are then organized by sections known as *Objective Domains*. Each question can be identified by the Objective Domain and the objective it covers. The question numbers follow this format:

Test Number.Objective Domain.Objective.Question Number

For example, question number 70-270.02.01.003 means this is question three (003) for the first objective (01) in the second Objective Domain (02) of the Installing, Configuring, and Administering Microsoft Windows XP Professional exam (70-270). Refer to the "Exam Objectives Summary" section later in this introduction to locate the numbers associated with particular objectives. Each question is numbered based on its presentation in the printed book. You can use this numbering system to reference questions on the electronic assessment or in the Readiness Review book. Even though the questions in the book are organized by objective, questions in the electronic assessment and actual certification exam are presented in random order.

Notational Conventions

- Characters or commands that you type appear in **bold lowercase** type.

- Variable information and URLs are *italicized*. *Italic* is also used for book titles.

- Acronyms, filenames, and utilities appear in FULL CAPITALS.

Notes

Notes appear throughout the book.

- Notes marked *Caution* contain information you will want to know before continuing with the book's material.

- Notes marked *Note* contain supplemental information.

- Notes marked *Tip* contain helpful process hints.

Using the Readiness Review Electronic Assessment

The Readiness Review electronic assessment simulates the actual MCP exam. Each iteration of the electronic assessment consists of 50 questions covering all the objectives for the Installing, Configuring, and Administering Microsoft Windows XP Professional exam. (MCP certification exams consist of approximately 50 questions.) Just like a real certification exam, you see questions from the objectives in random order during the practice test. Similar to the certification exam, the electronic assessment allows you to mark questions and review them after you finish the test.

To increase its value as a study aid, you can take the electronic assessment multiple times. Each time you are presented with a different set of questions in a revised order; however, some questions might be repeated.

If you have used one of the certification exam preparation tests available from Microsoft, the Readiness Review electronic assessment will look familiar. The difference is that this electronic assessment gives you the opportunity to learn as you take the exam.

Installing and Running the Electronic Assessment Software

Before you begin using the electronic assessment, you need to install the software. You need a computer with the following minimum configuration:

- Multimedia PC with a 75 MHz Pentium or higher processor

- 16 MB RAM for Windows 95 or Windows 98, or

- 32 MB RAM for Windows NT or Windows Me, or

- 64 MB RAM for Windows 2000 or Windows XP

- Internet Explorer 5.01 or later

- 17 MB of available hard disk space

- A double-speed CD-ROM drive or better

- Super VGA display with at least 256 colors

▶ **To install the electronic assessment**

1. Insert the Readiness Review companion CD-ROM into your CD-ROM drive.

   A starting menu displays automatically, with links to the resources included on the CD-ROM.

2. Click Install Readiness Review.

   A dialog box appears, indicating that you will install the MCSE Readiness Review to your computer.

3. Click Next.

   The License Agreement dialog box appears.

4. To continue with the installation of the electronic assessment engine, you must accept the License Agreement by clicking Yes.

5. The Choose Destination Location dialog box appears showing a default installation directory. Either accept the default or change the installation directory if needed. Click Next to copy the files to your hard disk.

6. A Question dialog box appears asking whether you want Setup to create a desktop shortcut for this program. If you click Yes, an icon is placed on your desktop.

7. The Setup Complete dialog box appears. Select whether you want to view the README.TXT file after closing the Setup program, and then click Finish.

The electronic assessment software is completely installed. If you chose to view the README.TXT file, it launches in a new window. For optimal viewing, enable word wrap.

▶ **To start the electronic assessment**

1. From the Start menu, point to Programs, point to MCSE Readiness Review, and then click MCSE RR Exam 70-270.

   The electronic assessment program starts.

2. Click Start Test.

   Information about the electronic assessment program appears.

3. Click OK.

Taking the Electronic Assessment

The Readiness Review electronic assessment consists of 50 multiple-choice questions, and as in the certification exam, you can skip questions or mark them for later review. Each exam question contains a question number that you can use to refer back to the Readiness Review book.

Before you end the electronic assessment, make sure to answer all the questions. When the exam is graded, unanswered questions are counted as incorrect and lower your score. Similarly, on the actual certification exam complete all questions or they are counted as incorrect. No trick questions appear on the exam. The correct answer is always among the list of choices. Some questions might have more than one correct answer, and this will be indicated in the question. A good strategy is to eliminate the most obvious incorrect answers first to make it easier for you to select the correct answer.

You have 75 minutes to complete the electronic assessment. During the exam you see a timer indicating the amount of time you have remaining. This will help you gauge the amount of time you should use to answer each question and to complete the exam. The amount of time you are given on the actual certification exam varies with each exam. Generally, certification exams take approximately 100 minutes to complete.

Ending and Grading the Electronic Assessment

When you click the Score Test button, you have the opportunity to review the questions you marked or left incomplete. (This format is not similar to the one used on the actual certification exam, in which you can verify whether you are satisfied with your answers and then click the Grade Test button.) The electronic assessment is graded when you click the Score Test button, and the software presents your section scores and your total score.

Note You can always end a test without grading your electronic assessment by clicking the Home button.

After your electronic assessment is graded, you can view the correct and incorrect answers by clicking the Review Questions button.

Interpreting the Electronic Assessment Results

The Score screen shows you the number of questions in each Objective Domain section, the number of questions you answered correctly, and a percentage grade for each section. You can use the Score screen to determine where to spend additional time studying. On the actual certification exam, the number of questions and passing score depend on the exam you are taking. The electronic assessment records your score each time you grade an exam so you can track your progress over time.

▶ **To view your progress and exam records**

1. From the electronic assessment Main menu, click View History. Each test attempt score appears.

2. Click a test attempt date/time to view your score for each Objective Domain.

    Review these scores to determine which Objective Domains you must study further. You can also use the scores to determine your progress.

Using the Readiness Review Book

You can use the Readiness Review book as a supplement to the Readiness Review electronic assessment, or as a stand-alone study aid. If you decide to use the book as a stand-alone study aid, review the Contents or the list of objectives to find topics of interest or an appropriate starting point for you. To get the greatest benefit from the book, use the electronic assessment as a pretest to determine the Objective Domains for which you must spend the most study time. Or, if you want to research specific questions while taking the electronic assessment, you can use the question number on the question screen to reference the question number in the Readiness Review book.

One way to determine areas in which additional study might be helpful is to carefully review your individual section scores from the electronic assessment and note objective areas where your score can be improved. The section scores correlate to the Objective Domains listed in the Readiness Review book.

Reviewing the Objectives

Each Objective Domain in the book contains an introduction and a list of practice skills. Each list of practice skills describes suggested tasks you can perform to help you understand the objectives. Some of the tasks suggest reading additional material, while others are hands-on practices with software or hardware. You must pay particular attention to the hands-on practices, because the certification exam reflects real-world knowledge you can gain only by working with the software or technology. Increasing your real-world experience with the relevant products and technologies will improve your performance on the exam.

After you choose the objectives you want to study, turn to the Contents to locate the objectives in the Readiness Review book. You can study each objective separately, but you might need to understand the concepts explained in other objectives.

Make sure you understand the key terms for each objective—you need a thorough understanding of these terms to answer the objective's questions correctly. Key term definitions are in the Glossary of this book.

Reviewing the Questions

Each objective includes questions followed by the possible answers. After you review the question and select a probable answer, turn to the Answer section to determine whether you answered the question correctly. (For information about the question numbering format, see "Question Numbering System," earlier in this introduction.)

The Readiness Review briefly discusses each possible answer and explains why each answer is correct or incorrect. After reviewing each explanation, if you feel you need more information about a topic, question, or answer, refer to the Further Readings section for that domain for more information.

The answers to the questions in the Readiness Review are based on current industry specifications and standards. However, the information provided by the answers is subject to change as technology improves and changes.

Exam Objectives Summary

The Installing, Configuring, and Administering Microsoft Windows XP Professional certification (70-270) exam measures your ability to implement, administer, and troubleshoot Windows XP Professional. Before taking the exam, you must be proficient with the job skills presented in the following sections. The sections provide the exam objectives and the corresponding objective numbers (which you can use to reference the questions in the Readiness Review electronic assessment and book) grouped by Objective Domains.

Objective Domain 1: Installing Windows XP Professional

The objectives in Objective Domain 1 are as follows:

- Objective 1.1 (70-270.01.01)—Perform an attended installation of Windows XP Professional.

- Objective 1.2 (70-270.01.02)—Perform an unattended installation of Windows XP Professional.

- Objective 1.3 (70-270.01.03)—Upgrade from a previous version of Windows to Windows XP Professional.

- Objective 1.4 (70-270.01.04)—Perform post-installation updates and product activation.

- Objective 1.5 (70-270.01.05)—Troubleshoot failed installations.

Objective Domain 2: Implementing and Conducting Administration of Resources

The objectives in Objective Domain 2 are as follows:

- Objective 2.1 (70-270.02.01)—Monitor, manage, and troubleshoot access to files and folders.

- Objective 2.2 (70-270.02.02)—Manage and troubleshoot access to shared folders.

- Objective 2.3 (70-270.02.03)—Connect to local and network print devices.

- Objective 2.4 (70-270.02.04)—Configure and manage file systems.

- Objective 2.5 (70-270.02.05)—Manage and troubleshoot access to and synchronization of offline files.

- Objective 2.6 (70-270.02.06)—Configure and troubleshoot fax support.

Objective Domain 3: Implementing, Managing, Monitoring, and Troubleshooting Hardware Devices and Drivers

The objectives in Objective Domain 3 are as follows:

- Objective 3.1 (70-270.03.01)—Implement, manage, and troubleshoot disk devices.

- Objective 3.2 (70-270.03.02)—Implement, manage, and troubleshoot display devices.

- Objective 3.3 (70-270.03.03)—Configure Advanced Configuration Power Interface (ACPI).

- Objective 3.4 (70-270.03.04)—Implement, manage, and troubleshoot input and output (I/O) devices.

- Objective 3.5 (70-270.03.05)—Manage and troubleshoot drivers and driver signing.

- Objective 3.6 (70-270.03.06)—Monitor and configure multiprocessor computers.

Objective Domain 4: Monitoring and Optimizing System Performance and Reliability

The objectives in Objective Domain 4 are as follows:

- Objective 4.1 (70-270.04.01)—Monitor, optimize, and troubleshoot performance of the Windows XP Professional desktop.

- Objective 4.2 (70-270.04.02)—Manage, monitor, and optimize system performance for mobile users.

- Objective 4.3 (70-270.04.03)—Restore and back up the operating system, system state data, and user data.

Objective Domain 5: Configuring and Troubleshooting the Desktop Environment

The objectives in Objective Domain 5 are as follows:

- Objective 5.1 (70-270.05.01)—Configure and manage user profiles.

- Objective 5.2 (70-270.05.02)—Configure support for multiple languages or multiple locations.

- Objective 5.3 (70-270.05.03)—Manage applications by using Windows Installer packages.

- Objective 5.4 (70-270.05.04)—Configure and troubleshoot desktop settings.

- Objective 5.5 (70-270.05.05)—Configure and troubleshoot accessibility services.

Objective Domain 6: Implementing, Managing, and Troubleshooting Network Protocols and Services

The objectives in Objective Domain 6 are as follows:

- Objective 6.1 (70-270.06.01)—Configure and troubleshoot the TCP/IP protocol.

- Objective 6.2 (70-270.06.02)—Connect to computers by using dial-up networking.

- Objective 6.3 (70-270.06.03)—Connect to resources using Internet Explorer.

- Objective 6.4 (70-270.06.04)—Configure, manage, and implement Internet Information Services (IIS).

- Objective 6.5 (70-270.06.05)—Configure, manage, and troubleshoot remote desktop and remote assistance.

- Objective 6.6 (70-270.06.06)—Configure, manage, and troubleshoot an Internet connection firewall.

Objective Domain 7: Configuring, Managing, and Troubleshooting Security

The objectives in Objective Domain 7 are as follows:

- Objective 7.1 (70-270.07.01)—Configure, manage, and troubleshoot Encrypting File System (EFS).

- Objective 7.2 (70-270.07.02)—Configure, manage, and troubleshoot local security policy.

- Objective 7.3 (70-270.07.03)—Configure, manage, and troubleshoot local user and group accounts.

- Objective 7.4 (70-270.07.04)—Configure, manage, and troubleshoot a security configuration.

- Objective 7.5 (70-270.07.05)—Configure, manage, and troubleshoot Internet Explorer security settings.

Getting More Help

A variety of resources are available to help you study for the exam. Your options include instructor-led classes, seminars, self-paced kits, or other learning materials. The materials described here are created to prepare you for MCP exams. Each training resource fits a different type of learning style and budget.

Microsoft Official Curriculum (MOC)

Microsoft Official Curriculum (MOC) courses are technical training courses developed by Microsoft product groups to educate computer professionals who use Microsoft technology. The courses are developed with the same objectives used for Microsoft certification, and MOC courses are available to support most exams for the MCSE certification. The courses are available in instructor-led, online, or self-paced formats to fit your preferred learning style.

Self-Paced Training

Microsoft Press self-paced training kits cover a variety of Microsoft technical products. The self-paced kits are based on MOC courses, feature lessons, hands-on practices, multimedia presentations, practice files, and demonstration software. They can help you understand the concepts and get the experience you need to take the corresponding MCP exam.

To help you prepare for the Installing, Configuring, and Administering Microsoft Windows XP Professional 70-270 MCP exam, Microsoft has written the *Microsoft Windows XP Professional* training kit. With this official self-paced training kit, you can learn the fundamentals of using Windows XP Professional. This kit gives you training for the real world by offering hands-on training through CD-ROM–based exercises.

MCP Approved Study Guides

MCP Approved Study Guides, available through several organizations, are learning tools that help you prepare for MCP exams. The study guides are available in a variety of formats to match your learning style, including books, compact discs, online content, and videos. These guides come in a wide range of prices to fit your budget.

Microsoft Seminar Series

Microsoft Solution Providers and other organizations are often a source of information to help you prepare for an MCP exam. For example, many solution providers will present seminars to help industry professionals understand a particular product technology, such as networking. For information on all Microsoft-sponsored events, visit *http://msevents.microsoft.com/isapi/events/usa/enu/searchglobal.asp*.

Installing Windows XP Professional

The process of installing Microsoft Windows XP Professional is easier than the installation process for previous Windows operating systems, but you still must verify that the computer meets the minimum hardware requirements and that Windows XP Professional supports the hardware. You also have to perform a full backup, uncompress drives, and verify that the computer is free of viruses. This objective domain assesses your ability to prepare for and perform both attended (that is, manual) and unattended (that is, automated) installations. You must determine whether existing operating systems and applications will be upgraded or removed and replaced with new installations. There are several methods for automated installations of Windows XP Professional and you must be familiar with them all: the System Preparation utility (SYSPREP.EXE), Remote Installation Services (RIS), WINNT.EXE, and WINNT32.EXE. Your ability to deploy service packs, diagnose installation failures, and correct installation failures will also be assessed. You will do a number of case studies that check your ability to identify the appropriate installation method when presented with detailed information about various computing environments. You will also need to understand the difference between activation and registration of Windows XP Professional and how to complete the activation process through all available methods.

Tested Skills and Suggested Practices

The skills that you need to successfully master the Installing Windows XP Professional objective domain on the *Installing, Configuring, and Administering Microsoft Windows XP Professional* exam include

- **Confirming that the target computer meets the requirements for a new installation or upgrade to Windows XP Professional.**

  - Practice 1: Verify that the target computer meets the minimum hardware requirements necessary to install and operate Windows XP Professional. Check the processor, memory, free hard drive space, video display, keyboard, and pointing device. Also make sure that there is a CD-ROM available for CD-based installations and a network adapter for network installations.

■ Practice 2: Verify that the hardware in the target computer is compatible with Windows XP. You can perform an automated check using the installation program WINNT32.EXE with the /checkupgradeonly switch. Note that the setup program has a new feature called Dynamic Update, which collects hardware information about the target computer and then anonymously downloads upgrade files from Microsoft's Web site. You can check manually by downloading the latest Hardware Compatibility List from *http://www.microsoft.com/hcl.*

■ **Performing an attended installation of Windows XP Professional.**

  ■ Practice 1: Familiarize yourself with the various stages of the installation process by installing Windows XP Professional on computers with no operating system and with existing 32-bit Windows operating systems such as Microsoft Windows NT Workstation 4 and Microsoft Windows Me.

  ■ Practice 2: Install Windows XP Professional on a computer running MS-DOS using the 16-bit installation program (WINNT.EXE).

  ■ Practice 3: Activate Windows XP Professional over the Internet.

■ **Performing an unattended installation of Windows XP Professional.**

  ■ Practice 1: Learn the command-line switches available with WINNT32.EXE.

  ■ Practice 2: Launch Setup Manager and create an answer file for an unattended installation of a single computer. Run Setup Manager again but create a Uniqueness Database File (UDF) for automating the installation of Windows XP Professional on multiple computers. Verify that the answer file and UDF file created by Setup Manager work by running a Windows XP Professional installation using them.

  ■ Practice 3: Learn about cloning Windows XP Professional computers using the SysPrep utility. Use the image created to install Windows XP Professional.

  ■ Practice 4: Build a RIS infrastructure by installing and configuring a Microsoft Windows 2000 Server with RIS and Dynamic Host Configuration Protocol (DHCP). Build a Windows XP Professional system, use the Remote Installation Preparation Wizard (RIPREP.EXE) to prepare the system, and then use third-party software to create an image of the system. Upload the image to the RIS server. Create a Remote Boot Disk or use a Pre-Boot eXecution Environment (PXE)–capable computer to boot to the network and run a RIS-based installation. If you don't have access to third-party imaging software, you can copy the Windows XP Professional installation CD-ROM to the RIS server and the setup process will be similar to a normal CD-ROM–based installation.

- **Upgrading to Windows XP Professional and deploying service packs.**

  - Practice 1: Perform upgrades from Microsoft Windows 2000 Professional and Windows Me to Windows XP Professional. The simplest way to do this is to insert the Windows XP Professional installation CD-ROM into the target computer's CD-ROM drive and follow the prompts to upgrade the operating system. You can also run WINNT32.EXE from the \I386 directory of the CD-ROM.

  - Practice 2: Get a copy of the latest service pack for Windows XP Professional and run UPDATE.EXE to install the service pack. Also run UPDATE.EXE with the -? switch and review the available command-line switches.

  - Practice 3: Use the Files and Settings Transfer Wizard to migrate the settings from one computer to another. The originating computer can be running Windows XP Professional, Microsoft Windows 98, Windows Me, Windows NT Workstation 4, or Windows 2000 Professional; the destination computer must be running Windows XP Professional.

  - Practice 4: Use the User State Migration Tool (USMT) to implement an automated migration of a user's settings from one computer to another. Customize the USMT process by making some changes to the .inf files used by the tool.

- **Troubleshooting Windows XP Professional installation errors.**

  - Practice 1: Locate and examine the log files created during installation in the computer's operating system folder (*%systemroot%*).

  - Practice 2: Enable the highest level of error reporting during an install by using the /debug4 switch with WINNT32.EXE. Examine the log file after installation is complete. The default location and filename is *%systemroot%/* WINNT32.LOG.

  - Practice 3: Visit computer hardware vendors' Web sites and locate their support section. Study basic input/output system (BIOS) update procedures for motherboards, disk controllers, and other types of hardware that commonly have BIOS chips onboard.

Further Reading

This section lists supplemental readings by objective. We recommend that you study these sources thoroughly before taking exam 70-270.

Objective 1.1

Microsoft Corporation. *MCSE Training Kit: Microsoft Windows XP Professional*. Redmond, Washington: Microsoft Press, 2001. Read and complete Lessons 1, 2, and 3 in Chapter 2, "Installing Windows XP Professional."

Microsoft Corporation. *Microsoft Windows XP Professional Resource Kit Documentation*. Redmond, Washington: Microsoft Press, 2001. Read Chapter 1, "Planning Deployment," for an explanation of how to plan and prepare for deploying Windows XP Professional to meet the business needs of various types of organizations. Read Chapter 4, "Supporting Installations," which provides additional setup information. In particular, read the first two sections "The Setup Process" and "Support Tools."

Objective 1.2

Microsoft Corporation. *MCSE Training Kit: Microsoft Windows XP Professional*. Redmond, Washington: Microsoft Press, 2001. Read and complete Lessons 1, 2, and 3 in Chapter 19, "Deploying Windows XP Professional."

Read *Microsoft Windows XP Corporate Deployment Tools User's Guide* (DEPLOY.CHM), located on the installation CD-ROM or DVD in \Support\ Tools\Deploy.cab. This file is formatted as a Windows Help file and contains extensive information about automating the deployment of Windows XP Professional in enterprise environments.

Microsoft Corporation. *Microsoft Windows XP Professional Resource Kit Documentation*. Redmond, Washington: Microsoft Press, 2001. Read Chapter 2, "Automating and Customizing Installations." This chapter gives detailed information about creating unique automated installation routines.

Objective 1.3

Microsoft Corporation. *MCSE Training Kit: Microsoft Windows XP Professional*. Redmond, Washington: Microsoft Press, 2001. Read and complete Lesson 4 in Chapter 2, "Installing Windows XP Professional."

Microsoft Corporation. *Microsoft Windows XP Professional Resource Kit Documentation*. Redmond, Washington: Microsoft Press, 2001. Read Chapter 1, "Planning Deployment." Focus on the third section, "Assessing Your Current Configuration."

Objective 1.4

Microsoft Corporation. *MCSE Training Kit: Microsoft Windows XP Professional*. Redmond, Washington: Microsoft Press, 2001. Read and complete Lesson 4 in Chapter 2, "Installing Windows XP Professional." Read and complete Lesson 4 in Chapter 19, "Deploying Windows XP Professional."

Microsoft Corporation. *Microsoft Windows XP Professional Resource Kit Documentation*. Redmond, Washington: Microsoft Press, 2001. Read Chapter 1, "Planning Deployment." Focus on the third section, "Assessing Your Current Configuration." Read Chapter 4, "Supporting Installations." This chapter provides additional setup information. Read the third and fourth sections "Installing Service Packs and Hotfixes" and "Uninstalling a Service Pack or Hotfix."

Read the online article "Deploying Windows XP Part I: Planning," available at: *http://www.microsoft.com/windowsxp/pro/techinfo/deployment/planning/default.asp*. Pay particular attention to page three, "Evaluating Current Network and Desktop Environments."

Read the online article "Step-by-Step Guide to Migrating Files and Settings," available at: *http://www.microsoft.com/windowsxp/pro/techinfo/deployment/filesettings/default.asp*. This article discusses the File and Settings Transfer Wizard included with Windows XP Professional that is designed for moving user settings and data from one computer to another.

Read the online article "User State Migration in Windows XP," available at: *http://www.microsoft.com/windowsxp/pro/techinfo/deployment/userstate/default.asp*. This article examines the User State Migration Tool, which is designed for administrators who are migrating multiple users between computers.

Objective 1.5

Microsoft Corporation. *MCSE Training Kit: Microsoft Windows XP Professional*. Redmond, Washington: Microsoft Press, 2001. Read and complete Lesson 5 in Chapter 2, "Installing Windows XP Professional."

Microsoft Corporation. *Microsoft Windows XP Professional Resource Kit Documentation*. Redmond, Washington: Microsoft Press, 2001. Read Chapter 4, "Supporting Installations." This chapter provides additional setup information. Read the fifth and sixth sections "Troubleshooting Windows XP Professional Setup" and "Additional Resources."

OBJECTIVE 1.1

Perform an attended installation of Windows XP Professional.

You must prepare for installing Windows XP Professional by verifying that the target computer's hardware and software is compatible with Windows XP Professional. Although it is not mandatory, all hardware should appear on the **Hardware Compatibility List (HCL)**. You can download the current version of the HCL from *http:// www.microsoft.com/hcl*. You also need to ensure that the computer's **basic input/output system (BIOS)** chip is compatible with Windows XP Professional. Apply a BIOS update if required. Most vendors make BIOS updates available on their public Web sites. Another important Web site you can refer to when checking compatibility of hardware and software is *http://www.microsoft.com/windowsxp/pro*. You can also find additional information about upgrading to Windows XP Professional from previous versions of Windows. You can run the Windows XP Professional setup program, WINNT32.EXE, with the /checkupgradeonly switch to create a detailed report on the hardware and software present on the target computer.

Note Even though you have verified that all the hardware in the target computer is compatible with Windows XP Professional, you might find that the installation CD-ROM does not contain all the required drivers. The Windows XP Professional setup routine can attempt to download the latest installation files, including updated drivers, from the Windows Update Web site (*http://windowsupdate.microsoft.com/*). Contact the hardware manufacturer for any necessary driver updates that aren't available from this site.

At a minimum, you need the following hardware resources available on the computer where Windows XP Professional is to be installed.

- Pentium II processor running at 233 megahertz (MHz) or faster.

- 128 megabytes (MB) of RAM (64 MB of RAM minimum).

- 1.5 gigabytes (GB) of free hard disk space for the boot partition. Additional space will be required for optional components and additional applications. Even more will be needed if installing over a network.

- Video card and monitor running at Video Graphics Adapter (VGA) resolution or higher.

- Keyboard and pointing device.

- CD-ROM or DVD drive for CD-ROM–based and DVD-based installations.

- Network card that is PXE-enabled or a network boot disk and network card for network-based installations.

After you have verified hardware and software compatibility, back up any important files and check the system for viruses. You must then decide how you will partition the hard disk and select the appropriate file system for the boot **partition**. There are both 64-bit and 32-bit versions of Windows XP Professional. The 64-bit version is designed to run on Itanium processors and it requires **globally unique identifier (GUID) partition table (GPT)** disks and cannot install on **master boot record (MBR)** disks. MBR disks must be converted to GPT disks before the installation of 64-bit Windows XP Professional can proceed. For more information about GPT disks, visit *http:// www.microsoft.com/hwdev/storage/Whistler-GPT_FAQ.htm*. The 32-bit version of Windows XP Professional uses MBR disks. If you are performing a new installation, Setup can format disk partitions with the **NT File System (NTFS)**. If you are upgrading, you can choose to convert partitions to NTFS or retain your existing **File Allocation Table (FAT)** or **File Allocation Table-32 (FAT32)** file systems.

If there is an existing operating system on the target computer, you must decide whether it will be retained for dual-booting, upgraded, or removed. If there is no operating system on the target computer, you will perform a clean installation. You must decide where you will install Windows XP Professional from: either the Windows XP Professional installation CD-ROM or a **distribution folder** on the network. Setup is launched from one of two programs: WINNT.EXE when running a 16-bit operating system such as DOS 6.22 or Microsoft Windows 3.*x*, or WINNT32.EXE when running a 32-bit operating system such as Windows 2000 Professional or Windows Me.

Setup is divided into three phases: the **Setup Loader phase**, the **Text-Mode Setup phase**, and the **GUI-Mode Setup phase**. During these phases, you make choices about retaining, replacing, or upgrading existing operating systems, configuring hard disk partitions, installing optional components, and configuring the network. You also enter information such as a unique computer name, regional settings, date and time settings, and whether the computer will belong to a **workgroup** or **domain** on the network.

To successfully answer questions in this objective, you must be adept at manually installing Windows XP Professional on a range of computer systems. You must know how to prepare for the installation of Windows XP Professional and the phases of installation. You must also understand the differences between the various installation methods and how to use each method to install Windows XP Professional.

Objective 1.1 Questions

70-270.01.01.001

You want to perform a clean install of Windows XP Professional on a computer running Microsoft Windows NT Workstation 3.51. The computer contains a Pentium II processor running at 350 MHz, 48 MB of RAM, a 4-GB hard disk formatted as two 2-GB FAT partitions (drive C has 1.5 GB of free space, while drive D has 900 MB of free space), a 24x CD-ROM drive, a mouse, a keyboard, and a Super Video Graphics Array (SVGA) video subsystem. All the hardware is on the HCL. Your desired results are to

- Replace the existing operating system with Windows XP Professional

- Choose a file system that will enable you to ensure the greatest level of security possible

- Rejoin the computer to the Active Directory domain

- Retain the existing applications and user settings

You perform the following tasks.

1. Increase the amount of RAM to 128 MB.

2. While logged on to the existing installation of Windows NT Workstation 3.51, execute WINNT32.EXE from the Windows XP Professional installation CD-ROM and choose to perform a New Installation.

3. Answer the prompts during installation. When prompted, type the appropriate domain name.

Which goals does your proposed approach provide? (Choose two.)

A. Ensures that the computer meets the minimum hardware requirements for running Windows XP Professional

B. Replaces the existing installation of Windows NT Workstation 3.51 with a new installation of Windows XP Professional

C. Chooses a file system that enables you to ensure the greatest level of security possible

D. Rejoins the computer to the domain

E. Retains the existing applications and user settings

70-270.01.01.002

You want to perform a clean install of a Windows XP Professional computer running Windows NT Workstation 3.51. The computer contains a Pentium III processor running at 700 MHz, 32 MB of RAM, a 4-GB hard disk, a 24x CD-ROM drive, a mouse, a keyboard, and a SVGA video subsystem. The hard disk is formatted as two 2-GB partitions, both formatted with the FAT16 file system with 650 MB of free space. All the hardware is on the HCL. Your desired results are to

- Replace the existing operating system with Windows XP Professional

- Choose a file system that enables you to ensure the greatest level of security possible

- Rejoin the computer to the domain

- Retain the existing applications and user settings

- Allow for more efficient use of hard disk space by creating a single 4-GB partition

You perform the following tasks.

1. While logged on to the existing installation of Windows NT Workstation 3.51, execute WINNT32.EXE from the Windows XP Professional installation CD-ROM and choose to perform a New Installation.

2. Answer the prompts during installation but make certain to convert the existing boot partition to NTFS.

3. When prompted, type the appropriate domain name, and then add the computer account to the domain by providing logon credentials for an account belonging to the Domain Administrators group.

4. After setup completes, open the Computer Management Microsoft Management Console (MMC) snap-in, and then open the Disk Management snap-in and perform the appropriate actions to convert the second partition to NTFS.

Which goals does your proposal achieve? (Choose three.)

A. Ensures that the computer meets the minimum hardware requirements for running Windows XP Professional

B. Replaces the existing installation of Windows NT Workstation 3.51 with a new installation of Windows XP Professional

C. Chooses a file system that enables you to ensure the greatest level of security possible

D. Rejoins the computer to the domain

E. Retains the existing applications and user settings

F. Allows for more efficient use of hard disk space by creating a single 4-GB partition

70-270.01.01.003

An account executive on your company's outside sales team just returned from a major networking conference. His laptop was stolen from him while he was passing through airport security. You have a new replacement computer available. His data was backed up to a network server before he left for the conference so it is possible to restore a recent copy of his data to the new computer. You are more concerned that the thief might have compromised proprietary and sensitive information. You want to safeguard your firm's confidential data against potential theft in the future.

Which of the following steps do you take to protect the account executive's replacement computer when you install Windows XP Professional on it? (Choose two.)

A. You configure the computer so that the Welcome Screen is enabled.

B. During the installation of Windows XP Professional, you specify the FAT32 file system for the single partition on the hard disk.

C. You add the computer to the corporate domain and issue user certificates for Secure/Multipurpose Internet Mail Extensions (S/MIME) and EFS from the Active Directory–integrated Certificate Services Certificate Authority. You install the certificates onto a PC Card Smart Card that is compatible with Windows XP Professional and Windows 2000 Server Certificate Services. You install the Smart Card into the new laptop computer and verify that suitable device drivers are installed.

D. Using EFS and the user's logon credentials, you encrypt the user's My Documents folders and other folders where the user stores data. You also enable S/MIME in e-mail client software and teach the user how to use both features.

E. You install the Recovery Console and configure it for automatic administrative logon.

70-270.01.01.004

Your current laptop computer is running Windows XP Professional but you believe that its performance is unacceptable due to the speed of its CPU and the amount of RAM installed. You acquire a new computer with significantly more RAM and a much faster CPU to replace your existing system. What tool can you use to migrate your data and user settings from the old computer to the new one?

A. The Setup Wizard

B. SysPrep

C. USMT

D. RIS

Objective 1.1 Answers

70-270.01.01.001

▶ **Correct Answers: A and B**

    A. **Correct:** By increasing the system RAM to 128 MB from 48 MB, you have guaranteed that the computer has enough memory for Windows XP Professional to install and run correctly. The computer already met all the other hardware requirements for Windows XP Professional and you already knew that all the hardware was on the HCL.

    B. **Correct:** Although you cannot upgrade directly from Windows NT Workstation 3.51 to Windows XP Professional, you can perform a clean install. By selecting a New Installation, you are able to replace the existing copy of Windows NT Workstation 3.51.

    C. **Incorrect:** You can install Windows XP Professional onto a partition formatted with the FAT 16 file system, but that file system does not allow for file and folder level access controls. To ensure the greatest level of security possible, you need to convert each partition to NTFS. The version of NTFS included with Windows XP Professional also supports the Encrypting File System (EFS). EFS enables a user to encrypt files so that the data they contain is protected even if a hostile intruder obtains physical access to the hard disk. Nothing in the lists of tasks indicates that you converted each partition to NTFS.

    D. **Incorrect:** Before a computer can join a domain, a computer account must be created in the domain. If a computer account already exists with the same name, it needs to be reset or deleted first. This can be accomplished before setup by adding the computer account into the Active Directory service—a domain administrator is able to do this. It can also be achieved during the installation of Windows XP Professional by anyone who has the right to add workstations to the domain. Nothing in the lists of tasks indicates that you created the account in the domain.

    E. **Incorrect:** Performing a new installation on a computer with an existing operating system causes the loss of all user settings and forces you to reinstall all the applications. Performing an intermediate upgrade to Windows NT Workstation 4 or Windows 2000 Professional could have retained these.

70-270.01.01.002

▶ **Correct Answers: B, C, and D**

    A. **Incorrect:** The computer does not have the minimum recommended 64 MB of RAM for Windows XP Professional to install and run correctly. The computer already met all the other hardware requirements for Windows XP Professional and you already knew that all the hardware was on the HCL.

    B. **Correct:** Although you cannot upgrade directly from Windows NT Workstation 3.51 to Windows XP Professional, you can perform a clean install. By selecting a New Installation, you are able to replace the existing copy of Windows NT Workstation 3.51.

    C. **Correct:** You can install Windows XP Professional onto a partition formatted with the FAT 16 file system, but that file system does not allow for file and folder level access controls. To ensure the greatest level of security possible, you need to convert each partition to NTFS. The list of completed tasks indicates that you converted the boot partition to NTFS during installation. You also converted the second partition to NTFS after setup was complete. You cannot convert boot partitions from FAT16 or FAT32 to NTFS after setup using the tools included with Windows XP Professional.

D. **Correct:** Before a computer can join a domain, a computer account must be created in the domain. If a computer account of that name already exists in the domain, it must be reset or deleted first. The list of tasks indicates that you provided logon information for an account with sufficient privileges to create a new computer account during the installation of Windows XP Professional and that you completed the required actions to add the computer to the domain.

E. **Incorrect:** Performing a new installation on a computer with an existing operating system causes the loss of all user settings and forces you to reinstall all the applications. In contrast, performing an intermediate upgrade to Windows NT Workstation 4 or Windows 2000 Professional could have retained these.

F. **Incorrect:** Nothing in the list of tasks performs indicates that the hard disk partitions were replaced with a single partition or somehow combined.

70-270.01.01.003

▶ **Correct Answers: C and D**

A. **Incorrect:** Windows XP Professional can be configured to automatically display the Welcome Screen at bootup. The Welcome Screen lists the local user accounts so that users have to type only their password, not their user name when logging in. When the computer displays the user names, people who have gained physical access to it have useful information if they try to break into the installation of Windows XP Professional. It is more secure to require users to type both their user name and password when they log on to a computer.

B. **Incorrect:** NTFS supports folder and file level access controls. By carefully setting permissions on operating system and data files, you can ensure that only authenticated users are able to view files on the computer whether logged on locally or over the network. The FAT32 file system does not have any built-in security and therefore is a bad choice for computers that will contain sensitive data.

C. **Correct:** Smart Cards for public key encryption can greatly enhance security, especially for mobile users. Smart Cards are a more secure method for storing user certificates because it is extremely difficult to extract the certificates from the Smart Card before destroying the card itself.

D. **Correct:** By encrypting the user's data files, you ensure that if the replacement laptop computer is stolen and the hard disk is moved to another computer, the thief is unable to view confidential information. S/MIME further enhances security by allowing the account executive to digitally sign sent e-mail and receive encrypted e-mail messages.

E. **Incorrect:** The Recovery Console can be a useful tool for diagnosing and repairing serious computer failures such as corrupted system files and unsupportable configuration changes. Configuring the Recovery Console for automatic logging on significantly decreases security on a system. This is especially true for mobile users whose laptop computers are at risk of theft. This configuration setting is appropriate only on computers that are physically secure or contain no sensitive data and are unable to access any other important computers over the network. Use this setting with caution.

70-270.01.01.004

▶ **Correct Answers: C**

A. **Incorrect:** The Setup Wizard is part of the attended installation process; it does not include any features for migrating user settings from another computer to the system where Windows XP Professional is being installed.

B. **Incorrect:** You use SysPrep to prepare a computer running Windows XP Professional for imaging so that the disk image can be used to automate the deployment of similarly configured systems. It does not include any features for migrating user settings from one computer to another.

C. **Correct:** The USMT is a set of tools to help transfer a user's data files and settings between computer systems or a new installation of Windows XP Professional on an existing computer. It can copy many different types of files and settings for such things as the Desktop, Display, and Microsoft Outlook. It is the ideal tool in the scenario.

D. **Incorrect:** You use RIS for automating the deployment of computers across the network. It leverages technologies such as Windows 2000 Server, Active Directory, Group Policy Objects, and Windows XP Professional. It does not include any features for migrating user settings between computers.

OBJECTIVE 1.2

Perform an unattended installation of Windows XP Professional.

Automation of the installation of Windows XP Professional, called **unattended installation**, is much more efficient and less prone to error when deploying large numbers of computers. To effectively automate the deployment of Windows 2000 Professional, you must know how to plan for deployment, build and configure the installation environment, create customized **answer files**, and distribute the operating system and applications to the target computers.

A number of methods for automating operating systems have been developed over time; consequently, there are several alternatives for preparing installation routines and deploying the installation packages. Preparation methods include

- Installation scripts that partially or completely automate setup:

    There are two types of scripts: answer files and **Uniqueness Database Files (UDF)**. An answer file can be named anything—UNATTENDED.TXT is typically used. However, you must name it WINNT.SIF when installing Windows XP Professional from a bootable CD-ROM or SYSPREP.INF when using the SysPrep tool. You use UDF files in conjunction with answer files to deploy the operating system to multiple computers. Answer files are text files containing section headers, keys, and values for each key. Every key requires a value, but some keys are optional. You can create an answer file using the Setup Manager Wizard or with a text editor such as Notepad.

- The /syspart switch available with WINNT32.EXE:

    This method is appropriate for clean installations to computers with different types of hardware.

- The SysPrep utility and disk imaging:

    This method is suitable when the reference system and the target computers have identical or nearly identical hardware. Use SysPrep to prepare the operating system on the reference computer for imaging. You can fully automate the installation routine by creating an answer file called SYSPREP.INF. Use a third-party imaging tool to copy the disk image to a network share or removable media.

- Images built with the RIS RIPrep tool

Distribution methods include

- Bootable CD-ROM:

  This approach is useful when deploying Windows 2000 Professional to remote sites with slow network links.

- Batch file and a network distribution folder

- RIS:

  RIS works with both CD-ROM–based and image-based installation preparation methods.

- Systems Management Server (SMS):

  SMS is useful when upgrading multiple computers from previous versions of Windows.

To successfully answer questions in this objective, you must know how to use the Setup Manager Wizard to prepare for a Windows XP Professional installation and to create answer files and UDF files. You must also know how to create and edit these installation scripts manually using a text editor. You need to be familiar with all the preparation and distribution methods and understand which ones are appropriate for different circumstances.

Objective 1.2 Questions

70-270.01.02.001

You are directed to install Windows XP Professional on 25 identical new desktop computers for the Accounts Receivable department in your firm. To date, your colleagues have been manually installing Windows XP Professional and the suite of applications on each computer as they arrive, carefully following written step-by-step instructions. The process has been tedious and slow; additionally, numerous configurations errors have been uncovered on existing systems after they've been turned over to the end users. You want to deploy the computers as efficiently as possible with all the desktop applications that are required by the staff in Accounts Receivable installed and configured. You also want to ensure that all 25 computers are configured consistently.

You propose to do the following:

- Manually install and configure Windows XP Professional and the required applications on one of the new computers, meticulously following the existing step-by-step instructions.

- Use Setup Manager to fully automate the installation routine by creating an answer file called SYSPREP.INF.

- Use a third-party tool to create an image of the reference computer.

- Use the third-party tool to copy the image from the reference computer to the remaining computers.

What critical step is missing from your proposal?

A. Use Setup Manager to create a UDF file with unique settings for each of the 25 computers.

B. Create RIS boot disks so that the computers can connect to the RIS server to download the disk image.

C. Use the SysPrep utility to prepare the reference computer for imaging.

D. Install PXE-compliant network cards into each computer so that they can connect to the RIS server to download the disk image.

70-270.01.02.002

You are creating an automated installation of Windows XP Professional for 30 computers. You want to accomplish the following.

- Assign a unique computer name to each computer

- Ensure that all computers have the same display settings, time zone configured, default user name, and organization name entered

- Install Microsoft Office XP Professional on all the computers

- Configure the local Administrator account with a unique password on each system

- Modify the user interface so that the desktop icons are no longer visible

You plan to use Setup Manager to create a fully automated installation combining an answer file and a UDF file with the preceding settings. Which goals does your approach achieve? (Choose three.)

A. You can assign a unique computer name to each computer.

B. You can ensure that all computers have the same display settings, time zone configured, default user name, and organization name entered.

C. You can install Office XP Professional on all the computers.

D. You can configure the local Administrator account with a unique password on each system.

E. You can modify the user interface so that the desktop icons are no longer visible.

F. Your solution does not achieve any of the desired goals.

70-270.01.02.003

You want to perform an unattended installation of Windows XP Professional onto a computer with a bootable CD-ROM drive. You have already verified that the computer meets the minimum hardware requirements for Windows XP Professional and all the hardware is on the HCL. You also have a bootable version of the Windows XP Professional installation CD-ROM.

Which of the following is correct?

A. Ensure that the answer file has a section called [Winnt32] that contains the required keys and values. Save the answer file as SYSPREP.INF and copy it to a floppy disk. Configure the target computer's BIOS so that it will boot from the CD-ROM drive, and then insert the Windows 2000 Professional installation CD-ROM and reboot the computer. Insert the floppy disk as soon as the computer boots from the CD-ROM.

B. Ensure that the answer file has a section called [Winnt32] that contains the required keys and values. Save the answer file as WINNT.SIF and copy it to a floppy disk. Configure the target computer's BIOS so that it boots from the CD-ROM drive, and then insert the Windows 2000 Professional installation CD-ROM and reboot the computer. Insert the floppy disk as soon as the computer boots from the CD-ROM.

C. Ensure that the answer file has a section called [Data] that contains the required keys and values. Save the answer file as SYSPREP.INF and copy it to a floppy disk. Configure the target computer's BIOS so that it boots from the CD-ROM drive, and then insert the Windows 2000 Professional installation CD-ROM and reboot the computer. Insert the floppy disk as soon as the computer boots from the CD-ROM.

D. Ensure that the answer file has a section called [Data] that contains the required keys and values. Save the answer file as WINNT.SIF and copy it to a floppy disk. Insert the floppy disk into the target computer. Configure the target computer's BIOS so that it boots from the CD-ROM drive, and then insert the Windows 2000 Professional installation CD-ROM and reboot the computer.

70-270.01.02.004

During an unattended installation of Windows XP Professional, keys may have values set in the answer file, the UDF file, in both files, or in neither file. How does Setup handle the following scenarios? (Choose four.)

A. If a section or key is present in the UDF file but there is no section or key of the same name in the answer file, Setup creates and uses the UDF section.

B. If a key is specified in the answer file and referenced by the unique ID in the UDF file, the value specified in the answer file is used.

C. If a key is specified in the answer file and referenced by the unique ID in the UDF file, the value specified in the answer file is used.

D. If a key is specified in the UDF file but not in the answer file, the value specified in the UDF file is used.

E. If a key is not specified in the answer file, and it is in the UDF file but the value is left blank, the default value is supplied automatically by Setup.

F. If a key is not specified in the answer file, and it is in the UDF file but the value is left blank, no value is set.

G. If a key is specified in the answer file but not in the UDF file, the value specified in the answer file is used.

Objective 1.2 Answers

70-270.01.02.001

▶ **Correct Answers: C**

    A. **Incorrect:** When using disk imaging to deploy Windows XP Professional, you do not need to create UDF files.

    B. **Incorrect:** RIS is another possible approach to deploying multiple computers but you have already proposed using disk images. Copying the images to the disk drives of the new computers does not require RIS.

    C. **Correct:** Before you create an image of the reference computer, you must use SysPrep to remove security and user information unique to the system. SysPrep erases the computer's name and its Globally Unique Identifier (GUID) and all other settings that might cause problems if they appear on multiple computers on the same network.

    D. **Incorrect:** RIS is another possible approach to deploying multiple computers but you have already proposed using disk images. Copying the images to the disk drives of the new computers does not require RIS or PXE-enabled network cards. Additionally, the entire computer needs to be PXE-compliant, not just the network cards. Merely installing PXE-enabled network cards into a computer does not guarantee that it will be able to boot directly from the network.

70-270.01.02.002

▶ **Correct Answers: A, B, and D**

    A. **Correct:** With Setup Manager, you can create UDF files that can be used in conjunction with answer files. The settings in a UDF file take precedence over those in an answer file. You can specify unique values for many settings such as computer names so that each computer deployed has a distinct name.

    B. **Correct:** Setup Manager can create or modify answer files that can contain all the settings listed. An answer file is a customized script used to run an unattended installation of Windows XP Professional.

    C. **Incorrect:** Setup Manager cannot automate the installation of any version of Office XP on its own. You can use Setup Manager to launch other programs and scripts, but you have to create an automated installation for Office XP Professional with other tools such as those found in the Office XP Resource Kit.

D. **Correct:** With Setup Manager, you can create UDF files that can be used in conjunction with answer files. The settings in a UDF file take precedence over those in an answer file. You can specify unique values for many settings such as the password for the Local Administrator account.

E. **Incorrect:** Setup Manager does not include tools to modify user interface properties such as the appearance of desktop icons. A different tool such as Active Directory's Group Policies is needed to accomplish this goal.

F. **Incorrect:** The proposed solution does assign a unique computer name and administrator password to each computer. It also ensures that all computers have the same display settings, time zone configured, default user name, and organization name entered.

70-270.01.02.003

▶ **Correct Answers: D**

A. **Incorrect:** The answer file must be named WINNT.SIF, not SYSPREP.INF. SYSPREP.INF is the name given to the answer file when using SysPrep to deploy Windows XP Professional via disk imaging. The section with the required keys for automating installation from the bootable installation CD-ROM must be called [Data].

B. **Incorrect:** The section with the required keys for automating installation from the bootable installation CD-ROM must be called [Data].

C. **Incorrect:** The answer file must be named WINNT.SIF, not SYSPREP.INF. SYSPREP.INF is the name given to the answer file when using SysPrep to deploy Windows XP Professional via disk imaging.

D. **Correct:** The [Data] section is an optional section needed only when installing Windows XP Professional in an unattended fashion directly from the product CD-ROM. If you use the Setup Manager Wizard to create the answer file and specify that the answer file will be used to install from a CD-ROM, it creates the [Data] section with the required keys and values: AutoPartition=1, MsDosInitiated="0", and UnattendedInstall="Yes". The answer file must be named WINNT.SIF; by default, Setup Manager offers to name the file UNATTENDED.TXT. Be sure to name the file WINNT.SIF before booting from the installation CD-ROM. Remember to insert the diskette into the floppy drive right after the computer boots from the CD-ROM.

70-270.01.02.004

▶ **Correct Answers: A, D, F, and G**

A. **Correct:** Setup automatically uses values within the UDF file when the corresponding values are not specified in the answer file.

B. **Incorrect:** The values specified in the UDF file take precedence over those in the answer file whenever they are in conflict.

C. **Incorrect:** The values specified in the UDF file take precedence over those in the answer file whenever they are in conflict.

D. **Correct:** Setup automatically uses values within the UDF file when the corresponding values are not specified in the answer file.

E. **Incorrect:** Setup does not automatically supply default values for any keys left blank. In this situation, it is possible that the user will be prompted for the missing information.

F. **Correct:** If a key has a blank value in the UDF file and the answer file has no value specified for that key, no value is set and it is possible that the user will be prompted for the missing information.

G. **Correct:** Any keys specified in the answer file that are not superseded by those in the UDF file are used.

OBJECTIVE 1.3

Upgrade from a previous version of Windows to Windows XP Professional.

Often, Windows XP Professional is needed on systems that already have a version of Windows installed. The best way to minimize the impact on the applications running on that system is to perform an **in-place upgrade** to Windows XP. In-place upgrades can be performed on systems that have Microsoft Windows 98, Windows Me, Windows NT Workstation 4 with Service Pack 3, or Windows 2000 Professional. This process is much more complex than performing a **clean installation**—fortunately, the Windows XP setup procedures include many tools to make this process as painless as possible.

Systems running older Windows operating systems can also be upgraded, but not directly. For example, Microsoft Windows 95 cannot be upgraded to Windows XP Professional simply by running WINNT32.EXE—it must be upgraded to Windows 98 first. Similarly, a computer with Windows NT 4 and Service Pack 3 installed must be upgraded to Service Pack 6 before the Windows XP Professional setup routine can be run successfully.

In addition to verifying that the system's hardware resources meet Microsoft's minimum requirements (as defined within Objective 1.1), you also need to verify that all applications installed on the system are compatible with Windows XP. To facilitate this process, Microsoft provides the Windows XP Application Compatibility Toolkit. This toolkit is available online at *http://msdn.microsoft.com/downloads/sample.asp?url=/msdn-files/027/001/685/msdncompositedoc.xml*.

Caution One class of programs that you must be particularly cautious with when upgrading to Windows XP Professional is antivirus utilities. Antivirus programs are operating-system specific; that is, they are written to work with a particular operating system. You must uninstall or upgrade any installed antivirus programs to a version compatible with Windows XP Professional before upgrading the operating system. Failing to do so can cause severe problems including loss of data or an unbootable computer.

During the first phase of an attended install, the Windows XP setup procedure automatically checks applications installed on the system for compatibility with Windows XP and notifies the installer of any potential incompatibilities. This phase is known as the report phase. To generate this report without performing an install, insert the Windows XP Professional installation CD-ROM and run WIN32.EXE with the /checkupgradeonly switch. For example, if your CD-ROM is the D: drive, type **D:\i386\Winnt32 /checkupgradeonly**.

The second phase of an attended install is the installation phase. This phase handles the actual migration to Windows XP Professional by transferring user, application, and system configuration settings from the previously installed operating system. Afterward, system files are updated and the newly installed operating system is booted for the first time.

If you have ever replaced your personal desktop or laptop computer that you have been using for months or years with a new one, you understand how challenging it can be to copy all your data and user preferences over to the replacement system. Windows XP Professional includes two methods for migrating users' configuration settings and data between systems. The **Files and Settings Transfer Wizard (FSTW)** is intended for home users, small office users, and lightly managed users in an enterprise environment. The **User State Migration Tool (USMT)** is a command-line tool created for migrating large numbers of users in a corporate setting. You launch FSTW from the Start menu by selecting All Programs, selecting Accessories, selecting System Tools, and then clicking Files And Settings Transfer Wizard. The USMT is located on the Windows XP Professional installation media in the folder called \VALUEADD\MSFT\USMT. You can run this tool from the installation CD-ROM or DVD or you can copy it to a local hard disk.

The FSTW provides clear instructions while walking you through the process to automatically gather files and settings from your old system and transferring them to the new one. You can use floppy disks or removable media to transfer the files, a direct cable connection, or a shared folder on the network. You can customize exactly what files and settings are transferred and what are left behind. To successfully complete this objective, you must know what types of application and operating systems can be transferred, what file types and locations are migrated by default, and how to specify additional files and locations for transfer.

The USMT is intended for network administrators; it is not an appropriate tool to use for migrating individual users. It includes several command-line programs, .dll files, and a handful of .inf files that most administrators will want to customize before implementing the migration process. The USMT ScanState (SCANSTATE.EXE) tool collects user data and settings by reading information contained in MIGMAP.INF, MIGSYS.INF, MIGUSER.INF, and SYSFILES.INF. The LoadState (LOADSTATE.EXE) tool stores the collected information on the freshly installation of Windows XP Professional. USMT does not work on an upgraded installation. ScanState and LoadState support command-line switches that you must be familiar with. You must also understand how to customize the .inf files in order to modify what data files and settings are collected by ScanState.

Objective 1.3 Questions

70-270.01.03.001

A newly hired CIO understands the benefits of using a single desktop operating system for the entire company, and has hired you to upgrade all networked systems to Windows XP. Previously, local administrators with varying policies and procedures had managed each remote office. Consequently, desktop systems have a mixture of Microsoft Windows for Workgroups 3.11, Windows 95, Windows NT Workstation 4, and Windows 2000 Professional. You want to minimize the impact on each user's applications by performing an in-place upgrade whenever possible.

Which of these operating systems can be upgraded to Windows XP in a single step? (Choose two.)

A. Windows for Workgroups 3.11

B. Windows 95

C. Windows NT Workstation 4 with no service pack

D. Windows NT Workstation 4 with Service Pack 6

E. Windows 2000 Professional

70-270.01.03.002

You are an administrator for a corporate network supporting 40 users. Your CEO recently learned about the many benefits that Windows XP Professional offers over the Windows 98 operating system that is currently installed on her laptop computer. You have been assigned the task of upgrading the CEO's laptop to Windows XP. It is critical that the computer be returned when the CEO returns from a business trip the following day, and all data, applications, and settings must be available.

Which is the best upgrade strategy?

A. Perform a full system backup, scan for viruses, and uncompress any compressed drives. Document the user preferences and applications installed on the system. Run the Windows XP Professional setup procedure and repartition all drives with NTFS. After setup has completed, restore the backup over the new installation. After setup has completed, verify the functionality of all hardware and applications.

B. Perform a full system backup, scan for viruses, and uncompress any compressed drives. Run the standard Windows XP Professional setup procedure and perform an in-place upgrade. After setup has completed, verify the functionality of all hardware and applications. If Windows XP was unable to install drivers for some hardware components, download and install updated drivers. If any of the applications do not function correctly, download and apply patches from the software vendors.

C. Perform a full system backup, scan for viruses, and uncompress any compressed drives. Generate a compatibility report by running the WINNT32.EXE /checkupgradeonly command. Download any drivers that the compatibility report indicates are not provided by Windows XP, and patch any applications that have not been certified. Run the standard Windows XP Professional setup procedure and perform an in-place upgrade, providing updated drivers as prompted. After setup has completed, verify the functionality of all hardware and applications.

D. Perform a full system backup, scan for viruses, and uncompress any compressed drives. Generate a compatibility report by running the WINNT32.EXE /checkupgradeonly command. Download any drivers that the compatibility report indicates are not provided by Windows XP, and patch any applications that have not been certified. Run the standard Windows XP Professional setup procedure and perform a new install with a different system directory (that is, C:\WinXP\), providing updated drivers as prompted. After setup has completed, verify the functionality of all hardware and applications. Once the system is functioning correctly, delete the directory containing Windows 98.

70-270.01.03.003

You have several identical computers that you want to upgrade from Windows Me to Windows XP Professional. You have already verified that all the computers meet the minimum hardware requirements and that they and their subcomponents appear on the Windows XP HCL. You have also verified that each computer already has the current BIOS installed. The computers have been in operation for several months and their users have installed their own applications. How can you quickly determine whether there will be any application compatibility issues before proceeding with the upgrade?

A. Run the setup program from the Windows XP Professional installation media with the /checkupgradeonly switch by typing **x:\i386\WINNT32.EXE /checkupgradeonly** from a command prompt where x: is the drive letter assigned to the CD-ROM drive on each computer.

B. Create a list of the applications installed on each computer and then visit the Web site of the vendor for each application to find out whether the versions installed on the computers to be upgraded are compatible with Windows XP Professional.

C. Purchase the latest versions of each installed application.

D. Perform a clean installation of Windows XP Professional on each system, and then reinstall all the applications.

70-270.01.03.004

You are the administrator of a network that includes 50 users running Windows 2000 Professional and 4 servers running Microsoft Windows 2000 Advanced Server and Active Directory in a domain setting. You are told to replace 20 of the users' desktop computers with new laptop computers that have Windows XP Professional preinstalled. You want to add the computers to the domain and transfer the users' data and settings from their current desktop computers to their new laptop systems. Which of the following solutions best accomplishes these goals?

A. Name each of the computers appropriately, and then join them to the domain. Install the appropriate applications. Copy each user's User Profile from his or her old computer to the new computer.

B. Give each of the computers a unique name and then join them to the domain. Write a script that copies each user's My Documents folder from the old computer to the replacement system, and schedule the script to run on each of the replacement computers.

C. Name each of the computers appropriately and then join them to the domain. Install the appropriate applications. Write a script that uses the USMT ScanState tool to copy all users' settings from their old computers to a shared drive on one of the domain controllers. Write a script that launches the LoadState tool with the required settings to copy the files and settings from the shared network drive and schedule the script to run on each laptop computer.

D. Schedule a task to launch the FSTW on each laptop computer and be sure the job is executed in the context of an account with local administrative access on all the computers.

70-270.01.03.005

You are the administrator for a network that includes 80 users and 3 servers running Windows 2000 Advanced Server and Active Directory in a domain setting. You are preparing to migrate 15 users from their existing laptop computers running Windows Me to new laptop systems that will be running Windows XP Professional. You have automated most of the process including installing Windows XP Professional, joining the computer to the domain, and installing the required applications. You are having trouble with the USMTs on your test system that is running Windows Me. How can you effectively troubleshoot the automated process of copying user data and settings to a shared folder on the network?

A. Run the ScanState tool with verbose error logging enabled by typing **/l scanstate.log /v 7 /u /f** to the command you use to run the tool.

B. Check the local system and application logs for error messages.

C. Run the LoadState tool with verbose error logging enabled by typing **/l scanstate.log /v 7** to the command you use to run the tool.

D. Check the application and system logs on the domain controller where the shared network folder is located.

Objective 1.3 Answers

70-270.01.03.001

▶ **Correct Answers: D and E**

A. **Incorrect:** Windows for Workgroups 3.11 cannot be upgraded directly to Windows XP Professional. After determining that the hardware and software are compatible with Windows XP, you must perform a full system backup and define a list of installed applications and document personalization settings such as wallpaper and color scheme. Then, perform a fresh install of Windows XP, reinstall all applications, and restore the user's data and settings. Alternatively, the system can be upgraded to Windows 95, and then Windows 98, and then Windows XP Professional.

B. **Incorrect:** You cannot upgrade directly from Windows 95 directly to Windows XP Professional. The suggested upgrade path is from Windows 95, to Windows 98, to Windows XP.

C. **Incorrect:** You cannot upgrade Windows NT Workstation 4 to Windows XP Professional unless Service Pack 3 or later is installed.

D. **Correct:** You can upgrade Windows NT Workstation 4 directly to Windows XP Professional, as long as Service Pack 6 is installed.

E. **Correct:** You can upgrade Windows 2000 Professional directly to Windows XP Professional.

70-270.01.03.002

▶ **Correct Answers: C**

A. **Incorrect:** Restoring Windows 98 system files over a Windows XP installation might return the system to its original state, or it might leave the system completely nonfunctional. Though at times it might be necessary to restore user data to a freshly upgraded system, applications and system settings cannot be transferred this way.

B. **Incorrect:** This is a commonly used method and will work on many systems. However, it is very risky because there is a distinct possibility that the system will not function at all after the upgrade. Additionally, if you discover after the upgrade that a critical application cannot be patched to work properly with Windows XP, your only method of recovery is to perform a full system restore. It is more time efficient to perform a WINNT32.EXE /checkupgradeonly procedure and resolve any issues before running the full setup procedure.

C. **Correct:** This method is the correct choice because it proactively identifies system incompatibilities. Generating a compatibility report before performing the upgrade greatly improves the chance of a successful upgrade. If a system component or application is completely incompatible with Windows XP, this method identifies that weakness ahead of time.

D. **Incorrect:** Performing a new install of Windows XP preserves the user's data, but not applications and system settings. Though applications are not available from the Start menu, the application files still consume hard disk space. Applications need to be reinstalled, and system settings are completely lost.

70-270.01.03.003

▶ **Correct Answers: A**

A. **Correct:** This procedure will generate an application compatibility report for Windows XP Professional without actually installing the operating system; it is the most efficient way to check for application compatibility.

B. **Incorrect:** Although you might have to contact some of the vendors for upgrades to their applications after running the application compatibility report described in answer A, it is unlikely you will need to visit all their Web sites. This approach is unnecessarily cumbersome and time consuming.

C. **Incorrect:** You might need to upgrade some of the installed applications, but it is unlikely that you will have to upgrade all, or even most of them. This approach is expensive and time consuming.

D. **Incorrect:** This approach fails to accomplish the basic objective of upgrading the existing operating system on each computer. Additionally, you have done nothing to verify that the applications are compatible with Windows XP Professional so you might find that you cannot install some of them.

70-270.01.03.004

▶ **Correct Answers: C**

A. **Incorrect:** The format and structure of user profiles are different between Windows 2000 and Windows XP. Copying a profile from a computer running one operating system to another will probably cause problems, perhaps serious, such as users being unable to log on or, after they have logged on, being unable to access certain applications.

B. **Incorrect:** Although efficient, this approach docs not migrate all the user settings, and any user data stored outside the My Documents folder will not be copied to the new laptop computers.

C. **Correct:** These procedures accomplish all the stated goals in an efficient manner. The steps to add the computers to the domain can be partially automated through a script, but the laptop computers were delivered with Windows XP Professional already installed, so it might be faster do that manually. When scheduling the execution of the USMT tools, make sure the scheduled job is executed in the context of an account that belongs to the local Administrators group.

D. **Incorrect:** The FSTW is an interactive tool that cannot be run silently from a command line. In other words, scheduling the tool in this manner does not accomplish the goal of copying user data and settings. Additionally, there is nothing in this answer to suggest that the computers were added to the Active Directory domain.

70-270.01.03.005

▶ **Correct Answers: A**

A. **Correct:** The /l switch enables logging for SCANSTATE.EXE; you must provide a filename for the log. The /v switch specifies the level of verbosity for the logging—7 is the most verbose setting. The /u and /f switches provide additional information about the resources to be scanned.

B. **Incorrect:** The USMT does not record detailed error messages to the system or application logs.

C. **Incorrect:** The question states that you are having problems on the computer running Windows Me, which implies that the trouble involves the ScanState tool, not the LoadState tool. The LoadState tool would be run on the target computer that has Windows XP Professional installed.

D. **Incorrect:** The ScanState tool is run locally on the computer where data and settings are being transferred from; it is not likely that it will record any events on the domain controller's application or system log. It might generate events in the security log on the domain controller if auditing were enabled and you were trying to access a shared folder with an account that did not have sufficient permission to write files to that location.

Perform post-installation updates and product activation.

All operating systems require patches to be applied on a regular basis to fix problems, provide compatibility with new hardware, and resolve newly discovered security vulnerabilities. Microsoft distributes these updates in the form of **service packs**. These updates can be retrieved from the Windows Update Web site, a portion of *http:// www.microsoft.com/* dedicated to providing information and software to keep Microsoft software current.

If the only Windows XP system you are responsible for managing is your own personal computer, you will probably choose to run Windows Update from the Start menu when updates are available. This method provides a quick, easy, and bandwidth-efficient method of keeping a single computer up to date. If you are responsible for managing a network of computers, you need to identify methods that scale to larger numbers of computers and give you tighter control over how patches are deployed.

Microsoft facilitates deploying patches to large numbers of computers by making available the complete set of service pack setup files. This complete service pack distribution is intended for creating a distribution point within your own network. After you have created a distribution point, the service pack can be deployed to systems within your network without contacting the Windows Update site.

Service packs can also be **slipstreamed** into a complete Windows XP Professional distribution point. Updating the Windows XP setup files with a service pack eliminates the need to install a service pack on a newly deployed system, because the slipstreaming process integrates service pack updates into the Windows XP Professional setup files. Future systems built from the slipstreamed distribution point will contain all updates included in the service pack and reflect the updated build number, but will not require the additional step of manually installing a service pack.

The UPDATE.EXE utility is included in the \update directory of all service packs to facilitate installing the update, creating a service pack distribution point, and slipstreaming a Windows XP distribution point. The UPDATE.EXE utility does not include a graphical user interface for executing these tasks, so you must understand the command-line arguments available. Perhaps the most useful argument available displays a list of all other available arguments, with a brief description of how to use them. Executing the command UPDATE -? is the fastest way to remind yourself of the specific syntax required for a task.

Windows XP Professional includes **Windows Product Activation (WPA)** except for versions sold through volume licensing arrangements. WPA is intended to reduce casual software piracy without compromising the rights of individual consumers to their privacy. WPA combines the product key entered during installation, the **product ID (PID)**, and the **hardware ID (HWID)** to create an installation ID. The PID is based on the name and version of the software being installed. The HWID is based on specific details of the hardware present in the target computer. After installation is complete the computer reboots and the Welcome to Microsoft Windows Page appears. This welcome wizard prompts the user to activate Windows XP Professional now, either over the Internet or by calling a toll-free telephone number. Activation over the Internet is far easier in most instances. During the activation process the Installation ID is sent to a Microsoft license clearinghouse, which verifies the PID and Installation ID and double-checks that that copy of Windows XP has not been installed on other hardware. If this process succeeds, your computer receives a confirmation ID that allows you use Windows XP Professional. You do not need to activate the operating system again unless you make significant hardware changes to the system. If you choose to skip product activation, you are able to continue using Windows XP Professional for 30 days. You can activate the product at any time during that period.

Objective 1.4 Questions

70-270.01.04.001

You are a systems administrator for a new application service provider. Your company plans to offer help desk services to 50 users. Though the users' desktop systems have been purchased, you need to install the latest version of Windows XP on each of them. Rather than installing Windows XP and then immediately upgrading to Service Pack 1, you want the initial deployment of Windows XP to include Service Pack 1.

Your Windows XP network distribution point is located at \\server\winxp\. Which command properly updates the distribution point to Service Pack 1?

A. Update -copydir:\\server\winxp

B. Update -syspart: \\server\winxp

C. Update -s: \\server\winxp

D. Update -o: \\server\winxp

70-270.01.04.002

You have a two-year-old computer from a well-known manufacturer. The computer is currently running Windows Me and several dozen applications. The computer has 128 MB of RAM, a 500-MHz Pentium III CPU, and a 12 GB hard disk with 7 GB of free space. You have verified that the computer and its sub-components are on the Windows XP HCL. You have also upgraded all the applications to versions that are compatible with Windows XP Professional except for the antivirus software you have temporarily uninstalled. You back up the current configuration to a removable hard drive and begin the upgrade process. The first phase of the upgrade appears to complete properly, but when the computer reboots it crashes before the second phase begins. You reboot the computer several times with the same result. What is the most likely cause of this problem?

A. The Windows XP Professional installation CD-ROM is corrupt.

B. One or more of the memory chips installed in the computer are faulty.

C. You entered an invalid product key.

D. The BIOS is incompatible with Windows XP Professional.

70-270.01.04.003

You have a home office with a cable modem connection to the Internet. You install and configure all of your own hardware and software. You have been using Windows XP Professional on a Pentium 4 computer for several months when the first service pack is released. You download and install the service pack from the Windows Update Web site and note that several minor problems have been resolved by the service pack. You decide to install another service to the existing installation of Windows XP Professional and insert the installation media when prompted. After the installation of the new service is complete what else must you do?

A. Run SETUPMGR.EXE.

B. Run SYSPREP.EXE.

C. Reapply the service pack.

D. Do nothing.

70-270.01.04.004

What types of information are transmitted to Microsoft during product activation when performed over an Internet connection?

A. The Windows XP Professional PID, the product key, and details about the hardware present in the computer where the operating system is installed.

B. The user's registration information including name, address, city, state, and zip code.

C. The user's credit card information.

D. The HKey Local Machine registry key and sub-keys.

Objective 1.4 Answers

70-270.01.04.001

▶ **Correct Answers: C**

   A. **Incorrect:** You use the /copydir argument with the Windows XP setup routine (WINNT32.EXE) to copy an additional, administrator-provided folder to a new instance of Windows XP.

   B. **Incorrect:** You only use the /syspart argument when preloading Windows XP setup on a hard drive before moving it to another computer.

   C. **Correct:** The -s: distribution_folder is the correct syntax for updating a Windows XP network distribution point. When this command is issued, the update procedure identifies outdated files in the Windows XP setup files and replaces them with versions included in Service Pack 1. As installations are performed from this distribution point, the updated files are automatically used. This process is known as slipstreaming.

   D. **Incorrect:** The -o argument is a valid argument for the update command, but it does not perform slipstreaming. The -o argument is used to bypass prompting to overwrite original equipment manufacturer (OEM) drivers during the service pack install.

70-270.01.04.002

▶ **Correct Answers: D**

   A. **Incorrect:** The first phase of the installation completed successfully which strongly suggests that the installation media is in good working order.

   B. **Incorrect:** Although this is a possible explanation, it is highly unlikely because the computer has been running for two years.

   C. **Incorrect:** If you had entered an invalid product key during the information gathering process, you would have seen an error message and been prompted to reenter the correct key. If you had entered a valid product key that had already been assigned to a different computer, you would not see an error until you tried to activate Windows XP.

   D. **Correct:** You performed most of the steps necessary before beginning the upgrade process, but you forgot to upgrade the BIOS with the latest version available from the manufacturer. An incompatible BIOS can render a computer unbootable. Recovering from this situation shouldn't be too difficult if you have another system running that is connected to the Internet. Visit the manufacturer's Web site and download the latest BIOS. Follow the manufacturer's instructions to upgrade the BIOS on the target computer; typically this involves copying the BIOS update to a bootable floppy disk and booting the target computer from it. After the BIOS is upgraded, remove the floppy disk and reboot—the Windows XP Professional installation should proceed without further problems.

70-270.01.04.003

▶ **Correct Answers: D**

A. **Incorrect:** Setup Manager is a tool for creating answer files to automate the installation of Windows XP Professional or to fully automate a SysPrep installation routine.

B. **Incorrect:** The SysPrep tool is used for deploying Windows XP Professional onto multiple computers using disk cloning. SysPrep assigns a unique security ID to each destination computer the first time the computer is restarted. This tool is not used for managing service packs or for adding and removing optional Windows components.

C. **Incorrect:** In previous versions of Windows, you had to reapply the most recent service pack after installing any additional components from the installation media. Windows XP Professional overcomes this limitation by ensuring that all the files included with a service pack are installed to the appropriate folders on the hard disk, even those that are not currently needed. When an optional component is added to a system with a newer service pack the most recent files are automatically retained, eliminating the need to reapply the service pack.

D. **Correct:** For the reasons noted in answer C, it is not necessary to reapply the service pack.

70-270.01.04.004

▶ **Correct Answers: A**

A. **Correct:** This is the only information sent to Microsoft.

B. **Incorrect:** Although this information is sent to Microsoft during the registration process, it is not sent during product activation. Registration is a voluntary step that users can choose to bypass— product activation is required to continue using Windows XP Professional for more than 30 days after installation.

C. **Incorrect:** This answer is incorrect for the reasons stated in answer B.

D. **Incorrect:** This answer is incorrect for the reasons stated in answer B.

O B J E C T I V E   1 . 5

Troubleshoot failed installations.

As you've learned, setting up an operating system is an extremely complex procedure. The rich variety of hardware components provides an unlimited number of combinations that the setup routine must be able to accommodate. To make these procedures even more complex, Windows XP Professional is often installed on hardware that was designed after the release of the operating system.

These complexities will lead to occasional failures of the setup routine. Though these failures are challenging to resolve, Windows XP Professional makes this a much simpler process by providing detailed logging and debugging information. Understanding how to interpret these log files is critical to quickly resolving failed installations. If you find that these log files are not providing enough information to effectively troubleshoot a failed installation, detailed debugging can be enabled.

The best way to prevent installation failures is to use only hardware listed on Microsoft's **Hardware Compatibility List (HCL)**. The complete HCL can be viewed online at *http://www.microsoft.com/hcl*. Although it is possible for Windows XP Professional to be successfully installed on software not listed in the HCL, using unsupported hardware greatly increases your chances of failure and nullifies Microsoft support agreements.

Even hardware listed on the HCL might need to receive an update of the **BIOS**. BIOS updates are generally available on the Web site of the vendor that manufactured the hardware. Often, updated versions of hardware BIOS are released in conjunction with the release of a new operating system. So, if you purchased a computer, network card, video card, sound card, or other accessory before the release of Windows XP Professional, there's a very good chance that the hardware vendor released a BIOS update to provide complete compatibility with the new operating system.

The setup routine has three installation phases: the **Setup Loader** phase, the **Text-Mode Setup** phase, and the **GUI-Mode Setup** phase. Understanding which installation steps occur during each of these three stages is critical to troubleshooting a failed install.

The Setup Loader phase copies installation files from the Windows XP Professional source to the local hard disk. A minimal version of Windows XP is loaded to detect the hardware and load the necessary drivers. The Setup Loader then modifies the **boot sector** to allow the Text-Mode Setup phase to begin after a reboot.

The Text-Mode Setup phase performs detailed detection and configuration of hardware drivers—and is the most likely place for the installation to fail. If fatal hardware incompatibilities exist, they generally surface during this phase. You are also given the option to create and format partitions during this phase, which might reveal disk problems that are not otherwise apparent. After another reboot, the GUI-Mode Setup phase begins.

The GUI-Mode Setup phase accepts input from the user regarding user preferences. Optional services and components are added to Windows XP Professional during this phase. Though failures during the GUI-Mode Setup phase are common, they are generally not fatal and will allow the installation procedure to complete and the operating system to boot. When the GUI-Mode Setup phase doesn't complete successfully, problems can be quickly resolved because the core Windows XP functionality will be available.

Throughout these setup phases, text-based log files are written to the local hard disk for later reference. These log files are located in the *%systemroot%* directory and end with a log file extension. After every successful and unsuccessful step of the installation routine, a detailed description of the action is appended to the various log files for later reference. Referring to these log files will uncover the nature of any problems experienced, even if the installation routine was able to complete successfully. If the installation routine fails, identifying the last log entries written will help isolate the nature of the failure.

Objective 1.5 Questions

70-270.01.05.001

You are attempting to perform a new, manual installation of Windows XP on a system that already has Windows Me installed. The setup routine fails, and you accidentally clear the error message box before reading it. Which log file do you view first to read the details of the error?

A. SETUPERR.LOG

B. COMSETUP.LOG

C. IIS6.LOG

D. TSOC.LOG

70-270.01.05.002

You are attempting to perform a new, manual installation of Windows XP on a system that already has Windows Me installed. The setup routine succeeds, but afterward you are unable to connect to the system with the Terminal Services client. Which log files do you view to determine whether errors were experienced during the installation of the terminal services? (Choose two.)

A. SETUPERR.LOG

B. COMSETUP.LOG

C. IIS6.LOG

D. TSOC.LOG

E. OEWABLOG.TXT

70-270.01.05.003

After several installation failures, you determine that you need to examine a debug log for the setup routine. You want the setup routine to create the most detailed debug log possible. Which command do you use?

A. Winnt32 /debug7:debug.log

B. Winnt32 /debug4:debug.log

C. Winnt32 /debug1:debug.log

D. Winnt32 /debug0:debug.log

70-270.01.05.004

After installing Service Pack 2 on a Windows XP Professional on a desktop system, you discover that a critical application doesn't work properly. The application vendor indicates that the application is not compatible with Service Pack 2, so you decide to uninstall the service pack. Which is a valid method?

A. From a command prompt, change to the *%systemroot%*\$NtServicePackUninstall$\spuninst folder. Type **spuninst.exe -u**.

B. From a command prompt, change to the *%systemroot%*\$NtServicePackUninstall$\spuninst folder. Type **spuninst.exe -f**.

C. From a command prompt, change to the *%systemroot%*\$NtServicePackUninstall$\spuninst folder. Type **Update -n**.

D. From a command prompt, change to the *%systemroot%*\$NtServicePackUninstall$\spuninst folder. Type **Update -u**.

Objective 1.5 Answers

70-270.01.05.001

▶ **Correct Answers: A**

A. **Correct:** The Windows XP setup routine creates the SETUPERR.LOG file during installation, and adds a description of every error encountered. This file is located in the *%systemroot%* directory.

B. **Incorrect:** The COMSETUP.LOG file contains a description of the progress of COM+ (Component Object Model) installation, but does not contain general error log information.

C. **Incorrect:** The IIS6.LOG file contains a description of the progress of the IIS6 installation, but does not contain general error log information.

D. **Incorrect:** The TSOC.LOG file contains a description of the progress of the installation of terminal services, but does not contain general error log information.

70-270.01.05.002

▶ **Correct Answers: A and D**

A. **Correct:** The Windows XP setup routine creates the SETUPERR.LOG file during installation, and adds a description of every error encountered. This file is located in the *%systemroot%* directory.

B. **Incorrect:** The COMSETUP.LOG file contains a description of the progress of COM+ (Component Object Model) installation, but does not contain general error log information.

C. **Incorrect:** The IIS6.LOG file contains a description of the progress of the IIS6 installation, but does not contain general error log information.

D. **Correct:** The TSOC.LOG file contains a description of the progress of the installation of terminal services. Examining this file in addition to the SETUPERR.LOG file might reveal more detailed information about the nature of the problem experienced.

E. **Incorrect:** The OEWABLOG.TXT file contains information about the Microsoft Outlook Express installation, but does not contain general error log information.

70-270.01.05.003

▶ **Correct Answers: B**

A. **Incorrect:** Though the /debug[level]:[filename] syntax is correct, debug level 7 is not a valid option.

B. **Correct:** The /debug[level]:[filename] syntax is correct, and debug level 4 is the highest level of debugging available. Possible options vary from 0 to 4; 0 represents severe errors, 1 represents errors, 2 represents warnings, 3 represents informational messages, and 4 represents very detailed information. Naturally, each higher level of debugging includes information from all lower levels.

C. **Incorrect:** Though the /debug[level]:[filename] syntax is correct, debug level 1 records only errors and severe errors.

D. **Incorrect:** Though the /debug[level]:[filename] syntax is correct, debug level 0 records only severe errors.

70-270.01.05.004

▶ **Correct Answers: A**

A. **Correct:** Unless specifically disabled, the service pack setup routine automatically creates the $NtServicePackUninstall$\spuninst\ folder. Within this folder are copies of all overwritten files, as well as the SPUNINST.EXE executable. This executable is used to uninstall the service pack and return the system to its previous state. The -u argument indicates an uninterrupted install.

B. **Incorrect:** SPUNINST.EXE is the correct command for removing a service pack from Windows XP Professional, but the -f argument is used to force all applications to close at shutdown, not to perform an uninstall.

C. **Incorrect:** The -n option is a valid argument to the Update command, but is used to stop backup files from being created. When the -n argument is used during the installation of a service pack, that service pack cannot be later uninstalled.

D. **Incorrect:** The -u argument is a valid response to the Update command, but -u is used to perform an unattended installation of the service pack.

Implementing and Conducting Administration of Resources

Since Microsoft Windows for Workgroups 3.11, the core functionality of peer-to-peer networking has been file and printer sharing. Though the Windows family of operating systems has evolved a great deal since then, file systems and printers remain the most critical aspects of the Microsoft desktop operating system. Likewise, understanding how Microsoft Windows XP interacts with disk volumes, file systems, file shares, and printers is a critical part administering Microsoft Windows XP Professional.

For the average user, managing disks, shared folders, and printers is self-explanatory because Windows XP does an excellent job of making these resources simple to administer. Administrators who are expected to troubleshoot these resources must understand it in more detail, however. For example, understanding the differences between **File Allocation Table (FAT)**, FAT32, and **NT File System (NTFS)** can mean the difference between having a system that successfully dual-boots between Microsoft Windows Me and Windows XP, and a system that must be rebuilt from scratch. Network connectivity is critical for most users, yet it's not always possible for users who travel with portable computers. **Offline Files** minimize the problems users experience when disconnected from the network or accessing files across an unreliable network connection. Files in a shared folder can be automatically **synchronized** with the local hard disk when connected to a network, and users can access these files transparently when the network is not available. Files even can be edited while offline and automatically synchronized later.

The desktop fax facility allows you to send and receive fax transmissions on the computer rather than through a fax machine. The **Fax Service** can be configured to archive and print received faxes, archive sent faxes, retry sending faxes that could not be transmitted, and automatically clean up unsent faxes after a specified period of time.

Tested Skills and Suggested Practices

The skills you need to successfully master the Implementing and Conducting Administration of Resources domain on the *Installing, Configuring, and Administering Microsoft Windows XP Professional* exam include

- **Implementing and administering Windows XP file system features.**

    - Practice 1: Create a partition using the Disk Management utility.

    - Practice 2: Convert a file system from FAT32 to NTFS using the CONVERT.EXE command-line utility.

    - Practice 3: Convert a basic disk to a dynamic disk using the DISKPART.EXE command-line utility.

    - Practice 4: Using the Disk Management administrative utility, experiment with the different options available when accessing basic and dynamic disks.

    - Practice 5: Create a striped disk by combining two dynamic disks.

    - Practice 6: Use mount points to graft a dynamic volume into the file system of an existing volume.

    - Practice 7: Use the FSUTIL.EXE VOLUME EXTEND command to extend an NTFS volume, and view the results with the Disk Management administrative utility.

    - Practice 8: Move files between compressed and uncompressed folders on an NTFS volume, and notice whether the compression status is inherited from the source or destination folder.

    - Practice 9: Move files between compressed and uncompressed folders on different NTFS volumes, and notice whether the compression status is inherited from the source or destination folder.

    - Practice 10: Compress different types of files, and determine which file types benefit the most from compression.

    - Practice 11: Create a share that only members of the Administrators group can access.

    - Practice 12: Create a shared folder using the NET.EXE SHARE command-line utility.

    - Practice 13: Remotely connect to a folder shared from a Windows XP Professional system. Then, from the system hosting the shared folder, open the Shared Folders MMC snap-in. Use this tool to send all connected users a message warning them that their session will be disconnected. Finally, forcibly disconnect the user's session.

- Practice 14: Grant a user Full Control using NTFS file permissions. Create a share, and grant that same user only Read access at a share level. Experiment with that user's ability to write files to the shared folder when accessing across the network. Do that user's rights differ when accessing the same folder when logged on locally?

- Practice 15: Stop the Workstation service and attempt to connect to a shared folder. Next, stop the Server service and attempt to create a shared folder.

- **Implementing and administering Windows XP printing.**

  - Practice 1: Add and share a new printer using the Add Printers Wizard.

  - Practice 2: Stop the Workstation service and attempt to connect to a shared printer. Next, stop the Server service and attempt to create a shared printer.

  - Practice 3: Remove the default right of the Power Users group to manage a printer.

  - Practice 4: Print to a shared printer and immediately remove the document using the Printers window.

  - Practice 5: Connect to a shared printer using a URL. Print a document, and use a browser to remove the document before it has completed printing.

- **Configuring offline files.**

  - Practice 1: Disable simple folder sharing—this is required for all following exercises.

  - Practice 2: Create a shared folder and enable automatic caching of documents.

  - Practice 3: Connect to a folder shared from a Windows XP system and pin individual documents to ensure synchronization.

  - Practice 4: Change the default synchronization behavior so that files are synchronized nightly instead of when users log on and log off.

  - Practice 5: Create a shared folder and configure it for automatic caching of programs. Connect to this share from a client system and pin files for synchronization. Disconnect from the network and modify the synchronized files. Reconnect to the network and attempt to synchronize the modified files to the shared folder.

- **Installing, configuring, and using the Windows XP Fax Service.**

    - Practice 1: Verify that the Fax Service and a Fax Printer are installed on a computer that has a fax-capable device installed.

    - Practice 2: Run the Fax Configuration Wizard by launching the Fax Console for the first time. The Fax Console is located in the All Programs\Accessories\ Communications\Fax folder. Complete the wizard by typing appropriate information.

    - Practice 3: Select Printers And Faxes from the Start menu and then right-click the fax device and select properties from the shortcut menu that appears. Select the Devices tab, and then click the Properties button to open the Device Information for the fax hardware device. Select the Receive tab from the dialog box that appears and verify that Enable Receive is enabled. Configure the receive options, close all the dialog boxes by clicking the OK buttons, and test your configuration by sending a fax from a different fax device.

    - Practice 4: Run the Fax Console from the Start menu; it is located in the All Programs\Accessories\Communications\Fax folder. Select Personal Cover Pages from the Tools menu and select the New button from the Personal Cover Pages dialog box to launch the Fax Cover Page Editor. Create a new cover sheet and save it.

    - Practice 5: Use the Fax Console to send a new fax to a different fax device. Verify that both the cover sheet and selected document arrive at the targeted fax device.

Further Reading

This section lists supplemental readings by objective. We recommend that you study these sources thoroughly before taking exam 70-270.

Objective 2.1

Microsoft Corporation. *MCSE Training Kit: Microsoft Windows XP Professional.* Redmond, Washington: Microsoft Press, 2001. Read and complete Lessons 1, 2, and 3 in Chapter 8, "Securing Resources with NTFS Permissions," and Lessons 1 and 4 in Chapter 14, "Managing Data Storage."

Microsoft Corporation. *Microsoft Windows XP Professional Resource Kit Documentation.* Redmond, Washington: Microsoft Press, 2001. Read Chapter 16, "Authorization and Access Control." This chapter provides an overview of file security concepts such as discretionary access control lists.

Objective 2.2

Microsoft Corporation. *MCSE Training Kit: Microsoft Windows XP Professional.* Redmond, Washington: Microsoft Press, 2001. Read and complete Lessons 1, 2, and 3 in Chapter 9, "Administering Shared Folders," and Lessons 1 and 2 in Chapter 15, "Monitoring, Managing, and Maintaining Network Resources."

Objective 2.3

Microsoft Corporation. *MCSE Training Kit: Microsoft Windows XP Professional.* Redmond, Washington: Microsoft Press, 2001. Read and complete Lessons 1 through 5 in Chapter 6, "Setting Up, Configuring, and Troubleshooting Common Setup and Configuration Problems for Network Printers," and Lessons 1 through 5 in Chapter 7, "Administering and Troubleshooting Common Administrative Problems for Network Printers."

Microsoft Corporation. *Microsoft Windows XP Professional Resource Kit Documentation.* Redmond, Washington: Microsoft Press, 2001. Read Chapter 11, "Enabling Printing and Faxing." This chapter provides detailed information about managing printers both locally and across a network.

Objective 2.4

Microsoft Corporation. *MCSE Training Kit: Microsoft Windows XP Professional.* Redmond, Washington: Microsoft Press, 2001. Read and complete Lesson 2 in Chapter 14, "Managing Data Storage."

Objective 2.5

Microsoft Corporation. *Microsoft Windows XP Professional Resource Kit Documentation.* Redmond, Washington: Microsoft Press, 2001. Read Chapter 5, "Managing Desktops," Chapter 6, "Managing Files and Folders," and Chapter 7, "Supporting Mobile Users." Pay particular attention to the sections that explain offline file synchronization and the suite of IntelliMirror technologies.

Objective 2.6

Microsoft Corporation. *Microsoft Windows XP Professional Resource Kit Documentation.* Redmond, Washington: Microsoft Press, 2001. Read Chapter 11, "Enabling Printing and Faxing." Focus on the section entitled "Faxing in Windows XP Professional," which explains how to install and configure Fax services in Windows XP Professional.

Select Help from the Fax Console and the Fax Cover Page Editor. Read all the articles available in each of these Help files.

O B J E C T I V E   2 . 1

Monitor, manage, and troubleshoot access to files and folders.

You never have enough disk space. This truth has been the driving factor behind the popularity of file compression in computer systems since they first had storage systems. Though file compression is nothing new to computer users, it has never been as simple and straightforward to use as with Windows XP. Users no longer need to access a third-party compression utility to reduce disk space utilization, because Windows XP integrates compression into **NTFS**.

Windows XP Professional administrators must understand the details behind NTFS compression precisely because it is so easy to use. As the feature increases in popularity, so will the number of users experiencing problems. Although any user can compress a folder using Microsoft Windows Explorer, only the system administrators will be able to explain exactly how compressed folders affect system performance and available disk space.

Though Windows Explorer provides the most user-friendly interface into the details of compression, the COMPACT.EXE utility is useful to administrators who need to compress multiple folders on a system, or compress folders on many different systems. COMPACT.EXE is a command-line utility designed to be included in batch files. Execute the command COMPACT.EXE /? to understand how COMPACT.EXE is used.

NTFS file compression does not obey the same rules of inheritance as other aspects of Windows XP. For example, files that are copied always inherit the compression state of the destination folder. However, if you move files within a single volume, the compression state of the file is retained. To make things more confusing, files moved between different volumes inherit the compression state of the destination folder.

Windows XP provides for file compression on **FAT** drives, also. When a user creates a compressed folder, Windows XP actually creates a **ZIP archive**. This archive can be accessed similar to standard folders; however, it is stored as a single compressed file.

Different types of files benefit differently from compression. The most compressible files have a great deal of repeated information within the file. For example, a bitmap image may have large field of white in the background. File compression can drastically reduce the size of this file by reducing the amount of duplicate information used to describe that white field. Similarly, Internet Information Services (IIS) log files consume less than half their normal disk space when compressed, because the entire file is text and many lines contain almost identical information.

Windows XP Professional includes the ability to restrict users' access to files and folders using NTFS file permissions. For example, a user that has Full Control permission to a file may alter other users' rights to that file by modifying the **discretionary access control list (DACL)**. The DACL is a list of **access control entries (ACEs)** that define rights assigned to users and groups. An ACE, for example, can explicitly grant members of the Power Users group Change access to a folder. Similarly, an ACE can explicitly deny members of the Guests group access to a folder by assigning the No Access permission. These capabilities are only available on partitions formatted with NTFS, however.

Note If your Windows XP Professional system is not in a domain, Windows Explorer does not display NTFS file permissions by default. To enable the Security tab when viewing a file or folder's permissions, open the Control Panel and double-click Folder Options. On the View tab, scroll down past Advanced Settings, and clear the Use Simple File Sharing checkbox. The next time you open Windows Explorer and view a file or folders properties, the Security tab will be available.

Similar to the way COMPACT.EXE provides a command-line alternative to enabling compressing within Windows Explorer, CACLS.EXE provides a command-line method for modifying file permissions. These tools are primarily used to assign permissions within batch files, but also provide greater flexibility than the Windows Explorer interface. For example, CACLS.EXE allows you to add an ACE to a folder and its subfolders without replacing the entire access control list—a valuable tool for environments with complex file permissions.

Objective 2.1 Questions

70-270.02.01.001

You are moving files from the folder \OLD to the folder \NEW on the same volume. The \OLD folder is compressed using Windows XP NTFS compression, but the \NEW folder is not. What will the compression status of the files be once the move has completed?

A. The files are uncompressed.

B. The files are compressed.

C. An error is returned because the files cannot be moved until their compression status matches that of the destination folder.

D. The destination files are not compressed because Windows XP automatically changes the type of file transfer to copy instead of move to allow the transfer to complete.

70-270.02.01.002

You are copying files from the folder \OLD to the folder \NEW on the same volume. The \OLD folder is compressed using NTFS compression, but the \NEW folder is not. What will the compression status of the files be once the copy has completed?

A. The files are uncompressed.

B. The files will be compressed.

C. An error is returned because the files cannot be copied until their compression status matches that of the destination folder.

D. The destination files are not compressed because Windows XP automatically changes the type of file transfer to move instead of copy to allow the transfer to complete.

70-270.02.01.003

You need to copy a log file that is compressed using NTFS compression to another volume. The file size of the log file is 2 GB, however, it consumes only 50 MB of the file system because it is compressed. The destination volume has only 1 GB of available space, so you enable compression on the folder that will receive the log file. During the file transfer, you receive an error indicating that there is not enough space to complete the copy. Which is the most likely explanation?

A. Files copied between volumes are always written as uncompressed, regardless of the compression state of the source file or the destination folder.

B. Files copied between volumes are first written to the disk uncompressed. NTFS then compresses the file only if the destination folder is compressed.

C. Files copied between volumes inherit the compression state of the base volume, not the destination folder. Because the volume itself is not compressed, NTFS attempts to write the file uncompressed.

D. Compressed files must be written to unfragmented areas of the disk. Though the destination disk might have sufficient free space, the free space is fragmented and therefore unusable for compressed files.

70-270.02.01.004

You need to increase the free space on a Windows XP Professional system. Which of the following folders are good candidates for NTFS compression? (Choose two.)

A. The system folder

B. A folder of archived IIS log files

C. A folder containing active IIS log files

D. A folder containing bitmap images

E. The temp folder

70-270.02.01.005

You need to grant Read access to files in the \Presentations folder for members of the Marketing user group in your Windows 2000 Active Directory. There is one exception, however, and his name is Todd. Todd is a member of the Marketing group, but must not be allowed access to your presentations. Which of these procedures provide the desired effect?

A. Within the shared folder share permissions, grant Read access to the Marketing Read group. Using Windows Explorer, edit the NTFS file permissions and remove all existing ACEs. Grant Change access to the Everyone group. Assign the members of the Marketing group Read access, and remove the rights from the user Todd.

B. Within the folder share permissions, grant Everyone Full Control access. Using Windows Explorer, edit the NTFS file permissions and remove all existing ACEs. Assign the No Access permissions to the Marketing group. Assign Read access to all members of the Marketing group with the exception of the user Todd.

C. Within the folder share permissions, grant Marketing Read access. Using Windows Explorer, edit the NTFS file permissions and remove all existing ACEs. Assign the No Access permissions to the user Todd.

D. Within the folder share permissions, grant Everyone Full Control access. Using Windows Explorer, edit the NTFS file permissions and remove all existing ACEs. Grant Read access to the Marketing group. Deny Read access permission to the user Todd.

Objective 2.1 Answers

70-270.02.01.001

▶ **Correct Answers: B**

A. **Incorrect:** Files that are moved within a single volume do not inherit the compression properties of the destination folder. This might seem confusing unless you understand that files are not rewritten when they are moved within a volume; only the pointer to the file is changed.

B. **Correct:** When files are moved within a single volume, the compression status of the files does not change.

C. **Incorrect:** Windows XP Professional does allow files to be moved to a destination folder that has a different compression status. However, the compression status of the files does not change and does not inherit the status of the destination folder.

D. **Incorrect:** Although files that are copied *always* inherit the compression status of the destination folder, Windows XP Professional does not automatically change the type of file transfer from move to copy.

70-270.02.01.002

► **Correct Answers: A**

A. **Correct:** Files that are copied within a single volume always inherit the compression properties of the destination folder. This is in contrast to files that are moved within a single volume, which retain their compression status.

B. **Incorrect:** When files are copied either within a single volume or between volumes, the compression status of the files is inherited from the destination folder.

C. **Incorrect:** Windows XP Professional does allow files to be copied to a destination folder that has a different compression status. The files inherit the compression status of the destination folder.

D. **Incorrect:** Windows XP Professional has the capability to move and copy files between folders that have different compression settings. When files are copied, they always inherit the compression status of the destination folder.

70-270.02.01.003

► **Correct Answers: B**

A. **Incorrect:** Files copied between volumes inherit the compression property of the destination folder.

B. **Correct:** Compression cannot occur on a file until the entire file has been received. Therefore, the file is written to the destination volume uncompressed. NTFS automatically compresses the file after the file transfer has completed. However, because the file is initially written uncompressed regardless of the compression state of the destination folder, the destination volume must have enough free space to store the entire uncompressed file.

C. **Incorrect:** Files copied between volumes inherit the compression property of the destination folder, regardless of the compression status of the volume.

D. **Incorrect:** Compressed files are written in blocks to the disk and can be fragmented like any other file. In fact, using compressed files necessitates more frequent disk defragmentation because of the way NTFS compresses files.

70-270.02.01.004

► **Correct Answers: B and D**

A. **Incorrect:** NTFS compression negatively affects system performance, so you must avoid compressing files that are accessed frequently, such as system files.

B. **Correct:** Old log files are an excellent candidate for NTFS compression. Log files compress significantly, and because they are not being regularly accessed, the compression won't negatively affect system performance.

C. **Incorrect:** Windows XP Professional must perform processor-intensive calculations when writing to compressed files. These calculations can negatively affect system performance in situations where the processor is the performance bottleneck. Active IIS log files are written to regularly, making them a poor candidate for compression.

D. **Correct:** BMP files compress extremely well because of the large amount of redundant information within a file. Unless bitmap files are being accessed continuously, they make an excellent candidate for compression.

E. **Incorrect:** Many applications for Windows XP Professional use the temp folder continuously. The processor overhead associated with reading from and writing to compressed files can negatively affect system performance, so it is never advisable to compress the temp folder.

70-270.02.01.005

▶ **Correct Answers: D**

A. **Incorrect:** This method does not accomplish the desired effect. Though the user Todd does not have explicit access to the folder, he has Change permissions because of his implicit membership in the Everyone group. His effective privileges are Read, because of the restriction placed on the share.

B. **Incorrect:** This method does not accomplish the desired effect. The No Access ACE always over-writes all other ACEs. So, all members of the Marketing group are restricted from accessing the files because the No Access right was assigned to the Marketing user group.

C. **Incorrect:** This method does not accomplish the desired effect. The Marketing group has been assigned Read access to the folder share permissions, but this is not sufficient to enable members of that group to access files on the file system. For access to be granted to files accessed through a network share, a user must have access to both the share and the underlying file system. In this scenario, adding the Read right to the Marketing group within NTFS permissions accomplishes the desired effect.

D. **Correct:** This method accomplishes the desired effect. Members of the Marketing group have access to the shared folder through their implicit membership in the Everyone group. They have been explicitly assigned Read access to the folder at the NTFS level. Finally, Todd's access was removed by explicitly assigning Deny Read access rights. Assigning the Deny Read access right overrides the Read access that was granted to the Marketing group.

OBJECTIVE 2.2

Manage and troubleshoot access to shared folders.

Windows XP Professional is more than a desktop operating system; it is a peer-to-peer networking platform. Using Windows XP Professional, users can give other users access to files and printers across the network. Although this functionality has changed very little from Microsoft Windows 2000, the user interface is significantly different. The Windows Explorer interface has been optimized to allow nonexpert users to share files. Experts can still have full control over granular share permissions, caching, and simultaneous incoming connections when simple file sharing is disabled.

Share permissions are similar to file permissions when simple file sharing is disabled, but there are several key differences. First, share permissions can be defined regardless of the underlying file system. Whether you choose **FAT32** or **NTFS**, you can define an **access control list (ACL)** to grant or deny user access to the share. When users create a share using the Windows Explorer interface, a single **access control entry (ACE)** is created for the Everyone local group. If the user selects the Allow Network Users To Change My Files check box, the Everyone group receives Full Control permissions. Otherwise, Everyone is assigned only Read access.

By default, Windows XP Professional creates a **hidden share** at the root of every drive. For example, the root folder of the C:\ drive is automatically shared as C$. The fact that the share name ends in a dollar ($) sign indicates that it does not appear when users browse the network from within My Network Places. To connect to a hidden share, a user must explicitly type the name of the share in the Map Network Drive dialog box, and must have an Administrator privilege to connect to a default hidden share such as C$. Although hidden shares reduce the chances of other users discovering your shared files, it must not be relied on as a security mechanism.

Tip You can view which users are connected to a share and which files they have open using the Shared Folders MMC snap-in. This snap-in is available in the Computer Management administrative utility, located underneath the Administrative Tools branch.

Sharing files and printers between Windows XP Professional systems is critical in many environments; however, in some environments it is a waste of resources and might even present a potential security vulnerability. For this reason, it is often desirable to disable file and printer sharing. The most complete way to do this is to stop and disable the Server service. Windows XP Professional relies on the Server service to accept incoming connections from other computers.

Besides traditional file sharing, Windows XP Professional users also have the option of creating **Web shares**. Users access Web shares in the same way as folder shares, or they can be accessed with a browser such as Microsoft Internet Explorer to present a more interactive Web interface. Web shares rely on the **World Wide Web Publishing service** instead of the Server service. The World Wide Web Publishing service is part of IIS, which is not installed during a standard Windows XP Professional installation.

Creating Web shares can be accomplished using the Windows Explorer interface, viewing the folder properties, and selecting the Web Sharing tab. This is where the similarities with traditional folder sharing end. Individual Web shares can be managed from Windows Explorer, but more detailed control of configuration must be done from the Internet Services Manager administrative tool or the IIS node under the Services And Applications branch of the Computer Management tool.

Objective 2.2 Questions

70-270.02.02.001

Which Windows XP Professional built-in user groups have permissions to create shared folders? (Choose two.)

A. Administrators

B. Network Configuration Operators

C. Backup Operators

D. Power Users

E. Users

70-270.02.02.002

You need to create a shared folder on your Windows XP Professional system, but you do not want users browsing the network to see the share. How do you name a share to ensure that it is not visible to users through My Network Places?

A. PRIVATE#

B. $PRIVATE

C. #PRIVATE

D. PRIVATE$

70-270.02.02.003

You are a domain administrator of your company's Windows 2000 Active Directory. You want to create a shared folder to allow one of your coworkers to view files on your Windows XP Professional system. You create an Active Directory user account named EricaE, and grant it Change permissions to your \Presentations folder using Windows Explorer. You then share the folder as Presentations, remove all default share permissions, and assign the EricaE user account Read permissions. What are EricaE's effective permissions when connecting to the share across the network?

A. No Access

B. Read

C. Change

D. Full Control

70-270.02.02.004

What is the maximum number of users that may connect to a single folder shared on a Windows XP Professional system?

A. 1

B. 5

C. 10

D. 20

Objective 2.2 Answers

70-270.02.02.001

▶ **Correct Answers: A and D**

A. **Correct:** Administrators, by default, can create shares on Windows XP Professional systems. Select the Computer Administrator account type to place a user only into the Administrators group when using the User Accounts Wizard. Grant this privilege only to users who understand the security implications associated with sharing folders across a network.

B. **Incorrect:** The Network Configuration Operators group provides a member user with the ability to modify network parameters such as IP address. However, it does not provide the ability to share folders.

C. **Incorrect:** Although Backup Operators can access the entire file system for the purpose of backing up files, they do not have the ability to share folders.

D. **Correct:** Power Users, by default, can create shares on Windows XP Professional systems. User accounts cannot be placed in the Power Users group directly from the Control Panel, however. To place a user account into the Power Users group, use the Computer Management administrative utility. Grant Power Users privilege only to users who understand the security implications associated with sharing folders across a network.

E. **Incorrect:** One of the differences between the Power Users and the Users groups is that the Users group lacks the ability to create shared folders. Creating a shared folder provides access to the contents of that folder across the network, and as a result, can weaken the security of a system if misused. Therefore, place users who do not understand the implications of shared folders only into the Users group. Select the Limited account type to place a user only into the Users group when using the User Accounts Wizard.

70-270.02.02.002

▶ **Correct Answers: D**

A. **Incorrect:** This answer is incorrect for the reasons stated in answer D.

B. **Incorrect:** This answer is incorrect for the reasons stated in answer D.

C. **Incorrect:** This answer is incorrect for the reasons stated in answer D.

D. **Correct:** Hidden shares are created by ending the share name with a $.

70-270.02.02.003

▶ **Correct Answers: B**

A. **Incorrect:** Users have No Access rights to the share only if they are explicitly assigned No Access or if they, or any group they belong to, are not named in the ACL. In this case, the user has been assigned Change file permissions and Read share permissions.

B. **Correct:** Share permissions override file permissions when the user accesses files across the network. Windows XP Professional restricts EricaE's access to read-only because that user has only Read share permissions. If EricaE were to log on locally to the system, she would be able to modify files because Change permissions are assigned at an NTFS level. In other words, when users access files using a network share, only the most restrictive permissions are granted.

C. **Incorrect:** Though EricaE has Change permissions at the NTFS level, the Read share permissions take precedence. This is because Windows XP Professional uses the most restrictive permissions when comparing access at both the share-level and file-level.

D. **Incorrect:** The user EricaE has Full Control permissions to the files in the shared folder only if the user had been explicitly granted Full Control permission in both the file ACL and the share ACL.

70-270.02.02.004

▶ **Correct Answers: C**

A. **Incorrect:** A maximum of 10 users may connect to a folder shared on a Windows XP Professional system.

B. **Incorrect:** A maximum of 10 users may connect to a folder shared on a Windows XP Professional system.

C. **Correct:** Only 10 users may simultaneously connect to a folder shared on a Windows XP Professional system. You need to use a member of the Microsoft Windows .NET Server family to provide access to more than 10 users simultaneously.

D. **Incorrect:** A maximum of 10 users may connect to a folder shared on a Windows XP Professional system.

OBJECTIVE 2.3

Connect to local and network print devices.

Windows XP Professional allows users on the network to access a printer attached to a remote system. This enables printers that cannot be directly attached to the network to be shared between multiple networked users. Sharing a printer is similar to sharing a folder: right-click the printer from within Printers And Faxes, select Sharing, and provide a share name.

Another similarity to file sharing is the ability to share a printer using Web protocols. When IIS is installed, users can print to a printer using **Hypertext Transfer Protocol (HTTP)**. HTTP is the most common protocol on the Internet, and allows users to access printers across firewalls and proxy servers. Installing IIS on a Windows XP Professional system with a shared printer also allows users to view the printer status using a Web browser. By default, printer status can be viewed by typing the URL *http:// server/printers* into a browser.

Controlling access to a shared printer is very different from controlling the security applied to file share. When Simple File Sharing is disabled, printer access is controlled through the printer's Properties dialog box by selecting the Security tab. The permissions that can be assigned to users differ, too. The primary rights available are Print, Manage Printers, and Manage Documents. By default, Everyone is allowed to print, and only Power Users and Administrators are granted access to manage documents and printers.

Connecting to remote printers is handled through the Add Printer Wizard—the same interface used to set up a directly connected printer. Users have the option of selecting the printer by browsing the network, typing a Universal Naming Convention (UNC) name in the form \\server\printer, or typing a URL in the form *http://server/printers/ printer/.printer*.

Objective 2.3 Questions

70-270.02.03.001

Which services must be running to connect to and print to network printers? (Choose two.)

A. Computer Browser

B. Net Logon

C. Network Connections

D. Print Spooler

E. Server

F. Workstation

70-270.02.03.002

Which services must be running to share a printer on a network and allow network users to print? (Choose two.)

A. Computer Browser

B. Net Logon

C. Network Connections

D. Print Spooler

E. Server

F. Workstation

Objective 2.3 Answers

70-270.02.03.001

▶ **Correct Answers: D and F**

   A. **Incorrect:** Though the Computer Browser service helps users find printers on a network, it isn't required to explicitly connect to shared network printers.

   B. **Incorrect:** The Net Logon service is used for pass-through authentication for computers in a domain, but is not required to connect to shared network printers.

C. **Incorrect:** The Network Connections services is used to manage objects in the Network and Dial-Up Connections folder, and does not need to be running to connect to shared network printers.

D. **Correct:** The Print Spooler service is responsible for receiving files from applications and forwarding them to printers. Any time a user needs to print from a Windows XP Professional system, the Printer Spooler service must be running—including printing to a network printer.

E. **Incorrect:** The Server service is required only on the system hosting the shared printer. Windows XP Professional systems connecting to the shared printer across the network do not need to have the Server service running.

F. **Correct:** The Workstation service is responsible for establishing connections to shared files and printers. Therefore, it is not required when printing to a local printer, but is required when printing to a shared network printer.

70-270.02.03.002

▶ ## Correct Answers: D and E

A. **Incorrect:** Though the Computer Browser service helps users find printers on a network, it isn't required to explicitly share printers.

B. **Incorrect:** The Net Logon service is used for pass-through authentication for computers in a domain but is not required to shared network printers. However, if the Net Logon service is not running, users must have an account on the Windows XP Professional system that is sharing the printer. For users authenticated using domain accounts, the Net Logon service is required because it enables pass-through authentication.

C. **Incorrect:** The Network Connections services is used to manage objects in the Network and Dial-Up Connections folder, and does not need to be running to share network printers.

D. **Correct:** The Print Spooler service is responsible for receiving files from applications and forwarding them to printers. Any time a user needs to print to a Windows XP Professional system, the Printer Spooler service must be running—including remote users printing to a shared printer.

E. **Correct:** The Server service is required on the system hosting the shared printer because it is responsible for receiving network connections from remote systems. The Server service interacts with the Workstation service, which acts as the client in the client-server relationship.

F. **Incorrect:** The Workstation service is responsible for establishing connections to shared files and printers. Although it is required for users connecting to a remote printer, it does not need to be running on the Windows XP Professional system sharing the printer.

OBJECTIVE 2.4

Configure and manage file systems.

Windows XP Professional supports both **basic disks** and **dynamic disks**. Basic disks are the only format available to Windows Me, Microsoft Windows NT 4, and earlier operating systems. If you need to access a disk from one of these operating systems, you have no choice but to use basic disks. Microsoft Windows 2000 and Windows XP support dynamic disks, which offer much greater flexibility for configuring volumes.

Dynamic disks support three different types of volumes: **simple volumes**, **spanned volumes**, and **striped volumes**. Simple volumes exist within a single disk. Spanned volumes concatenate multiple disks into a single volume. For example, a spanned volume can combine two 36 GB drives into a single 72 GB volume. Striped volumes are similar to spanned volumes in that they provide for combining multiple drives, however, striped volumes offer performance benefits when **Small Computer System Interface (SCSI)** drives are used because data is written to both disks simultaneously.

Volumes cannot be used until they have been formatted with a file system. Windows XP Professional supports a wide variety of file systems to allow access to the broadest range of media possible. Windows XP supports **FAT** and **NTFS** for accessing local disks. The FAT16 and FAT32 file systems allow for dual-booting with Microsoft Windows 95, Microsoft Windows 98, or Windows Me. NTFS is the preferred file system, however, and adds user-level file permissions, compression, encryption, disk quotas, volume mount points, directory junctions, and more.

Tip If you want to add disk space without creating a spanned volume, Windows XP Professional supports using mount points to graft a new volume into the folder structure of an existing volume.

Windows XP provides the ability to convert from FAT to NTFS for users upgrading from previous operating systems. The tool for converting file systems is the CONVERT.EXE command-line utility. Issue the command CONVERT.EXE /? to view parameters for this tool.

Although CONVERT.EXE is the only utility provided with Windows XP Professional that can be used to convert file systems, many other functions can be accessed either through the graphical Disk Management utility or command-line utilities. File system changes using command-line utilities are available to facilitate automated installation and administrative tasks. One of these command-line utilities is **DISKPART.EXE**— a tool available in previous versions of Windows only when accessing the Recovery Console. Executing the command DISKPART.EXE without any parameters provides access to a set of commands useful for managing volumes and partitions. To view a list of commands DISKPART.EXE provides access to, issue the command DISKPART.EXE to open the DISKPART.EXE shell. Then, at the DISKPART> prompt, issue the command HELP.

FSUTIL.EXE is a command-line utility useful for managing NTFS. Unlike DISKPART.EXE, FSUTIL.EXE does not start its own shell—FSUTIL.EXE is controlled using command-line parameters. For example, execute the command FSUTIL VOLUME DISMOUNT D: to dismount the D: volume from a command line. For a complete list of FSUTIL.EXE parameters, execute the command FSUTIL.EXE by itself at a command line.

Several additional file systems are available for accessing removable media. Floppy disks are formatted with FAT12, a version of FAT optimized for low-capacity media. The **CD-ROM File System (CDFS)** is the standard format for CD-ROMs. **Universal Disk Format (UDF)** is primarily used for **digital video disc (DVD)** access.

Objective 2.4 Questions

70-270.02.04.001

You are building a new Windows XP Professional system for a user in the imaging department of a publishing firm. Knowing that disk input/output (I/O) is critical for image editing, you decide to create a single volume striped across two SCSI disks. Which disk and volume type must you use?

A. Basic disks with spanned volumes

B. Basic disks with striped volumes

C. Dynamic disks with spanned volumes

D. Dynamic disks with striped volumes

70-270.02.04.002

You are installing both Windows Me and Windows XP Professional onto a system with a single 36 GB hard disk. You need to dual-boot between the two operating systems. Which file system must you use?

A. FAT

B. FAT32

C. CDFS

D. NTFS

70-270.02.04.003

On which operating systems can you create a RAID 5 volume? (Choose four.)

A. Windows Me

B. Microsoft Windows NT Workstation 4

C. Microsoft Windows NT Server 4

D. Microsoft Windows 2000 Professional

E. Microsoft Windows 2000 Server

F. Windows XP Professional

G. Windows .NET Server family

70-270.02.04.004

Which tools can be used to convert a disk from basic to dynamic? (Choose two.)

A. Disk Management snap-in

B. FSUTIL.EXE

C. FORMAT.EXE

D. DISKPART.EXE

E. Disk Defragmenter snap-in

Objective 2.4 Answers

70-270.02.04.001

▶ **Correct Answers: D**

A. **Incorrect:** Basic disks cannot support spanned volumes. Regardless, spanned volumes do not improve disk I/O because data on the disk is not generally written to or read from multiple disks simultaneously.

B. **Incorrect:** Although striped volumes are the correct choice for improving disk I/O when accessing multiple disks, basic disks cannot support striped volumes.

C. **Incorrect:** Although dynamic disks can support spanned volumes, spanned volumes do not improve disk I/O because data on the disk is not generally written to or read from multiple disks simultaneously.

D. **Correct:** Dynamic disks support striped volumes, while basic disks do not. Striped volumes combine multiple disks into a single logical volume. When files are written to or read from the volume, both disks are accessed simultaneously. When SCSI disks are used, this improves disk I/O performance.

70-270.02.04.002

▶ **Correct Answers: B**

A. **Incorrect:** Although both Windows Me and Windows XP Professional can access FAT partitions, FAT is not optimized for such large disk partitions.

B. **Correct:** Both Windows Me and Windows XP Professional can access FAT32 partitions, and FAT32 can efficiently address 36 GB hard disks. For these reasons, FAT32 is the best choice for dual-booting between Windows Me and Windows XP Professional.

C. **Incorrect:** CDFS is a file system used only for CD-ROMs. It is not an option for hard disk drives.

D. **Incorrect:** Although NTFS is an excellent choice for Windows XP Professional systems, NTFS partitions cannot be accessed from Windows Me.

70-270.02.04.003

▶ **Correct Answers: B, C, E, and G**

A. **Incorrect:** Windows Me cannot support RAID 5, nor any NTFS volume.

B. **Correct:** Windows NT Workstation 4 supports RAID 5 volumes across three or more disks using NTFS partitions. Windows NT Workstation 4 was the last desktop operating system from Microsoft to support RAID 5.

C. **Correct:** Windows NT Server 4 supports RAID 5 volumes across three or more disks using NTFS partitions.

D. **Incorrect:** Windows 2000 Professional supports NTFS, but does not support RAID 5 volumes.

E. **Correct:** Windows 2000 Server supports RAID 5 volumes across three or more disks using NTFS partitions.

F. **Incorrect:** Windows XP Professional supports NTFS, but does not support RAID 5 volumes.

G. **Correct:** The Windows .NET Server family supports RAID 5 volumes across three or more disks using NTFS partitions.

70-270.02.04.004

▶ **Correct Answers: A and D**

A. **Correct:** The Disk Management snap-in is the preferred way to upgrade a disk from basic to dynamic. To do this, open the Disk Management snap-in or launch the Computer Management tool and select Disk Management. Right-click the disk to be upgraded, and select Convert To Dynamic Disk. Complete the process by following the instructions that appear.

B. **Incorrect:** FSUTIL.EXE is useful for modifying aspects of the file system, but it cannot be used to modify disk properties.

C. **Incorrect:** The FORMAT.EXE utility is used to add a file system to a disk that has already been configured. It cannot be used to change properties of a disk, such as whether the disk is basic or dynamic.

D. **Correct:** DISKPART.EXE provides command-line access to functionality normally accessed using the Disk Management snap-in. To upgrade disk 0 from basic to dynamic, you must first open the DISKPART.EXE shell by executing the command DISKPART.EXE. At the DISKPART> prompt, type the command SELECT DISK 0 to indicate that future disk-related commands will affect disk 0. Then, type the command CONVERT DYNAMIC to convert the disk from basic to dynamic.

E. **Incorrect:** The Disk Defragmenter utility is used to reorganize files segments on a disk to improve performance. It does not have the ability to upgrade disks from basic to dynamic.

O B J E C T I V E   2 . 5

Manage and troubleshoot access to and synchronization of offline files.

Enterprise workers rely on the network to access information and exchange files. Users who always work from the office take this access for granted—but roaming users cannot. When a user with a portable computer disconnects from the network, their access to business critical information is also disconnected. To ease the pain of separation, Windows XP includes the ability to **synchronize** files for offline use.

Synchronizing files requires the cooperation of both the client and the server. The server must be configured to share the folder on the network, and must be configured to support one of three types of **caching**. Caching type can only be controlled when simple file sharing is disabled. The **Manual Caching Of Documents** setting is enabled by default and allows the client connecting to the shared folder to determine which files and folders will be synchronized. The **Automatic Caching Of Documents** setting behaves slightly differently; when a client accesses a file, the client attempts to cache that file locally. This method has the advantage of not requiring the end user to specify which files are synchronized. However, only those files that have been recently accessed will be available. The **Automatic Caching Of Programs And Documents** setting is very similar to the Automatic Caching Of Documents setting, except that the client does not attempt to update the files in the shared folder if they have been modified offline.

Users control when their computer synchronizes files using the **Synchronization Manager**. The synchronization manager is available by selecting the Start button, navigating to the All Programs\Accessories folder, and selecting Synchronize. This utility is useful for troubleshooting offline file problems because it displays when folders were last synchronized. It can also be used to configure offline files for synchronization when users log on or log off, while the computer is idle, or at specific times.

Offline files, also known as **Client Side Cache (CSC)**, are encrypted by default. This was not possible with previous versions of Windows. As a result, an unauthorized user could access confidential files normally secured by a file server directly from a portable computer.

Objective 2.5 Questions

70-270.02.05.001

What caching options are selected by default for folders shared from a Windows XP Professional system?

A. Caching on shared folders is disabled by default.

B. Manual Caching Of Documents is selected by default.

C. Automatic Caching Of Documents is selected by default.

D. Automatic Caching Of Programs And Documents is selected by default.

70-270.02.05.002

You have configured a shared network folder for offline use with your Windows XP Professional system. While you were disconnected from the network, you edited one of the synchronized files. At the same time, another user modified the network copy of this document. What happens when you reconnect your system to the network?

A. The copy of the document on the network share is automatically overwritten with your cached copy.

B. Changes you made to the cached document are automatically merged into the shared networked document.

C. Windows XP Professional prompts you to choose which version to keep, and allows you to rename one of the copies of the document.

D. The copy of the document that was modified most recently is kept. Changes to the older version of the document are discarded.

70-270.02.05.003

The vice president of marketing at your organization uses a Windows XP Professional laptop computer. While traveling, she needs to update a set of presentations located on a shared network folder. She will intermittently dial into your corporate network, but also plans to make updates while offline. Which synchronization strategy meets her needs?

A. Disable simple file sharing. Enable Automatic Caching Of Documents by clicking the Caching button on the server's shared folder properties. From the Items To Synchronize settings, select When I Log On To My Computer and When I Log Off My Computer for automatic synchronization for both her local area network (LAN) and dial-up connections.

B. Disable simple file sharing. Enable Automatic Caching Of Programs And Documents by clicking the Caching button on the server's shared folder properties. From the Synchronization Manager settings, select When I Log On To My Computer and When I Log Off My Computer for automatic synchronization for both her LAN and dial-up connections.

C. Disable simple file sharing. Enable Manual Caching Of Documents by clicking the Caching button on the server's shared folder properties. From Microsoft Windows Explorer, right-click the files and select Make Available Offline to pin the files that she needs to access offline. From Items To Synchronize settings, select When I Log On To My Computer and When I Log Off My Computer for automatic synchronization for both her LAN and dial-up connections.

D. Disable simple file sharing. Enable Manual Caching Of Documents by clicking the Caching button on the server's shared folder properties. From Windows Explorer, right-click the files and select Make Available Offline to pin the files that she needs to access offline. From the Items To Synchronize settings, deselect When I Log On To My Computer and When I Log Off My Computer for automatic synchronization for both her LAN and dial-up connections. Instead, select the Synchronize The Selected Items While My Computer Is Idle checkbox.

Objective 2.5 Answers

70-270.02.05.001

▶ **Correct Answers: B**

A. **Incorrect:** Caching is enabled by default for folders shared from Windows XP Professional systems.

B. **Correct:** By default, shared folders on a Windows XP Professional system have manual caching for documents enabled. Users connecting to the share must then specifically mark files as being available offline for the caching to be effective—no files are automatically cached with this setting.

C. **Incorrect:** The Automatic Caching Of Documents setting on a shared folder causes the client system to cache documents in the folder after they have been accessed. Older and less frequently accessed cached documents are automatically removed to save space on the connecting user's hard disk. This option is not enabled by default.

D. **Incorrect:** The Automatic Caching Of Programs And Documents setting on a shared folder is similar to the Automatic Caching Of Documents setting, but it does not allow files on the shared folder to be overwritten. This setting enables caching for read-only documents and applications, and ensures changes made to a document offline are not synchronized back to the shared folder. This option is not enabled by default.

70-270.02.05.002

▶ **Correct Answers: C**

A. **Incorrect:** Windows XP never automatically overwrites a document that has been updated since synchronization, even if changes were made to a cached version of the document.

B. **Incorrect:** Windows XP lacks the capability to merge changes. However, you can manually merge changes between multiple versions of documents.

C. **Correct:** Windows XP Professional provides the user with the option of overwriting one version of the document. Avoid this, however, because changes to the discarded document are lost. Instead, choose the option of renaming one of the documents and manually merge the document's changes.

D. **Incorrect:** Windows XP never automatically overwrites a document that has been updated since synchronization.

70-270.02.05.003

▶ **Correct Answers: C**

A. **Incorrect:** The automatic caching of documents setting meets the user's needs, but this synchronization strategy does not include pinning the files for offline use. Pinning files ensures they are always synchronized. With this strategy, files are available offline only when the user accessed those files prior to disconnecting from the network.

B. **Incorrect:** The Automatic Caching Of Programs And Documents setting does not meet the user's needs because this is a read-only caching strategy. Files accessed through this type of shared folder cannot be edited offline and automatically synchronized the next time the user connects.

C. **Correct:** This synchronization strategy meets the user's needs. When manual caching is enabled on a folder, the user must pin files for them to be synchronized. Manual caching is enabled on shared folders by default, and Items To Synchronize is configured to synchronize files when users log on and log off by default.

D. **Incorrect:** The manual caching of documents setting meets the user's needs, except that the synchronization strategy was changed to happen when the computer was idle. This setting must not be used with users who are intermittently connected to the network, because the computer is unlikely to be both connected and idle.

OBJECTIVE 2.6

Configure and troubleshoot fax support.

Windows XP Professional includes software for sending and receiving fax documents through compatible fax modems attached to your computer. While drivers are installed automatically for most modems, you must manually install the **Fax Service** included with Windows XP Professional. To do so,

1. Open the Add Or Remove Programs program in Control Panel.

2. Click Add/Remove Windows Components.

3. Select the Fax Services checkbox. Click Next, and then click Finish.

After the Fax Service is installed, a new printer called Fax appears on the list of installed printers. To configure Fax Service options,

1. From the Start menu, point to All Programs\Accessories\Communications\Fax, and then click Fax Console.

2. Provide information to the Fax Configuration Wizard as requested. When you have completed the form, the Fax Console will launch.

3. In the Fax Console, click Tools, and then click Fax Printer Configuration.

4. Set your preferences here such as archiving, notification, retries, and automatic cleanup of unsent faxes.

There are several other tools in the Fax program group:

- *Fax Configuration Wizard*   This wizard configures user information, Transmission Station Identifier (TSID), and fax devices for sending and receiving faxes. It launches automatically the first time you try to send a fax if you have not already provided this information.

- *Fax Cover Page Editor*   This tool creates, edits, and deletes fax cover pages.

Existing applications can take advantage of the Fax Service simply by sending a print job to the Fax Printer. When you send a print job to the Fax Printer, the Send Fax Wizard is launched. The wizard prompts you for details of where and when to send the fax, whether to include a cover sheet, and whether to provide notification of a successful or failed transmission. The fax job is then queued by the Fax Service for transmission.

Note The Fax Printer cannot be shared with other users on the network.

The Windows XP Professional Fax Monitor watches for incoming fax documents. When an incoming fax transmission is answered, the Fax Monitor stores the document as a Tagged Image File (.tif). The image file can be saved to a folder, sent via e-mail to a configured e-mail profile, or sent to a printing device. Any combination of these three options is possible, but the default is to save the image file to the Received Faxes folder. To route faxes to a network printer, the Fax Service must be configured with a logon account with the necessary rights to access that printer. To forward faxes to an e-mail profile, the Fax Service must be configured with a logon account with sufficient privileges to access the user's e-mail profile. By default, the Fax Service is configured with the Local System account, which does not have access to either network printing or local e-mail profiles.

Objective 2.6 Questions

70-270.02.06.001

A user has been successfully sending and receiving fax documents by using the Fax Service included with Windows XP Professional. The user is frustrated that incoming fax documents are stored as .tif files and wants to be able to edit the documents using WordPad without having to manually retype them. What do you do to allow the user to save fax documents in a format editable by WordPad?

A. Configure Fax Monitor to save incoming fax documents as Rich Text Format (.rtf) documents instead of .tif files.

B. Use the Windows Picture and Fax Viewer to scan each .tif file for text and then save them as .rtf files.

C. Configure Fax Monitor to save incoming fax documents as Unicode Text Documents instead of .tif files.

D. Explain to the user that this is not possible with the features built into Windows XP Professional and the Fax Service.

70-270.02.06.002

You want to send and receive fax documents on your computer. You have just finished installing Windows XP Professional on a new computer. All the components in the system including the fax modem are on the HCL. What do you do?

A. Open the Printers And Other Hardware program in Control Panel and double-click Add New Printer to install a new fax printer that sends print jobs to the fax modem.

B. Use the Add Or Remove Programs program in Control Panel to install the Fax Service from the Windows XP Professional installation media.

C. Log on to the computer with an account that has administrative privileges and make sure that the account with user privileges that you normally use has permissions to submit and view documents to and from the Fax Service.

D. Do nothing because the fax modem should have been detected during the Windows XP Professional setup routine. Appropriate drivers as well as the Fax Service should have been installed automatically.

70-270.02.06.003

You are an independent computer consultant who has recently completed installing Windows XP Professional on all the employees' computers at a small real estate firm. You noticed that one of the agents has a fax-capable modem installed in her computer so you installed and configured the Fax Service. A few days later the agent asks you to return and configure the fax modem so that other users can send fax documents over the network. What do you do?

A. Open the Fax Console to configure permissions to the Fax Service so that network users can access it.

B. From the Start menu, point to All Programs\Accessories\Communications\Fax, and then click Fax Console. From the Fax Console, click Tools and then click Fax Printer Configuration to enable network access to the Fax Service.

C. Explain to the agent that it is not possible to share fax devices across networks with Windows XP Professional.

D. Select Printers And Faxes from the Start menu, right-click the fax device and then select properties from the context menu that appears and enable sharing of the device. If you do not see the Sharing tab in the fax device's properties dialog box, you must uninstall and then reinstall the Fax Service because the original installation has failed.

70-270.02.06.004

You install a new fax modem in your Windows XP Professional computer. You then install and configure the Fax Service so that you can send and receive fax documents locally. You want to have incoming faxes automatically printed but your computer does not have a printer directly attached to it. Your computer belongs to your organization's Active Directory domain and you are able to print other documents on the network printer down the hall from your office. How do you configure the Fax Service so that incoming fax documents are automatically printed on the network printer?

A. Change the logon account for the Fax Service to an account that has permissions to send print jobs to the printer and has sufficient rights to log on to your computer and run the Fax Service. Use the Fax Console to configure the Fax Service to automatically print received faxes to the network printer.

B. Configure the shared network printer to allow anonymous access to creating and managing print jobs. Use the Fax Console to configure the Fax Service to automatically print received faxes to the network printer.

C. Configure the shared network printer to allow the local System account on your computer to create and manage print jobs. Use the Fax Console to configure the Fax Service to automatically print received faxes to the network printer.

D. Because the Fax Service is a local system service rather than a network service, it is impossible to configure it to automatically forward incoming fax documents to a network printer. Use the Fax Console to configure the Fax Service to automatically print received faxes to the network printer.

Objective 2.6 Answers

70-270.02.06.001

▶ **Correct Answers: D**

A. **Incorrect:** Fax Monitor can save fax documents only as .tif files; it does not have the ability to translate text within the image file into other formats.

B. **Incorrect:** The Windows Picture and Fax Viewer program can be used to view and edit .tif files but it does not include any optical character recognition (OCR) features.

C. **Incorrect:** Fax Monitor can save fax documents only as .tif files as explained in answer A.

D. **Correct:** The Fax Service can save fax documents only as image files—this is known and expected behavior. One possible solution is to install OCR software from a third-party vendor to scan for text in the image files.

70-270.02.06.002

▶ **Correct Answers: B**

A. **Incorrect:** You are not able to add any printers that point to a fax-capable device until after you manually install the Fax Service as described in answer B. Normally, you won't have to manually add a printer that points to the fax-capable device because the setup routine for the Fax Service automatically creates a new printer called Fax that sends print jobs to the fax-capable device.

B. **Correct:** Although the Windows XP Professional setup routine normally detects fax-capable devices and installs the appropriate drivers, the Fax Service is not installed automatically. You must manually install the Fax Service unless you have created a custom unattended installation routine for Windows XP Professional that includes the Fax Service. This behavior is slightly different from Windows 2000 Professional's setup routine, which automatically installs the Fax Service during setup if a fax-capable device was detected.

C. **Incorrect:** You are not able to edit security for the Fax Service until after you have manually installed it as described in answer B.

D. **Incorrect:** Answer B explains why the Fax Service must be manually installed on Windows XP Professional.

70-270.02.06.003

▶ **Correct Answers: C**

A. **Incorrect:** As described in answer C, the Fax Service is not a sharable network service.

B. **Incorrect:** As described in answer C, the Fax Service is not a sharable network service.

C. **Correct:** The Fax Service is not a sharable network service; it is only available to locally logged-on users. The real estate agent in this scenario has to buy third-party fax server software. Fax server products usually require Windows 2000 Server or Windows 2000 Advanced Server, so you might want to suggest that the real estate firm install a fax modem on a file or print server to fulfill this need.

D. **Incorrect:** As described in answer C, the Fax Service is not a sharable network service.

70-270.02.06.004

▶ **Correct Answers: A**

A. **Correct:** By default, the Fax Service is configured to log on with the local System account—this account does not have any domain privileges and therefore cannot send jobs to the printer unless the shared printer is configured to allow anonymous connections. Allowing anonymous access to shared network resources is very insecure, therefore the better approach is to configure the Fax service to log on with a domain account. The account needs Read & Execute access to the program files used by the Fax service and Change access to the folders where fax documents are managed. A quick way to give a domain account sufficient access to the local file system is to add it to the local Power Users or Administrators group. That account also needs some additional user rights on your computer: the right to log on locally and the right to log on as a service.

B. **Incorrect:** As noted in answer A, this is an insecure approach to solving this need.

C. **Incorrect:** It is not possible to give local computer accounts on member computers privileges in the domain.

D. **Incorrect:** As noted in answer A, this scenario can be implemented.

Implementing, Managing, Monitoring, and Troubleshooting Hardware Devices and Drivers

Installing new hardware in a computer requires connecting it to the computer's bus and then installing the appropriate device driver so that it can interact with the operating system. After installation, it must be configured and managed. Management tasks differ between classes of devices. Consider a network card and a removable hard disk. A network card must have a suitable connection to the network and network software compatible with the other computers on that network. The network software must be configured with an accurate name and address and other protocol-specific information. A removable hard disk must be formatted and monitored for available storage space. Hardware that performs incorrectly or not at all requires troubleshooting. Effective troubleshooting combines determination, imagination, and technical knowledge of the system, subcomponents, and the way they interact.

Computer motherboards and many other hardware devices have **firmware** that contain code independent of the operating system needed for startup, **power-on self tests (POST)**, and initialization of the device. On x86-based computers such as Pentium IIIs and Pentium IVs this firmware is known as **basic input/output system (BIOS)**, while on Itanium-based computers it is called **Extensible Firmware Interface (EFI)**. If problems with setup or stability affect only a few Microsoft Windows XP Professional computers in your network, verify that the firmware on the motherboard and peripherals is up to date and configured properly.

Tested Skills and Suggested Practices

The skills that you need to successfully master the Installing Windows XP Professional objective domain on the *Installing, Configuring, and Administering Microsoft Windows XP Professional* exam include

- **Installing, upgrading, and configuring hardware devices.**

  - Practice 1: Install Plug and Play hardware such as a digital camera, scanner, and network card into an existing Windows XP Professional computer.

  - Practice 2: Install legacy hardware such as an Industry Standard Architecture (ISA)–based modem into an existing Windows XP Professional computer.

  - Practice 3: Replace an existing video adapter with an Accelerated Graphics Port (AGP) or Peripheral Component Interconnect (PCI) video card. Install a second video adapter and video monitor; configure the computer for multiple monitors.

  - Practice 4: Download updated drivers for each of the hardware devices you have been practicing with and install them. Try installing updated drivers from the Windows Update Web site; also check the manufacturer's Web site of the hardware device.

  - Practice 5: Install and configure a PC Card device, and then stop and eject it.

- **Installing, upgrading, and configuring Advanced Configuration Power Interface (ACPI) hardware.**

  - Practice 1: Check to see whether your computer is an ACPI system. Compare an ACPI-compatible with one that is not.

  - Practice 2: Review the various Power Schemes; create and test a custom Power Scheme.

  - Practice 3: Enable hibernation.

- **Troubleshooting hardware devices.**

  - Practice 1: Open Device Manager and inspect the properties of all the objects displayed there. Run the hardware troubleshooter for some of the devices by clicking the Troubleshoot button on the General tab of the device's Properties window.

  - Practice 2: Familiarize yourself with the other tools available for troubleshooting hardware such as DRIVERS.EXE, DXDIAG.EXE, WINMSD.EXE, SIGVERIF.EXE, VERIFIER.EXE, and DMDIAG.EXE.

- **Installing and monitoring multiple central processing units (CPUs).**

    - Practice 1: Install a second processor into an APIC-compatible computer. Use Device Manager to upgrade the hardware abstraction layer (HAL).

    - Practice 2: Run the Performance snap-in to view and analyze data relating to the CPUs.

Further Reading

This section lists supplemental readings by objective. We recommend that you study these sources thoroughly before taking exam 70-270.

Objective 3.1

Microsoft Corporation. *Microsoft Windows XP Professional Resource Kit Documentation*. Redmond, Washington: Microsoft Press, 2001. Read Chapter 12, "Disk Management." This chapter explains the various storage types and partition styles available in Windows XP Professional, the Disk Management snap-in, and the command-line utilities you can use to manage storage devices. Review Chapter 27, "Troubleshooting Disks and File Systems." This chapter outlines the troubleshooting tools available in Windows XP Professional, many common problems relating to disk devices, and how to correct them. Read Chapter 9, "Managing Devices," to learn about installing and configuring hardware devices.

Microsoft Corporation. *MCSE Training Kit: Microsoft Windows XP Professional*. Redmond, Washington: Microsoft Press, 2001. Read and complete Lesson 4 in Chapter 14, "Managing Data Storage." This lesson describes some of the tools used for managing storage devices in Windows XP Professional.

Objective 3.2

Microsoft Corporation. *Microsoft Windows XP Professional Resource Kit Documentation*. Redmond, Washington: Microsoft Press, 2001. Read Chapter 9, "Managing Devices," focusing on the sections about installing and configuring hardware and device drivers. Also read the sections called "Configuring the Display" and "Using Multiple Monitors." Review the list of error messages described in Appendix F, "Device Manager Error Codes."

Microsoft Corporation. *MCSE Training Kit: Microsoft Windows XP Professional*. Redmond, Washington: Microsoft Press, 2001. Read and complete Lesson 1 in Chapter 10, "Configuring Windows XP Professional." This lesson discusses configuring and troubleshooting the display subsystem. Read and complete Lessons 1 and 2 in Chapter 11, "Installing, Managing, and Troubleshooting Hardware Devices and Drivers" to learn about automatic and manual installation and troubleshooting of hardware in Windows XP Professional.

Objective 3.3

Microsoft Corporation. *Microsoft Windows XP Professional Resource Kit Documentation*. Redmond, Washington: Microsoft Press, 2001. Read Chapter 7, "Supporting Mobile Users," for a thorough look at all the challenges unique to managing mobile computers. Read Chapter 9, "Managing Devices" and review the section called "Power Management." Read Chapter 26, "Troubleshooting Concepts and Strategies." This chapter provides a generalized troubleshooting methodology, steps to take for gathering information, additional online and print resources for technical information, and step-by-step troubleshooting instructions for a variety of common issues.

Microsoft Corporation. *MCSE Training Kit*: *Microsoft Windows XP Professional*. Redmond, Washington: Microsoft Press, 2001. Read and complete Lesson 2 in Chapter 10, "Configuring Windows XP Professional." This lesson discusses Power Management.

Objective 3.4

Microsoft Corporation. *Microsoft Windows XP Professional Resource Kit Documentation*. Redmond, Washington: Microsoft Press, 2001. Read the sections called "Other Hardware Support" and "Hardware Troubleshooting" in Chapter 9, "Managing Devices." Read Chapter 10, "Managing Digital Media" and review the "Digital Media Components Overview" section to ensure that you understand what features Windows XP Professional includes for creating and managing digital media. Read the "Troubleshooting Digital Media" section to learn about solving a wide range of typical problems. Read Chapter 26, "Troubleshooting Concepts and Strategies." This chapter provides a generalized troubleshooting methodology, steps to take for gathering information, additional online and print resources for technical information, and step-by-step troubleshooting instructions for a variety of common issues.

Microsoft Corporation. *MCSE Training Kit*: *Microsoft Windows XP Professional*. Redmond, Washington: Microsoft Press, 2001. Read and complete Lessons 2 and 3 in Chapter 11, "Installing, Managing, and Troubleshooting Hardware Devices and Drivers." These lessons discuss the tasks relating to managing hardware devices in Windows XP Professional.

Objective 3.5

Microsoft Corporation. *Microsoft Windows XP Professional Resource Kit Documentation*. Redmond, Washington: Microsoft Press, 2001. Read Chapter 9, "Managing Devices," paying close attention to the sections titled "Device Drivers" and "Installing Drivers."

Microsoft Corporation. *MCSE Training Kit: Microsoft Windows XP Professional*. Redmond, Washington: Microsoft Press, 2001. Read and complete Lessons 3 and 4 in Chapter 11, "Implementing, Managing, and Troubleshooting Hardware Devices and Drivers." These lessons cover configuring and updating hardware and device driver software.

Objective 3.6

Microsoft Corporation. *Microsoft Windows XP Professional Resource Kit Documentation*. Redmond, Washington: Microsoft Press, 2001. Read Chapter 9, "Managing Devices," to learn about installing and configuring hardware devices. Read Chapter 26, "Troubleshooting Concepts and Strategies." Study the "Check Firmware Versions" section.

Microsoft Corporation. *MCSE Training Kit*: *Microsoft Windows XP Professional*. Redmond, Washington: Microsoft Press, 2001. Read and complete Lesson 5 in Chapter 11, "Installing, Managing, and Troubleshooting Hardware Devices and Drivers." This lesson explains how to configure computers with multiple CPUs.

Implement, manage, and troubleshoot disk devices.

Windows XP Professional supports a wide range of fixed and removable storage devices. Common fixed disk technologies include **Small Computer Systems Interface (SCSI)**, **Advanced Technology Attachment (ATA)** or **Advanced Technology Attachment Packet Interface (ATAPI)**, and **Intelligent Drive Electronics** or **Integrated Drive Electronics (IDE)** drives. **DVD**, floppy, **CD-ROM**, and tape drives are popular removable storage devices. Storage devices are physically connected to a suitable controller, which is attached to the computer's bus. As with other hardware devices, a software driver establishes and maintains communication between the storage hardware and Windows XP Professional.

After installation you use the Disk Management snap-in, by typing **diskmgmt.msc** at a command prompt, to convert storage types, create and extend volumes, and perform other disk management tasks. Windows XP Professional includes a command line tool, DISKPART.EXE, for creating and managing partitions and volumes from a command prompt or script. Typing **winmsd** at a command prompt opens the System Information tool, which contains detailed diagnostic data about installed hardware and software. This tool displays information about the physical and logical configuration of each storage device. The Event Logging Service, accessible through **eventvwr.msc**, records critical errors relating to hardware devices in the System and Application logs. To review, update drivers for, or troubleshoot storage media and controllers, you use Device Manager, by typing **devmgmt.msc** at command prompt. Use the Performance Logs And Alerts snap-in to monitor the use of system resources. You can monitor both physical and logical performance counters for storage devices; however, the default configuration of Windows XP enables only the physical counters. To enable or disable the physical or logical counters, use the DISKPERF.EXE tool. Type **diskperf /?** to view the options for this command line tool. Any changes made with diskperf take effect after the computer is rebooted.

Windows XP Professional supports two types of fixed disk storage: **basic disks** and **dynamic disks**. Basic disks are the traditional type of storage available in earlier versions of Windows. If you want to dual-boot Windows XP Professional with Microsoft Windows NT 4, Microsoft Windows Me, or earlier Windows operating systems, you must use basic disks. Microsoft Windows XP Home Edition is also unable to recognize dynamic disks. Basic disks divide physical disks into partitions, also known as **basic volumes**, with logical disks. Dynamic disks are divided into **dynamic volumes**. Dynamic disks support many advanced features such as volume spanning, volume extending, and unlimited volumes per disk. A command-line tool called DMDIAG.EXE is now available that displays the location and layout of dynamic disks and volumes. Microsoft Windows XP 64-Bit Edition supports a new partition style called **GUID partition table (GPT)**. GPT disks contain redundant partition tables for improved partition structure integrity.

Regularly backing up the operating system, applications, and data is an important task in managing computers. Windows XP Professional includes a full-featured backup utility, NTBACKUP.EXE, that can be run interactively through its graphical interface or from a command line or script. You can schedule backup jobs using the Schedule Jobs tab in the backup utility. Windows XP Professional introduces volume snapshots, a technology that allows you to back up all files on a volume, even those held open exclusively by another application. This backup tool also includes the Automated System Recovery (ASR) Wizard, a two-part recovery system that allows you to restore the operating system state from files backed up to tape and hard disk configuration information saved to a floppy disk.

Over time, the files on disks tend to become more and more fragmented. Windows XP Professional includes the Disk Defragmenter snap-in and a new command-line version of the tool called DEFRAG.EXE. Certain files are always excluded from being defragmented: BOOTSECT.DOS, SAFEBOOT.FS, SAFEBOOT.CSV, SAFEBOOT.RSV, HIBERFIL.SYS, MEMORY.DMP, and the paging file.

To successfully answer questions in this objective, you must be familiar with the common types of fixed and removable storage and how to install, manage, and troubleshoot each. You need to know how to use the tools included with Windows XP Professional for creating, managing, and modifying dynamic disks and basic disks. You must know how to enable and disable the different types of performance counters with DISKPERF.EXE and how to view performance data in the Performance Logs and Alerts snap-in. You must also know how to use the backup and defragmentation utilities included with Windows XP Professional and understand their unique limitations.

Objective 3.1 Questions

70-270.03.01.001

Which of the following multiboot scenarios results in each operating system listed being fully functional with access to at least one hard disk? (Choose two.)

A. Hard disk 1 configured as a basic disk with a single partition formatted as the NT File System (NTFS) with Windows XP Professional and Windows Me installed on it. Hard disk 2 configured as a basic disk with a single partition formatted as the 32-bit version of File Allocation Table (FAT32).

B. Hard disk 1 configured as a basic disk with a single partition formatted as FAT32 with Windows XP Professional and Windows Me installed on it. Hard disk 2 configured as a basic disk with a single partition formatted as NTFS.

C. Hard disk 1 configured as a dynamic disk with a single volume formatted as NTFS with Windows XP Professional installed on it. Hard disk 2 configured as a dynamic disk with a single volume formatted as NTFS with Microsoft Windows 2000 Professional installed on it.

D. Hard disk 1 configured as a dynamic disk with a single volume formatted as NTFS with Windows XP Professional and Windows 2000 Professional installed on it. Hard disk 2 configured as a basic disk with a single volume formatted as NTFS.

E. Hard disk 1 configured as a dynamic disk with a single partition formatted as NTFS with Windows XP Professional and Windows XP Home Edition installed on it. Hard disk 2 configured as a basic disk with a single partition formatted as FAT32.

70-270.03.01.002

Your company uses a flexible workspace approach to organizing office space. You are replacing 30 desktop computers for the telemarketing department. You want to ensure that no individual user can monopolize local storage on these new computers so you decide to apply disk quotas to them all. What file system supports disk quotas?

A. FAT

B. UDF

C. FAT32

D. NTFS

E. CDFS

70-270.03.01.003

You have a 700 MHz Pentium III computer with 256 megabytes of RAM running Windows 2000 Professional. You want to retain the existing operating system while installing Windows XP Professional. You successfully configure the computer for dual-booting and run a full backup using NTBACKUP.EXE. You also create a new Emergency Repair Disk (ERD) and manually edit the BOOT.INI file to change the order of the operating systems when you boot the computer. In doing so, you don't realize that you accidentally deleted the BOOT.INI file.

The next time you start the computer, you receive an error message and then it stops responding. What do you do to restore the computer to full functionality with the least amount of effort while retaining existing configuration settings?

A. Reinstall Windows 2000 Professional and all the applications, and then reinstall Windows XP Professional.

B. Use the Recovery Console to copy the BOOT.INI file from a Windows XP Professional installation CD-ROM.

C. Use the ERD to create a new BOOT.INI file.

D. Use the Recovery Console to copy the BOOT.INI file from a Windows 2000 Professional installation CD-ROM.

70-270.03.01.004

One of the graphics artists in your company's marketing department needs to access some multimedia files that were archived on an old removable storage device several years ago. You verify that the device is on the Windows XP Professional Hardware Compatibility List (HCL) and attach it to the artist's computer. You use the Add/Remove Hardware Wizard to install it but receive a message that Windows was unable to detect it. You choose to manually select it from the list of hardware in the Add/Remove Hardware Wizard but you cannot locate it.

What do you do to install it?

A. Click Have Disk on the Install New Hardware dialog box and specify the path to the driver files.

B. Change the Driver Signing File signature verification setting to Ignore.

C. Change the Driver Signing File signature verification setting to Block.

D. The device cannot be installed.

E. Reboot in Safe Mode and install the appropriate drivers.

Objective 3.1 Answers

70-270.03.01.001

▶ **Correct Answers: B and C**

A. **Incorrect:** Windows Me cannot read NTFS volumes, therefore formatting disk 1 as NTFS would make it impossible to run the operating system on that computer.

B. **Correct:** Both Windows Me and Windows XP Professional recognize partitions formatted with the FAT32 file system; therefore both operating systems can be installed onto disk 1 in this scenario. Although Windows XP Professional can read NTFS drives, Windows Me cannot. Therefore Windows Me does not recognize disk 2 in this scenario; however, the requirement was for each operating system to be able to recognize at least one disk, not necessarily both disks.

C. **Correct:** Both Windows XP Professional and Windows 2000 Professional support dynamic disks, but they store information about the disks in their Registry. If both operating systems are installed on the same disk and you use one to convert the disk to dynamic, the registry of the other operating system becomes out of date and it no longer boots. The proper method to use dynamic disks in a multiboot configuration with these operating systems is to install them on separate disks. For example, install Windows XP Professional on disk 1 and Windows 2000 Professional on disk 2. Use Windows XP Professional to convert disk 1 to dynamic, and then use Windows 2000 Professional to convert disk 2 to dynamic.

D. **Incorrect:** Although both Windows XP Professional and Windows 2000 Professional support dynamic disks, they store information about the disks in their Registry. If both operating systems are installed on the same disk and you use one to convert the disk to dynamic, the Registry of the other operating system becomes out of date and it no longer boots.

E. **Incorrect:** Windows XP Home Edition does not recognize dynamic disks and therefore it cannot be installed on a dynamic disk.

70-270.03.01.002

▶ **Correct Answers: D**

A. **Incorrect:** The 16-bit FAT file system was created when disk drives were relatively small. FAT16 does not support large partitions, file and folder level security, disk quotas, and other advanced features.

B. **Incorrect:** The Universal Disk Format (UDF) was introduced in Microsoft Windows 2000. It is a standards-based file system for DVD and CD-ROM. You cannot format a hard disk with the UDF file system.

C. **Incorrect:** The 32-bit version of the FAT file system supports large partitions, but not other advanced features such as security, auditing, and disk quotas.

D. **Correct:** NTFS is a high-performance file system designed for modern computer systems. It supports per user disk quotas, folder and file-level security, auditing, reparse points, and other advanced features.

E. **Incorrect:** The CD-ROM File System (CDFS) is the ISO-9660 compliant precursor to the UDF file system. It cannot be used to format a hard disk.

70-270.03.01.003

▶ **Correct Answers: C**

A. **Incorrect:** It is not necessary to reinstall the operating systems; there is a much quicker way to resolve this problem. Reinstalling the operating systems allows the computer to boot, but configuration settings are lost.

B. **Incorrect:** The Windows XP Professional installation CD-ROM does not contain a BOOT.INI file. If no BOOT.INI file is on a computer, it is created automatically by the setup program; if one already exists, the setup program automatically edits it.

C. **Correct:** You can boot from the Windows XP Professional installation CD-ROM and attempt to repair the existing installation. Selecting the Inspect Startup Environment option verifies and, if necessary, repairs the Windows XP Professional files in the system partition. A new BOOT.INI file is automatically created. You are then able to boot from the hard disk into Windows XP Professional and manually edit the BOOT.INI file to add Windows 2000 Professional to the boot menu.

D. **Incorrect:** The Windows 2000 Professional installation CD-ROM does not contain a BOOT.INI file. If no BOOT.INI file is on a computer, it is created automatically by the setup program; if one already exists, the setup program automatically edits it.

70-270.03.01.004

▶ **Correct Answers: A**

   A. **Correct:** You need to acquire device driver files compatible with Windows XP Professional from the vendor and then use them to install the device. In this particular scenario, the most likely location for those files is on the vendor's Web site.

   B. **Incorrect:** The issue is not Driver Signing; changing this setting does not correct the problem.

   C. **Incorrect:** The issue is not Driver Signing; changing this setting does not correct the problem.

   D. **Incorrect:** If the device appears on the HCL, it should be possible to install it.

   E. **Incorrect:** Safe Mode is used for resolving problems caused by installing drivers that lead to system instability. You don't use Safe Mode for installing new hardware devices.

O B J E C T I V E 3 . 2

Implement, manage, and troubleshoot display devices.

The video display subsystem of a computer running Windows XP Professional includes a video monitor connected to a video adapter which is attached to the computer bus and interfaces with a device driver communicating with the operating system. Recently manufactured video adapters are usually **Plug and Play (PnP)**–capable and connect to the motherboard via PCI or AGP bus technology. Older video adapters that are not PnP-capable typically use either PCI, **ISA**, or **Extended Industry Standard Architecture (EISA)** bus technology to connect to the motherboard. Legacy video adapters often require you to physically manipulate dual inline package (DIP) switches or jumper pins to assign resources such as **interrupt request (IRQ)** line, **Direct Memory Access (DMA)** channels, **input/output (I/O)** addresses, and **memory addresses**. IRQ conflicts are one of the most common problems encountered in computers with legacy hardware devices; conflicting demands on the other types of resources are also fairly frequent. PnP technology was designed to resolve these problems by allowing the operating system to automatically manage these limited resources in the background; nevertheless, you must be aware of how to use Device Manager to manually assign resources to different hardware devices.

Note Windows XP Professional supports PnP for video monitors only if the monitor, video adapter, and device driver for the adapter are all PnP; otherwise the monitor is detected as "Default Monitor." Also note that if you plug the monitor into a Keyboard-Video-Mouse (KVM) switch box, the PnP attributes of the monitor might be lost.

Another common configuration error is caused by a mismatch between the display settings configured for the video adapter and what the video monitor is capable of displaying. For example, many new video adapters can simultaneously support extremely high resolutions, high color depth, and a high refresh rate while monitors from only a couple of years ago might not be able to handle those settings. When you try to change these settings using the Display program in Control Panel, Windows XP Professional minimizes mismatch errors of this type by first limiting the list of supported configurations (for PnP hardware, where monitor's configurations are matched against the video adapter), next by testing the new settings and then asking you to confirm that you want to use them. If you render the display unreadable, you will not see the confirmation dialog box and the previous settings will be restored after 15 seconds.

Incompatible or unstable device drivers are also a primary cause of problems with video subsystems. If you install new video drivers and are no longer able to view the desktop or if the computer no longer boots, restart the computer in Safe Mode and select either Last Known Good or Enable VGA Mode. If you are in Enable VGA Mode, use the Display program in Control Panel to reconfigure the video adapter, and then restart. If you are able to log in to Windows XP Professional after selecting Last Known Good, a restart is not necessary.

Windows XP Professional supports a total of up to 10 video monitors attached to one computer. All the video adapters must be connect to the system bus via either PCI or AGP technology. If you plan to enable multiple monitors for a computer, install Windows XP Professional with only one adapter present. After installation of the operating system is complete, you can install and configure the additional video adapters and video monitors. On computers with a motherboard that includes an embedded video adapter, that adapter is usually detected first and automatically configured as the primary adapter. The logon prompt is displayed on the video monitor attached to the primary adapter. After you have completed the installation of the additional video adapters and video monitors, you use the Settings tab in the Display Program in Control Panel to configure multiple monitor support.

To successfully answer questions in this objective, you must know how to use the Add Hardware Wizard, Device Manager, and the Display program in Control Panel to install, configure, and troubleshoot both legacy and PnP video adapters and monitors. You must be able to install multiple video adapters and monitors, change the primary adapter, and move items between monitors.

Objective 3.2 Questions

70-270.03.02.001

Your computer is already running Windows Me; you upgrade the operating system to Windows XP Professional. After installation is finished, you log on and open the Display program in Control Panel. You want to increase the screen resolution but are unable to because the display is configured with the default Video Graphics Adapter (VGA) settings. You select the Advanced button from the Settings tab and then select the Adapter tab and find that Windows XP Professional did not recognize the EISA-based video adapter. You know that the card is a few years old and not PnP compatible, however it is on the HCL.

How do you fix the computer so that you will be able to select a higher screen resolution?

A. Reinstall Windows Me on the computer.

B. Reinstall Windows XP Professional so that setup can properly detect the video adapter.

C. Acquire updated drivers for the video adapter and use the Hardware Update Wizard to install them.

D. Physically move the video adapter to a different slot, and then run the Add Hardware Wizard to have Windows XP Professional recognize the device and install suitable drivers for it.

E. Enable the video card in Device Manager.

70-270.03.02.002

You bought a new computer with recently released multimedia hardware including a video adapter with many advanced features. The computer was shipped with Windows XP Professional preinstalled but the vendor's documentation indicates that the external television port on the video adapter was not functional at the time of shipping and that you must check with its Web site for updates. Two weeks later, you find and download new drivers for the video adapter from the vendor's Web site. You install them and reboot when told to do so. The system restarts normally and you log on. You see an error message indicating that the display settings have been restored to their defaults. You try to open the Display program in Control Panel but the system freezes.

What is the best way to return the computer to full functionality?

A. Turn the computer off, unplug the power cord, and disconnect it from the video monitor. Physically move the video adapter to a different slot, and then reconnect the cables and restart the computer.

B. Restart the computer and select Safe Mode. Use the Roll Back Driver button from the video adapter's properties dialog box to restore the original device drivers for the video adapter.

C. Restart the computer and use the ERD to restore the original drivers.

D. Restart the computer using the Recovery Console to delete the new video device drivers.

70-270.03.02.003

You buy a new Pentium IV computer with an AGP video adapter. You install Windows XP Professional from the installation CD-ROM and the video adapter is automatically configured. You use the computer for several days and decide that you want to change the font size to 125 percent of its normal size. What do you do?

A. Edit the size manually in the system registry using the Registry Editor tool.

B. Open Device Manager from the Computer Management console.

C. Select the List All Modes button from the Adapter tab of the display adapter's advanced properties dialog box.

D. Adjust the DPI setting from the General tab of the Display Adapter Advanced Properties dialog box.

70-270.03.02.004

You install Windows XP Professional on a Pentium 200 computer that has an EISA-based video adapter. During setup, the video adapter is not recognized and the display is set to VGA resolution. You know that the adapter and video monitor support higher resolutions—what do you do to fully enable the video adapter?

A. Use the Registry Editor tool to manually modify the display settings in the system registry.

B. Use DXDIAG.EXE to install the specified drivers from a floppy disk or CD-ROM.

C. Windows XP Professional is not compatible with legacy hardware devices such as EISA video adapters; therefore, you must replace the video adapter with either a PCI or AGP adapter.

D. Obtain and manually install the correct device driver for the video adapter.

Objective 3.2 Answers

70-270.03.02.001

▶ **Correct Answers: C**

A. **Incorrect:** You know that the video adapter is on the HCL and therefore it will work with Windows XP Professional. It is not necessary to revert to Windows Me to use the adapter at higher resolutions.

B. **Incorrect:** Reinstalling Windows XP Professional takes an unnecessarily long time and might not fix the problem because it is likely that setup will once again be unable to detect the legacy video adapter.

C. **Correct:** Windows XP Professional did not recognize the video adapter and is using the default VGA driver. You can contact the vendor for updated drivers and launch the Hardware Update Wizard from Device Manager to install them.

D. **Incorrect:** Most computers that support EISA devices contain only a single EISA slot, so moving the card might not be an option. Even if you can move the card to a different slot, it is unlikely that doing so will resolve the problem because Windows XP Professional will probably still not recognize it.

E. **Incorrect:** The video card is already enabled, but it is running in VGA mode. You need to acquire and install updated drivers for the card to resolve this problem.

70-270.03.02.002

▶ **Correct Answers: B**

A. **Incorrect:** These steps will not resolve the problem. If the video monitor is not displaying the Windows XP Professional desktop or if the image is flickering, the video adapter might not be seated properly in its slot or the slot's connectors might be damaged. If that is the case, moving the video adapter might resolve the problem. But the question stated that the image is viewable so moving the card will not help.

B. **Correct:** This is the best way to repair the computer. In Safe Mode, Windows XP Professional starts with only basic files and drivers. If your computer fails to start in Safe Mode, you might need to use the Recovery Console to repair it. After the computer has booted into Safe Mode, you can launch Device Manager, double-click the video adapter to open the properties dialog box, and select Roll Back Driver to restore the original drivers. In case of incorrect configuration you may also use Last Known Good Configuration, however other successful system changes since the last startup will be lost.

C. **Incorrect:** The ERD can be used to repair basic system files, the boot sector, and the startup environment, but it cannot help you to repair bad video drivers.

D. **Incorrect:** If you know the exact names and versions of each file that you need to delete and restore, it might be possible to manually correct this problem. This is a time-consuming and error-prone approach though; booting into Safe Mode and using the graphical tools to repair the computer are much more likely to succeed.

70-270.03.02.003

▶ **Correct Answers: D**

A. **Incorrect:** You don't need to manually edit the registry to change the appearance of fonts on the Windows XP Professional desktop.

B. **Incorrect:** You use Device Manager to manage system resource configuration for hardware devices but you cannot change the other video adapter and video monitor settings.

C. **Incorrect:** Use the Adapter tab to view detailed information about the display adapter, the list of modes that the adapter can display, and the adapter's properties. You cannot change the size of the fonts displayed on the Windows XP Professional desktop from the Adapter tab.

D. **Correct:** You can scale the fonts displayed in the Windows XP Professional desktop from 20 percent to 500 percent of their default size by selecting the DPI list and choosing Custom Setting from the General Tab on the display adapter's advanced properties dialog box, available from the Display Properties Settings tab. The specific font sizes available are determined by which fonts you have installed on your system. When you change the font size, you have to reboot for the new settings to take effect.

70-270.03.02.004

▶ **Correct Answers: D**

A. **Incorrect:** Some of the earlier versions of Windows required you to manually edit the system registry to resolve certain software problems; however, it is much easier to make a mistake and render Windows XP Professional unusable when you manually edit the Registry. Windows XP Professional allows you to manage virtually all aspects of the system through graphical tools and command-line tools. Whenever possible, use these built-in management tools to resolve issues such as this.

B. **Incorrect:** The DirectX Diagnostic Tool can be launched from a command line by typing DXDIAG.EXE. This tool is used review, configure, and troubleshoot the hardware in a computer that interacts with DirectX. The DirectX Diagnostic Tool is not used to install or update drivers for hardware devices.

C. **Incorrect:** Windows XP professional is compatible with numerous legacy hardware devices. If the specific device does not appear on the list in the Add/Remove Hardware Wizard, verify that it is on the HCL. If it is, contact the vendor to obtain up-to-date device drivers for Windows XP Professional.

D. **Correct:** Windows XP Professional is compatible with many EISA video adapters even though they are not PnP compatible. During the installation of Windows XP Professional, the setup program can detect many legacy hardware devices and then install appropriate drivers to enable them. However, setup does not always recognize every installed hardware device. If appropriate drivers are not on the Windows XP Professional installation CD-ROM, you might be able to locate compatible drivers on the vendor's Web site. Open Device Manager, right-click the video adapter, and choose Update Driver to launch the Hardware Update Wizard. Choose Install from a list or specified location and specify what folder contains the device driver. You can allow the wizard to search local drives for updated device drivers if you prefer.

O B J E C T I V E   3 . 3

Configure Advanced Configuration Power Interface (ACPI).

There are two ways to extend battery life in mobile computers: enhancing battery technology and decreasing power utilization. The vendors of batteries have been slowly improving their products since mobile computers were first introduced but the greatest gains over the past few years have come from making mobile computer hardware and software more energy efficient. **Advanced Configuration Power Interface (ACPI)** allows computers running Windows XP Professional to use electricity more efficiently than previous technologies. Windows XP Professional supports the ACPI for sophisticated power management. Windows XP Professional also supports the older and less effective standard **Advanced Power Management (APM)**. You can check to see whether your computer is ACPI-compliant in Device Manager by double-clicking Computer. You customize the power configuration by using the Power Options program in Control Panel; there are different options available depending on whether your computer has an ACPI or APM **BIOS**. Windows XP Professional supports power management of video monitors and hard disks on all computer platforms, even those with a BIOS with neither APM nor ACPI. If you are upgrading a computer that is already running third-party power management tools, uninstall or disable it before running the Windows XP Professional setup program.

On an ACPI system, power consumption is determined by the power settings configured in the Power Options, the requirements of running services and applications, and the capabilities of the installed hardware. To put it another way, Windows XP Professional fully supports the ACPI standard, but applications and hardware must be designed to work with ACPI and PnP for the power management system to be as effective as possible.

Windows XP Professional support of the APM standard is aimed at supporting legacy notebook computers—desktop support is extremely limited. The goal of APM in Windows XP Professional is to provide battery status and support for suspend, resume, and hibernation. You can check for APM BIOS compatibility using the AMPSTAT.EXE command-line tool; it is an optional utility that you install from the \SUPPORT\TOOLS folder on the Windows XP Professional installation **CD-ROM** by running SETUP.EXE.

Note Hibernation is supported on both ACPI- and APM-enabled systems; it saves the current state of Windows XP Professional including all open programs and documents to a file called HIBERFIL.SYS. This file can be quite large—be sure that your hard disk has sufficient free space before enabling hibernation in the Power Options program located in Control Panel.

To successfully answer questions in this objective, you must know how to create, modify, and select power schemes. You need to know how to enable and disable hibernation and configure power alarms, standby mode, and advanced power settings. You must be able to install, configure, and troubleshoot PC Cards. You need to be able to unplug or eject hardware from the taskbar.

Objective 3.3 Questions

70-270.03.03.001

You have installed Windows XP Professional on your laptop computer. You often carry the laptop around your campus while working, and periodically have to leave it unattended for extended periods of time. You want to be able to resume your work as quickly as possible when you return, yet you also want to extend the battery life. What do you do?

A. Shut down the computer.

B. Enable Hibernation in the Power Options program in Control Panel. Then create a power scheme that causes the laptop computer to hibernate whenever the computer is not used for a suitable period of time.

C. Use the Power Options in Control Panel to create a custom power scheme.

D. Use the Power Options in Control Panel to select the Max Battery power scheme.

70-270.03.03.002

Under which of the following scenarios do you not see the APM tab in the Power Options program located in Control Panel? (Choose two.)

A. The APM-based BIOS is failing.

B. The computer's BIOS is ACPI-compliant.

C. The external Uninterruptible Power Supply (UPS) is not properly connected to the serial port of the computer.

D. The computer's battery has been improperly charged.

E. The computer's BIOS is not APM-based.

70-270.03.03.003

A user in your organization has installed Windows XP Professional on his notebook computer. The notebook computer supports APM. When the user tries to shut down the computer and it freezes during the shutdown process, pressing the power button does not resolve the problem. He has to unplug the computer and remove the battery to completely shut it off. How do you check to see whether the APM-based BIOS is the cause of the problem?

A. Restart the computer and run ACLDIAG.EXE.

B. Install a new copy of Windows XP Professional so that the APM-based BIOS can be properly detected and installed.

C. Restart the computer in Safe Mode and disable as many of the power management options as possible.

D. Turn the computer on and, after the desktop has appeared, run the APMSTAT.EXE tool.

70-270.03.03.004

Your manager asks you to install Windows XP Professional on his notebook computer that is already running Microsoft Windows NT Workstation 4. The computer's BIOS is APM-compatible, but before you start the installation process you want to quickly verify that the BIOS has no known compatibility issues with Windows XP Professional. What do you do?

A. Run the APMSTAT.EXE tool.

B. Contact the manufacturer of the notebook computer.

C. Run the Microsoft Windows NT Diagnostics administrative tool on the notebook computer.

D. Create a Microsoft Windows NT Hardware Detection Tool–bootable floppy disk by running \SUPPORT\HQTOOL\MAKEDISK.BAT from the Windows NT Workstation 4 installation CD-ROM and then booting the notebook computer from the floppy disk to generate the NTHQ report.

OBJECTIVE 3.4

Implement, manage, and troubleshoot input and output (I/O) devices.

Many of the hardware devices you might use with Windows XP Professional can be considered **I/O** devices. Other objectives in this domain discuss several classes of I/O devices: network adapters, **PC Cards**, display adapters and monitors, and disks. This objective reviews many other I/O devices including modems, **smart card** readers and cards, **Universal Serial Bus (USB)**, wireless devices, and multimedia hardware. Multimedia hardware encompasses a broad array of devices such as **DVD** readers, Musical Instrument Digital Interface (MIDI) devices, scanners, digital cameras, digital video recorders, sound cards, and **CD-ROM** readers and writers. From a high level the process of installing and managing each type of I/O device is similar: physically connect the device to the computer's bus; install software drivers; configure the device; maintain and troubleshoot the device as needed. The details vary between devices, especially when comparing PnP devices to older models that do not fully support PnP. Windows XP Professional usually detects PnP hardware devices and automatically installs suitable drivers for them.

You use the Add Hardware Wizard to install devices that are not automatically detected and installed. You can also use this wizard to uninstall, unplug, and troubleshoot I/O devices. If a hardware installation wizard fails to install a device that you believe should be compatible with Windows XP Professional, verify that the **BIOS** is configured to support that class of device. For example, make sure that Infrared (IrDA) is enabled on your motherboard's BIOS if you are unable to install any IrDA devices. You use Device Manager for updating drivers, managing resource allocation (that is, IRQ and direct memory access [DMA] assignment), and troubleshooting installed devices. If you are not able to locate an installed device in Device Manager, open the View menu and select Show Hidden Devices. You can view, delete, and uninstall devices that are not currently attached to your computer by setting the following environmental variable at the command line: set devmgr_show_nonpresent_devices=1. Then run Device Manager from the same command line by typing **devmgmt.msc**. After Device Manager launches, open the View menu and select Show Hidden Devices.

Tip You can permanently enable this variable by opening the System program in Control Panel. Select the Advanced tab, click Environmental Variables, and then click New in the System Variables section. Type **devmgr_show_nonpresent_devices** as the variable name and the number **1** as the variable value. Click OK to accept the settings and close each of the dialog boxes by clicking OK.

You use the Wireless Link program in Control Panel to configure and troubleshoot IrDA ports. You use the Scanners and Cameras program in Control Panel to configure and troubleshoot digital scanners, cameras, and video devices. You use the Sounds and Audio Devices program in Control Panel to specify the kind of speakers you are using; create and select Sound Schemes; specify devices for sound and voice recording and playback and MIDI playback; view the properties of installed sound devices; trouble-shoot installed sound devices; and set speaker volume. You can also set speaker volume using the Volume program by going to the Start menu, choosing All Programs, and then Accessories, and then choosing Entertainment. You use the Phone and Modem Options program in Control Panel.

Note Note that Control Panel in Windows XP Professional has two views: Classic View lists all the Control Panel programs in a single pane; Category View is the default and it organizes the programs into 10 groups. This grouping creates an additional layer of navigation—if you are familiar with earlier versions of Windows, you might want to switch to Classic View.

Cardbus and **PC Card** devices, formally **Personal Computer Memory Card International Association (PCMCIA)** cards, are commonly used in mobile computers. PC Card and Cardbus devices are inserted into the PC Card slot. For the device to be recognized via PnP, the device, the PC Card slot, and the drivers for the PC Card slot must all be PnP compatible. PnP PC Card and Cardbus devices contain unique information that Windows XP Professional uses to create the card information structure (CIS). After the CIS is created, Windows XP Professional installs a driver to support the card. There are three types of drivers that you can use: (1) standard PnP drivers such as miniport drivers for **SCSI** devices and Network Driver Interface Specification (NDIS) version 5.*x* drivers for network cards, (2) generic device drivers supported for devices such as modems and disk drives, and (3) vendor-supplied drivers for devices that Windows XP Professional does not natively support. Normally the new device will be enabled without rebooting the computer; however, if the computer is not ACPI-complaint, the device might not be functional until after the computer is restarted.

There are several other important hardware troubleshooting utilities included with Windows XP Professional. DRIVERS.EXE lists information about all the drivers running. The **DirectX Diagnostic tool (DXDIAG.EXE)** is used to review, configure, and troubleshoot the hardware in a computer that interacts with DirectX. The **System Information tool (WINMSD.EXE)** shows detailed information about the installed hardware and software and the allocation of resources such as IRQ, DMA, I/O ports, and memory. The **File Signature Verification tool (SIGVERIF.EXE)** is used to scan the computer for critical files that have not been digitally signed by Microsoft.

To successfully answer questions in this objective, you must be able to use the Add Hardware Wizard and Device Manager to install, manage, and troubleshoot I/O devices. You must also be able to use the individual device management applications in Control Panel such as Phone and Modem Options, Scanners and Cameras, Sounds and Audio Devices, and Wireless Link.

Objective 3.4 Questions

70-270.03.04.001

A puzzled user in your organization asks you why he cannot install a flatbed scanner on his system. Previously he had successfully installed other hardware such as his handheld Microsoft Windows CE device that is connected to the USB port and a digital camera that communicates via the IrDA port. He tells you that he disconnected his personal laser printer, and then connected the scanner to the parallel port, turned it on, and launched the Add Hardware Wizard. He seems to think that Windows XP Professional might have detected the scanner but he receives a series of error messages and is unable to install the Windows XP drivers he just downloaded from the vendor's Web site.

What is preventing this user from installing the scanner?

A. Someone who is a member of the local Administrators group on the computer must be logged on to install hardware devices that are not PnP.

B. The scanner is not compatible with Windows XP.

C. The parallel cable is damaged.

D. There is an IRQ conflict between the parallel port and another installed hardware device.

70-270.03.04.002

Your multimedia-capable computer seems to record and play back sound and voice at very low quality. When you try to conduct video conferences over the Internet, your colleagues are not able to understand you although they have no problems communicating with one another. You also notice that their voices sound distorted and you hear lots of pops and hisses.

When you use a different computer in your office, the video conferencing tools work great. You suspect that there is something wrong with your sound card or the drivers that interact with it; you want to examine the sound recording and playback devices installed in your computer. You also want to check driver versions and perform diagnostics. How do you do this?

A. You run SIGVERIF.EXE at a command prompt.

B. You open the Registry Editor tool (REGEDT32.EXE) and look for entries that might be related to audio devices installed in your computer.

C. You select the Hardware tab in the Sounds and Audio Devices program in Control Panel.

D. You open the DirectX Diagnostics tool.

70-270.03.04.003

You are listening to an audio CD on your desktop computer at work when you realize the music might be disturbing your colleagues who are holding a small meeting in the cubicle next to yours. You turn off the speakers, put on your stereo headphones, and insert the plug into the jack on the front of the CD-ROM drive but you hear no sound. You adjust the volume control on the front of the CD-ROM drive but still hear no sound. You turn the speakers back on and are able to hear the music again.

Why can't you hear music through your headphones?

A. The CD-ROM drive is defective and must replaced.

B. Digital audio playback is enabled for your CD-ROM drive.

C. One or more of the volume levels in the Volume Control program is muted or turned all the way down.

D. The Hardware Sound Acceleration Level is set to No acceleration on the Sound tab of the DirectX Diagnostics tool.

70-270.03.04.004

You install a pair of identical modems into your home computer. You enable multilink on your computer and dial into your company's Routing and Remote Access Service (RRAS) server but only one modem connects. What do you do to enable multilink connections?

A. Log in with an account that is a member of the local Administrator group and then connect to the Routing and Remote Access Service.

B. Enable multilink on the Routing and Remote Access Service.

C. Disable Extensible Authentication Protocol security for each connection.

D. Double the length of time for the H.323 Call Alerting timeout.

70-270.03.04.005

You recently purchased an external USB hard disk. You plug the power cord in and connect the device to the USB hub that is already connected to your keyboard and Pocket PC. You insert the installation CD-ROM that came with the device, follow the prompts to install the device drivers, and reboot the computer when told to do so. You log back on to the desktop and open Windows Explorer. You don't see the new hard disk under My Computer where the other local disks are visible. You open Device Manager and cannot locate the new hard disk there either.

Which of the following are appropriate troubleshooting steps? (Choose three.)

A. Install the device into another computer.

B. You have attached too many USB devices; there is not enough power in the USB chain to support a mouse, Pocket PC, and disk drive simultaneously. Disconnect the Pocket PC and mouse whenever you want to use the hard disk.

C. Disconnect the new disk drive from the hub and plug it directly into a USB port on the computer.

D. Look for USB-related messages in the Application and System logs using Event Viewer.

E. Verify that USB support is enabled in your computer's BIOS.

F. Verify that you have not accidentally disabled USB support in Device Manager.

70-270.03.04.006

Which of the following are ways to install a modem in Windows XP Professional? (Choose three.)

A. Use the Phone and Modem Options program in Control Panel.

B. Use the Add Hardware program in Control Panel.

C. Use the Printer and Faxes program in Control Panel.

D. Boot into Safe Mode.

E. Attach a PnP modem.

F. From the Start menu, select Run and type **WINMSD.EXE**.

Objective 3.4 Answers

70-270.03.04.001

▶ **Correct Answers: A**

A. **Correct:** Windows XP Professional installs PnP devices automatically; an administrator does not need to be present. The puzzled user was able to use the PnP devices because they were automatically detected and appropriate drivers were installed for him. Non-PnP devices are installed in the context of the currently logged-on user, and only administrators are able to install device drivers and make other changes to critical system files and configuration settings. The user was not able to install the scanner because it is not PnP-capable.

B. **Incorrect:** The user told you that he downloaded Windows XP Professional drivers from the firm that built the scanner. It is possible that the user downloaded drivers for a different version of Windows but the Microsoft certification exams never contain false or misleading information in the questions so you can safely conclude that the drivers were indeed compatible with Windows XP.

C. **Incorrect:** The user believes that Windows XP Professional did detect the scanner and that he received the error messages after it had already been detected.

D. **Incorrect:** Nothing in the question suggests that there are any resource conflicts; additionally; the user had disconnected his personal laser printer from the parallel port before attempting to install the flatbed scanner. Because the user reported no problems with the printer, it is unlikely that there are resource conflicts between the parallel port and any other device.

70-270.03.04.002

▶ **Correct Answers: C**

A. **Incorrect:** The Signature Verification tool (SIGVERIF.EXE) is used to scan the computer for critical files such as device drivers and system DLLs. It checks to see whether each file has a valid digital signature from Microsoft; it is not used for hardware or driver troubleshooting. The Signature Verification Tool and driver signing is covered in detail in Objective Domain 4 within this book.

B. **Incorrect:** Manually searching the Registry is a haphazard and time-consuming approach to gathering the desired information. Launching the Sounds and Audio Devices program in Control Panel is much faster and more effective. Also, the Registry Editor tool does not include troubleshooting tools to help you resolve hardware and software problems.

C. **Correct:** You use the Sounds and Audio Devices program to adjust volume, specify the kind of speakers you are using, create and select Sound Schemes, select devices for sound and voice recording and playback, select devices for MIDI playback, view the properties of installed sound devices, and troubleshoot installed sound devices.

D. **Incorrect:** The DirectX Diagnostics tool is used to review, configure, and troubleshoot the hardware in a computer that interacts with DirectX. It does have a tab labeled Sound where you can test DirectSound, but it does not have detailed information about the sound card. You can launch the Sound Troubleshooter from the More Help tab in the DirectX Diagnostic tool or from the Hardware tab in the Sounds and Audio Devices program.

70-270.03.04.003

▶ **Correct Answers: B**

A. **Incorrect:** The CD-ROM drive plays audio CDs through the speakers and the question gives no indication of other problems with the drive so it is not clear that replacing it will solve the problem.

B. **Correct:** When digital playback of audio CDs is enabled, the headphone jack on the front of most CD-ROM drives is disabled. To use headphones to listen to audio CDs, you have to either connect the headphones to a jack attached to the sound card or to a headphone jack built into the speakers.

C. **Incorrect:** You can hear music through the speakers so the CD volume and master volume controls must not be muted or turned down. There is no volume control specific to headphone jacks so adjusting the volume levels in the Volume Control program won't resolve the problem.

D. **Incorrect:** The Hardware Sound Acceleration Level has no effect on the volume of audio CDs. Adjusting hardware acceleration on the Display and Sound tabs of the DirectX Diagnostic tools might help to resolve stability or performance issues relating to DirectX.

70-270.03.04.004

▶ **Correct Answers: B**

A. **Incorrect:** It is not necessary to be logged in to the computer with administrator privileges to utilize multilink functionality.

B. **Correct:** Multilink must be enabled on both computers, not just one of them. There are no more configuration changes required on your home computer in this scenario.

C. **Incorrect:** The Extensible Authentication Protocol (EAP) is compatible with multilink dial-up networking.

D. **Incorrect:** H.323 is a signaling and call control protocol that provides audiovisual conferencing over data networks such as the Internet. You configure H.323 settings by opening the Phone and Modem Options program in Control Panel, selecting the Advanced tab, selecting Microsoft H.323 Telephony Service Provider from the list, and clicking Configure. None of the settings relating to this protocol impact the multilink capabilities of your computer.

70-270.03.04.005

▶ **Correct Answers: A, C, and D**

A. **Correct:** If the problem reappears on a different computer system, it is likely that the USB hard disk is defective. If it performs as expected on the other computer, the problem is specific to the original computer.

B. **Incorrect:** There are limitations on how much power each individual USB device can draw from the USB chain; if a USB device tries to use more than 500 milliamps of current, the port is disabled until the system is rebooted. The total amount of power used by all the devices is also limited. The question states that you connected the USB disk drive's power plug, which means that it will not be using much current from the USB connection. Additionally, USB mice and Pocket PCs normally use a trivial amount of electric current from the USB connection.

C. **Correct:** If this step resolves the problem, you have determined that the issue was caused by the USB hub or its connection to your computer. Try power cycling the hub and plugging it into an alternate port on your computer.

D. **Correct:** When Windows XP Professional detects problems with USB devices, it writes error messages to the Application and System logs. These messages can provide useful troubleshooting information. Another important step to take when resolving USB-related issues is to examine all the devices under the USB controllers tree in Device Manager. If a yellow exclamation point appears before a device, verify that the system firmware is configured to allocate an interrupt request (IRQ) number to the USB controller.

E. **Incorrect:** The question stated that you had existing connections for your mouse and Pocket PC so USB support must already be enabled in your computer's BIOS.

F. **Incorrect:** The question stated that you had existing connections for your mouse and Pocket PC so USB support was not disabled in Device Manager. For the USB disk drive to have been specifically disabled in Device Manager, it first must be installed.

70-270.03.04.006

▶ **Correct Answers: A, B, and E**

A. **Correct:** After opening the Phone and Modem Options program, select the Modems tab and click Add to open the Install New Modem page in the Add New Hardware Wizard. The wizard tries to automatically detect and install the modem; if automatic detection fails, the wizard allows you to select the manufacturer and model of the new modem.

B. **Correct:** After the Add New Hardware Wizard launches, click Next and then select Add a new hardware device from the list and click Next. You are then able to either allow the wizard to automatically detect and install the modem or manually select it from a list. If automatic detection succeeds, the wizard installs the modem and the appropriate device drivers; if automatic detection fails, the wizard allows you to select the manufacturer and model of the new modem.

C. **Incorrect:** The Printer and Faxes program is used to manage existing Fax and Printer connections and to install, remove, and configure printers and fax printers. It is not used to install new modems.

D. **Incorrect:** Booting Windows XP Professional in Safe Mode is a method to resolve stability problems with services and hardware devices; it's not an effective approach to installing new hardware.

E. **Correct:** After you connect a PnP modem to the computer, the Install New Modem page in the Add New Hardware Wizard appears. The wizard tries to automatically detect and install the modem; if automatic detection fails, the wizard allows you to select the manufacturer and model of the new modem.

F. **Incorrect:** The System Information tool (WINMSD.EXE) is not used to install or configure any hardware devices including modems. The System Information tool shows detailed information about the installed hardware and software and the allocation of resources such as IRQ, DMA, I/O ports, and memory.

OBJECTIVE 3.5

Manage and troubleshoot drivers and driver signing.

Windows XP Professional includes several ways to update device drivers. The simplest is the Windows Update tool that is located in Help and Support on the Start menu. When launched, **Windows Update** connects to *http://windowsupdate.microsoft.com*. The first time this address is visited, the **Active Setup** ActiveX components are downloaded and installed. These components create a catalog of the hardware and software stored on the computer running Windows Update (no private information is sent to Microsoft). The Active Setup ActiveX components then query the Windows Update site for a list of available updates and cross-reference that list with the local inventory. A list of updates available for downloading is displayed. Microsoft digitally signs all updates posted to the Windows Update site, ensuring that they have passed the requirements for the **Windows Logo Program**. Windows XP supports **driver signing** to ensure users are aware of whether the **Windows Hardware Quality Lab (WHQL)** has certified a driver. When WHQL tests and approves of a driver for use with Windows XP, Microsoft creates a **digital signature** for the driver. When users install this driver, Windows XP recognizes it as being safe. Conversely, if Windows XP cannot find a valid signature for a driver, it warns the user. You can configure your computer to use Automatic Updates, a feature that automatically downloads updates from the Windows Update Web site as soon as they are available.

Warning users about unsigned drivers is the default behavior of Windows XP, but that behavior can be changed to suit individual needs. To change how Windows XP handles unsigned drivers, open the System Properties tool and select the Hardware tab. Click the Driver Signing button, and select Ignore, Warn or Block. Selecting Ignore causes Windows XP to install all drivers, regardless of whether a valid digital signature is available. Warn is the default setting, and it asks the user whether an unsigned driver should be installed. The Block setting ensures all drivers are certified by Microsoft by not allowing unsigned drivers to be installed.

These settings can also be modified using security policies. Using the Local Security Policy tool in the Administrative Tools folder, expand Local Policies and select Security Options. Driver signature verification is controlled using the Devices: Unsigned Driver Installation Behavior policy.

Note Windows Update can be disabled in Active Directory's Group Policy Objects. If your computer is a member of an Active Directory forest and you are unable to view Windows Update, check with your network administrator. Also keep in mind that Windows Update requires a working connection to the Internet; if no connection is available, Windows Update reports an error.

Drivers can also be updated in the Device Manager MMC snap-in. Navigate to the device you want to update, right-click it, and select Update Driver from the menu. This launches the Hardware Update Wizard; follow the prompts to either allow Windows XP Professional to automatically locate the update or manually specify its location. Another approach is to double-click the hardware device in Device Manager to open the device's properties dialog box. Click the Driver tab—there are buttons to view Driver Details, Update Driver, Roll Back Driver, and Uninstall. Click Update Driver to start the Hardware Update Wizard. For printers, you can update drivers by bringing up the properties dialog box of the printer you want to update, selecting the Advanced tab, and clicking the New Driver button. This launches the Add New Printer Driver Wizard.

Driver updates can be removed using Windows Update by following the instructions there. Another approach is to double-click the hardware device in Device Manager to open the device's properties dialog box. Select the Driver tab and click Uninstall to completely remove the driver. Windows XP Professional has a new system recovery tool called **Driver Rollback** that allows you to reinstall the last working driver prior to the current driver.

Note Administrator privileges are necessary for updating, uninstalling, and rolling back device drivers except when installing updates through Windows Update that require no user interaction.

To successfully answer questions in this objective, you must know how to configure and use Windows Update. You must be able to navigate to a specific hardware device in Device Manager, view its properties, and update, roll back, and uninstall its driver.

Objective 3.5 Questions

70-270.03.05.001

Members of which group can manually install, update, and roll back drivers on a computer running Windows XP Professional?

A. Network Configuration Operators

B. Debugger Users

C. Users

D. Administrators

70-270.03.05.002

You have been using a film scanner connected to the USB port of your computer for several months. You learn that the manufacturer has released new drivers for the scanner that allow it to make multiple passes of a single negative and generate a higher resolution digital image. You download the drivers from the vendor's Web site, install them using the Update Hardware Wizard, and reboot when prompted. Now the scanner no longer works.

What is the easiest way to resolve this problem?

A. Use the Roll Back Driver feature available on the device's properties page.

B. Uninstall the device drivers for the scanner, physically disconnect the printer, reboot, and then reconnect the printers and reinstall the new drivers when the Add Hardware Wizard prompts you.

C. Uninstall the device drivers for the scanner, physically disconnect the printer, reboot, and then reconnect the printers and reinstall the original drivers when the Add Hardware Wizard prompts you.

D. Use DRIVERS.EXE to roll back to the previous version of the device driver.

70-270.03.05.003

You want to update the driver for your 3D video adapter. Your computer has access to the Internet. Which of the following tools can you use to update the driver? (Choose two.)

A. Run DRIVERS.EXE from a command prompt.

B. Run Device Manager.

C. Use Windows Update.

D. Open the WMI Control console.

E. Open the System Information tool (WINMSD.EXE).

F. Launch the Add Hardware Wizard.

70-270.03.05.004

Which command launches the File Signature Verification tool that is used to identify unsigned drivers installed on a Windows XP Professional system?

A. WINMSD.EXE

B. FSUTIL.EXE

C. SIGVERIF.EXE

D. REGEDIT.EXE

Objective 3.5 Answers

70-270.03.05.001

▶ **Correct Answers: D**

A. **Incorrect:** By default, the members of the Network Configuration Operators group have limited administrative privileges which allow them to manage networking features.

B. **Incorrect:** By default, members of the Debugger Users group can debug processes on the computer.

C. **Incorrect:** By default, members of the Users group are restricted from making system-wide changes including installing, updating, or rolling back device drivers.

D. **Correct:** By default, members of the Administrators group have total control of the computer; therefore they can install, update, and roll back device drivers.

70-270.03.05.002

▶ **Correct Answers: A**

A. **Correct:** The ability to roll back device drivers is a new feature in Windows XP Professional. You access it by clicking the Roll Back Driver button in the device's properties page. You can view the properties of a device by double-clicking it in Device Manager.

B. **Incorrect:** You have already determined that the new drivers do not work with your system so this series of steps does not resolve the problem.

C. **Incorrect:** These procedures should resolve the problem but it is much faster and easier to use the Driver Rollback feature available in Windows XP Professional.

D. **Incorrect:** DRIVERS.EXE is a tool used for viewing information about the drivers currently running on a computer; it does not have the ability to roll back device drivers.

70-270.03.05.003

▶ **Correct Answers: B and C**

A. **Incorrect:** DRIVERS.EXE lists information about all the drivers running; it is not used for updating Device Drivers.

B. **Correct:** You can update device drivers from Device Manager in two ways. Navigate to the device and right-click it, and then select Update Driver from the menu. You can also double-click the device to open its properties dialog box, select the Driver tab, and click the Update Driver. Both methods launch the Hardware Update Wizard, which guides you through the process of updating the driver.

C. **Correct:** Windows Update is the simplest way to update device drivers; however it requires access to the Web. Windows Update is located in Help and Support on the Start menu.

D. **Incorrect:** Windows Management Instrumentation (WMI) provides a management infrastructure for monitoring and controlling system resources. WMI includes thoroughly documented application programming interfaces (API) that can be accessed with VBScript, C++, and other programming languages, facilitating the creation of management tools for Windows-based computers. The WMI Control console is used for configuring and controlling the WMI service; it is not used for managing device drivers.

E. **Incorrect:** The System Information tool shows detailed information about the installed hardware and software and the allocation of system resources; it does not have the ability to update device drivers.

F. **Incorrect:** The Add Hardware Wizard is used to install new hardware devices and to troubleshoot existing devices. It is not used to update drivers for existing devices.

70-270.03.05.004

▶ **Correct Answers: C**

A. **Incorrect:** WINMSD.EXE launches the Help And Support Services tool, which provides useful information about the system's configuration. Although this tool cannot be used to find unsigned drivers, it can be used to launch the File Signature Verification tool. To launch this tool, select File Signature Verification Utility from the Tools menu.

B. **Incorrect:** Running the FSUTIL.EXE command-line utility is useful for modifying aspects of the file system. However, this tool cannot be used to verify driver signatures.

C. **Correct:** SIGVERIF.EXE is the correct command to launch the File Signature Verification utility. This tool can also be launched from the System Information program located in the Start menu in the folder called All Programs\Accessories\System Tools.

D. **Incorrect:** The REGEDIT.EXE command launches the Registry Editor, which is used to modify system configuration parameters. It cannot be used to verify driver signatures.

OBJECTIVE 3.6

Monitor and configure multiprocessor computers.

The operating system **kernel** in Windows XP can support multiple **CPUs**. Windows XP Professional works with one or two CPUs; the three server versions of Windows XP support varying numbers of CPUs while Windows XP Home Edition can handle only a single CPU. Windows XP leverages an operating system component called the **hardware abstraction layer (HAL)** to segregate the underlying hardware components from the remainder of the operating system. This fundamental architecture facilitates porting the operating system to different hardware platforms. The HAL for a multiprocessor system is distinct from that of a uniprocessor system; therefore when adding a second processor to an existing Windows XP Professional computer, you must upgrade the HAL as well. Computers might contain **Advanced Processor Interrupt Controller (APIC)** hardware; those that do not are referred to as a PIC PC and appear in Device Manager as a Standard PC. A computer might also contain **ACPI** hardware. The different HAL versions available for these different types of hardware are not interchangeable; if you accidentally upgrade to an incompatible HAL, the computer will probably be unable to boot. The only way to recover from this situation is to reinstall Windows XP Professional. You use the Hardware Update Wizard for the Computer device in Device Manager to upgrade the HAL.

During installation, the Windows XP Professional setup program automatically detects the system **firmware** to determine which HAL to install. It tests the firmware for ACPI compliancy; if the firmware does not pass all the tests, the ACP HAL will not be installed. If your computer is ACPI-compliant but setup does not install the ACPI HAL, contact the computer manufacturer for a **BIOS** update. You have to reinstall Windows XP Professional to use the ACPI features. If you try to override the ACPI settings implemented by the operating system, serious problems might occur and the only resolution supported by Microsoft is to reinstall Windows XP Professional.

You use the Performance snap-in to monitor system performance. On each computer you manage, you must establish a baseline of satisfactory performance and monitor the system for diminished performance in an ongoing way. The Performance snap-in has three modes of operation: real-time display of current system activity, ongoing logging of system performance, and alert. Select the System Monitor from the Console to select counters and view their performance in real-time. Select Counter Logs and Trace Logs to configure logging of performance data. Select Alerts to create, configure, and remove automated notification when specified performance limits are exceeded. The major processor-related objects you must understand and monitor are thread, process, system, processor, job object, and job object details.

To successfully answer questions in this objective, you must know the different HAL versions available; how to upgrade from a single processor to a dual processor configuration; how to downgrade to a single processor configuration; and how to monitor system operation using the Performance snap-in.

Objective 3.6 Questions

70-270.03.06.001

What is the suggested threshold for processor utilization on both uniprocessor and multiprocessor systems?

A. 55 percent

B. 25 percent

C. 100 percent

D. 85 percent

70-270.03.06.002

You manage the computers for the graphics artists in your company. Many of these artists regularly use 3-D rendering software to create computerized special effects for promotional videos. Their standard workstations include dual Pentium III CPUs running at 1 gigahertz, 1 gigabyte of RAM, and a high-end video card with built-in 3-D graphics acceleration. One of the artists complains that her workstation periodically performs poorly. You log performance data from several of the computers while the artist experiencing diminished performance continues to work. You see the following processor-related statistics for that system:

- The Processor object's % Processor Time averages 85 percent.

- The Server Work Queues object's Queue Length averages 2.8.

- The System object's Processor Queue Length averages 1.8.

- The Processor object's Interrupts per second averages 6,500.

Which of the following is the likeliest cause of diminished performance?

A. Processor object's % Processor Time

B. Server Work Queues object's Queue Length

C. System object's Processor Queue Length

D. Processor object's Interrupts per second

70-270.03.06.003

Which of the following configurations does Windows XP Professional support for multiple processors?

A. Symmetric multiprocessing (SMP)

B. Windows XP Professional does not support multiple processors

C. Asymmetric multiprocessing (ASMP)

D. Both SMP and ASMP

Objective 3.6 Answers

70-270.03.06.001

▶ **Correct Answers: D**

A. **Incorrect:** When the Processor object's % Processor Time steadily reaches 55 percent, the system is considered moderately busy but there is still adequate room for increased activity. If the % Processor Time has been steadily increasing and recently hit 55 percent, you might have reason to be concerned about the system reaching capacity soon.

B. **Incorrect:** A computer with the Processor object's % Processor Time averaging 25 percent is not very busy; there is plenty of room for growth.

C. **Incorrect:** 100 percent is far above the suggested threshold of 85 percent. The Processor object's % Processor Time periodically peaks at 100 percent but if it is averaging 100 percent, the computer has a serious issue. Either a process is out of control and must be terminated and if possible debugged and corrected, or the computer has reached capacity and must have a second CPU installed or have a faster CPU replace the existing one.

D. **Correct:** When the Processor object's % Processor Time steadily averages 85 percent, the system is considered extremely busy. Either a process has performance problems that need to be addressed, fewer applications should be running on the computer, or the computer is about to reach its capacity and should have a second CPU installed or have a faster CPU replace the existing one.

70-270.03.06.002

▶ **Correct Answers: C**

A. **Incorrect:** Although 85 percent is a very high value for this counter, the computer should continue to function acceptably. The average for the Interrupts per second suggests why the percent processor time might be running so high.

B. **Incorrect:** This counter should not exceed 4 very often; if it does so regularly, there might be a processor bottleneck.

C. **Incorrect:** For this counter 1.8 is an acceptable average; it's high, but the computer should continue to function in an acceptable manner.

D. **Correct:** You must establish an acceptable baseline for Interrupts per second on a system performing nominally while under load. A generally considered acceptable starting point is 1,000 interrupts per second—6,500 interrupts per second indicates a serious performance problem, most likely caused by a network adapter. Try updating the BIOS on the adapter and the Windows XP Professional drivers for the adapter. If that does not resolve the problem, replace the adapter.

70-270.03.06.003

▶ **Correct Answers: A**

A. **Correct:** The Windows XP Professional kernel supports this architecture only for computers with multiple processors. Under the SMP architecture, all processors share the same memory running a single copy of the operating system and applications.

B. **Incorrect:** Windows XP Professional does support up to two processors.

C. **Incorrect:** Windows XP Professional does not support the ASMP architecture. Under ASMP, each processor serves a specific function; typically the operating system runs on one processor while each of the others runs an application. It is possible that a computer manufacturer will build a computer that uses some ASMP functionality, but the support for that functionality has to be provided by the manufacturer's firmware and software; Windows XP would not be involved.

D. **Incorrect:** Windows XP Professional supports only SMP architecture for multiprocessor systems.

Monitoring and Optimizing System Performance and Reliability

Microsoft Windows XP Professional is more reliable than any previous Windows operating system. All users will benefit from the improved stability, because many of the reliability features are enabled by default. Other reliability features are more complex, and require an administrator to understand and implement them successfully. Administrators have a great deal of control over the reliability features of Windows XP Professional, including the ability to control changes to system files, monitor system performance, trace errors, and schedule maintenance.

Computers, like cars, require regular maintenance. However, manually performing maintenance on hundreds of systems is incredibly time-consuming. Windows XP provides the **Task Scheduler** to automate system maintenance and reduce the total cost of ownership. This graphical utility facilitates scheduling any type of task, and can even ensure that a user's session isn't affected.

Administrators also have the ability to carefully monitor and tune system performance. Tools such as the **Task Manager**, the **Performance utility**, and a suite of command-line utilities allow for both real-time and historical performance data analysis. **Trace logs** function very similarly, and are used to troubleshoot system problems and debug applications.Tuning the performance of portable computers is more complicated than tuning desktop systems because administrators must balance battery life with performance. Windows XP provides power schemes to allow users to quickly change a system's power consumption. Power schemes, combined with standby and hibernation features, dramatically increase battery life when a system is not in use.

Portable computers also have more complex hardware, and may boot in both docked and undocked configurations. **Plug and Play (PnP)** standards have dramatically simplified hardware configuration, but some legacy computers still require **hardware**

profiles. Hardware profiles allow a single instance of Windows XP to boot to one of several different hardware configurations, each with a different set of enabled drivers. PnP computers rarely require the use of hardware profiles, but the functionality is available if needed.

Sometimes, problems are unavoidable. Windows XP provides a full set of troubleshooting tools to resolve these problems when they arise. The **System Restore** tool captures system configuration information, and can reapply a working configuration if the system later becomes unreliable. Functionality such as the **Last Known Good Configuration** can allow Windows XP to boot even if a faulty driver was installed. **Safe Mode** and the **Recovery Console** provide administrators with the ability to repair even the most damaged Windows XP installations.

Tested Skills and Suggested Practices

The skills you need to successfully master the Monitoring and Optimizing System Performance and Reliability objective domain on the *Installing, Configuring, and Administering Microsoft Windows XP Professional* exam include

- **Performing preventative maintenance and backing up critical data.**

  - Practice 1: Perform a complete system backup using the Backup Utility.

  - Practice 2: Save the current system configuration using the System Restore tool.

  - Practice 3: Install the Recovery Console as an option on the boot menu.

  - Practice 4: Prepare a system for Automated System Recovery (ASR).

- **Troubleshooting system problems and restoring data.**

  - Practice 1: Boot the computer using the Last Known Good Configuration.

  - Practice 2: Boot the computer using Safe Mode.

  - Practice 3: Launch the Recovery Console using the Windows XP Professional CD and examine the available commands by executing the HELP command. Examine each command in detail by typing the name of each command followed by /?.

  - Practice 4: Replace the BOOT.INI system file using the Recovery Console.

  - Practice 5: Restore the system configuration to a previous state using the System Restore tool.

  - Practice 6: Perform a complete system restoration using the Backup Utility.

- **Scheduling tasks.**

  - Practice 1: Configure Task Scheduler to perform a complete disk defragmentation weekly.

  - Practice 2: Schedule a task to run daily using the AT command. Execute the AT command without any parameters to view scheduled tasks.

  - Practice 3: Use Task Scheduler to modify a task created with the AT. Execute the AT command without any parameters to view scheduled tasks, and make note of how modifying a task with Task Scheduler affects the ability of AT to view that task.

  - Practice 4: Configure a task to run weekly, but only if the computer is idle. Modify that task to wake the computer if available.

- **Tuning a system for a mobile user.**

  - Practice 1: On a portable computer, manually set the hardware profile for both docked and undocked configurations.

  - Practice 2: Create a new hardware profile, and disable noncritical drivers for that profile.

  - Practice 3: Adjust the power scheme on a computer to a variety of different settings, and observe how the computer's behavior is changed. Create a custom power scheme.

- **Monitoring system performance.**

  - Practice 1: Use the Task Manager to determine which process is currently consuming the most processor time.

  - Practice 2: Change the fields on the Processes tab of the Task Manager so that every possible field is visible.

  - Practice 3: Change the priority of an application so that it runs at high priority.

  - Practice 4: Use the Performance administrative tool to monitor real-time performance information about several different counters simultaneously.

  - Practice 5: Create and analyze counter logs with processor utilization information gathered over several hours.

  - Practice 6: Use the RELOG.EXE command-line utility to reduce the total amount of information in a counter log.

  - Practice 7: Create a trace log, and use the TRACERPT.EXE utility to create a trace analysis report.

Further Reading

This section lists supplemental readings by objective. We recommend that you study these sources thoroughly before taking exam 70-270.

Objective 4.1

Microsoft Corporation. *Microsoft Windows XP Professional Resource Kit Documentation*. Redmond, Washington: Microsoft Press, 2001. Read sections covering Task Manager, Performance Monitor and Disk Defragmenter in Appendix D, "Tools for Troubleshooting."

Microsoft Corporation. *MCSE Training Kit: Microsoft Windows XP Professional*. Redmond, Washington: Microsoft Press, 2001. Read and complete Lessons 4, 5, and 6 in Chapter 15, "Monitoring, Managing, and Maintaining Network Resources." These lessons cover scheduling tasks and using the performance console.

Objective 4.2

Microsoft Corporation. *Microsoft Windows XP Professional Resource Kit Documentation*. Redmond, Washington: Microsoft Press, 2001. Read Chapter 7, "Supporting Mobile Users," for information about power schemes, standby mode, and hibernation.

Microsoft Corporation. *MCSE Training Kit: Microsoft Windows XP Professional*. Redmond, Washington: Microsoft Press, 2001. Read and complete all lessons in Chapter 11, "Configuring Windows XP Professional."

Objective 4.3

Microsoft Corporation. *Microsoft Windows XP Professional Resource Kit Documentation*. Redmond, Washington: Microsoft Press, 2001. Read Chapter 4, "Supporting Installations," Chapter 7, "Supporting Mobile Users," and Chapter 14, "Backup and Restore."

Microsoft Corporation. *MCSE Training Kit: Microsoft Windows XP Professional*. Redmond, Washington: Microsoft Press, 2001. Read and complete all lessons in Chapter 16, "Backing Up and Restoring Data." This chapter explains every aspect of how to use the Backup utility, including restoring data and the use of the Automated System Recovery Wizard.

Monitor, optimize, and troubleshoot performance of the Windows XP Professional desktop.

Windows XP Professional has been designed to provide the optimum performance on any hardware configuration. In fact, most users never need to monitor or modify the performance of their Windows XP system. Users are given control over some aspects of system performance, such as the richness of the user interface. By opening Control Panel, selecting Performance And Maintenance, and clicking Adjust Visual Effect, users can launch the **Performance Options** tool. This tool provides users with the ability to control the compromise between user interface features and system responsiveness.

Note Windows XP Professional allows for customization of the Control Panel window. The Classic View displays all of the icons and the Category View groups Control Panel icons into categories. The Category View is the default view in Windows XP Professional. You can toggle between the views when the Show Common Tasks In Folders option is enabled within the Tasks group of the Folder Options pop-up.

There are also times when an administrator who has a detailed understanding of system performance monitoring and tuning can improve a system's performance. For these administrators, Windows XP provides a suite of tools useful for monitoring, analyzing, and tuning system performance characteristics.

The most commonly used tool is the **Task Manager**. The Windows XP Task Manager provides more detail than previous versions of Windows; it now displays real-time information about network utilization and users in addition to monitoring applications, processes, and performance. The Task Manager can be started by pressing Ctrl+Alt+Delete, or by right-clicking the task bar and selecting Task Manager.

The **Performance tool** is a more powerful utility for analyzing system performance. This tool can provide real-time information about hundreds of detailed aspects of the system's performance, including memory utilization, shared folders, and network errors. This same tool can also be used to log data for later analysis. To launch the Performance tool, open Control Panel, select Performance And Maintenance, click Administrative Tools, and double-click Performance shortcut. Alternatively, you can execute the command **PERFMON**.

The Performance administrative utility has the ability to create both **counter logs** and **trace logs**. Counter logs function by polling various performance counters at a specific interval, and logging that data to a file. Trace logs operate very differently—each time a specified event occurs, information about that event is added to a trace log. Administrators typically use counter logs to tune system performance. Trace logs are more likely to be used by developers to troubleshoot problems.

There are four command-line utilities designed to complement these graphical tools. The **LOGMAN** utility is used to start, stop, and schedule the gathering of performance and trace data. The **RELOG** tool processes and summarizes performance logs. The **TRACERPT** utility processes transaction-based **trace event logs** and produces a **trace analysis report**. Finally, the **TYPEPERF** command echoes raw performance data to the command window or a text file.

Windows XP Professional provides the **Task Scheduler** to allow tasks to be executed when the computer is not being actively used. The Task Scheduler provides a graphical, intuitive user interface for configuring any type of task to run at a specific time or at regular intervals. To further reduce the chances that scheduled maintenance tasks interfere with users, you can configure the tasks to execute only if the computer is idle. Task Scheduler can even stop processes that have already started if a user begins actively working with a computer.

Note Task Scheduler is also the name of the service used to launch the scheduled programs.

The AT command-line utility is available for created scheduled tasks when a graphical user interface is not available. The AT command provides most, but not all, of the Task Scheduler's capabilities. For example, the AT command can schedule a weekly disk defragmentation process, but it cannot stipulate that the process begins only when the computer has been idle for a specific amount of time. The Task Scheduler graphical user interface can be used to edit tasks created with the AT command, but the AT command cannot see tasks created or modified by Task Scheduler.

Objective 4.1 Questions

70-270.04.01.001

You are a systems administrator, and your responsibilities were recently increased to include a group of users at a remote office who have, up until now, been forced to maintain their own Windows XP computers. One of your users is complaining that his computer has grown slower over the past year. In particular, he notes that it takes Microsoft Word longer to open documents that have been recently created. Which of the following actions improve the performance of this user's desktop?

A. Decrease the size of the paging file.

B. Enable NTFS compression.

C. Run Disk Defragmenter on the system's hard disk.

D. Set the Performance Logs and Alerts service to start automatically.

70-270.04.01.002

Which of the following pieces of information can be gathered from the Windows Task Manager? (Choose three.)

A. CPU utilization

B. Network utilization

C. Page file utilization

D. Packet loss

E. Memory usage

F. Open files

70-270.04.01.003

A user is complaining of performance problems with his Windows XP Professional system, but he is not sure whether the problems are caused by an underpowered processor, a shortage of memory for the applications he uses, or a slow disk drive. To upgrade the system component that is limiting the system's performance, you need to log performance data over a period of several days while the user is working with the computer. Which of the following procedures begins the process of gathering performance data? (Choose two.)

A. Log on to the user's computer. Launch the Computer Management console, expand System Tools, and then expand Performance Logs And Alerts. Select Counter Logs in the left pane. In the right pane, right-click System Overview and click Start.

B. Log on to the user's computer. Launch Control Panel and select Performance And Maintenance. Click Administrative Tools, and then double-click Performance. Select System Monitor in the left pane. In the right pane, right-click System Overview and click Start.

C. Log on to the user's computer. Launch Windows Task Manager. From the File menu, select Log Data, and provide a filename.

D. Log on to the user's computer. From a command prompt, type **LOGMAN START 'System Overview'**.

E. Log on to the user's computer. From a command prompt, type **RELOG System_Overview.BLG -q -o System_Overview.TXT**.

70-270.04.01.004

Which of the following tools can be used to set the priority of a process?

A. System Monitor

B. Performance Logs and Alerts

C. Computer Manager

D. Task Manager

70-270.04.01.005

A user complains about slow system performance. You decide to improve performance by adjusting the Performance Options tool. You launch this tool by opening Control Panel, selecting Performance And Maintenance, and clicking Adjust Visual Effects task. Which of the following changes that can be applied to the Performance Options tool improves the system's responsiveness?

A. At the Visual Effects tab, click the Adjust For Best Appearance option.

B. At the Visual Effects tab, click the Adjust For Best Performance option.

C. At the Advanced tab, under Processor Scheduling, select optimization for Background Services.

D. At the Advanced tab, under Memory Usage, select optimization for System Cache.

E. At the Advanced tab, under Virtual Memory, reduce the paging file size by half.

70-270.04.01.006

You are the system administrator of a small network of end users who have both desktop and laptop Windows XP Professional systems. All systems participate in a Windows XP domain. You want to avoid the reduced performance that fragmented file systems cause by scheduling the disk defragmenter utility to run on all systems every Sunday at 1 A.M. This task is important enough that systems must be brought out of power-savings mode if necessary. However, you do not want the disk defragmentation to interfere with the users, nor do you want it to consume the batteries on laptop systems.

The proposed solution is as follows: Launch the Scheduled Tasks administrative utility, and choose New Scheduled Task from the File menu. Name the task File Defragmentation, and then right-click the new task and select Properties. From the Task tab of the Properties dialog box, type **defrag C:** in the Run field. In the Run As field, type the user name of a Domain Admin account that has local Administrator rights on all systems in the domain, and set the password using the Set Password button. From the Schedule tab, at the Schedule Task drop-down list, select Weekly. Set the Start Time to 1:00 AM, and select only Sunday from the Schedule Task Weekly section. Create this task to all Windows XP Professional systems.

Which of your desired results does the proposed solution accomplish? (Choose two.)

A. Schedule the Disk Defragmenter to run on Sundays at 1 A.M.

B. Execute the Disk Defragmenter with an account that has proper privileges on all systems.

C. Ensure the Disk Defragmenter does not interfere with user sessions.

D. Wake the computers from power-savings mode to run the Disk Defragmenter, if possible.

E. Ensure the Disk Defragmenter does not consume the battery on laptop computers.

70-270.04.01.007

Using the AT command-line utility, you schedule a task to run nightly on your Windows XP Professional system. Immediately afterward, you decide that the task must run only weekly, so you launch the Scheduled Tasks administrative utility and modify the task properties. The next time you execute the AT command from the command-line, what does it display about your scheduled task?

A. The scheduled task appears, and is scheduled to run daily.

B. The scheduled task appears, and is scheduled to run weekly.

C. The scheduled task appears twice, and is scheduled to run both daily and weekly.

D. The scheduled task does not appear.

Objective 4.1 Answers

70-270.04.01.001

▶ **Correct Answers: C**

A. **Incorrect:** Windows XP Professional uses the paging file to temporarily store data from the computer's memory. Decreasing the size of the paging file increases the free space on the system's hard disk, but it does not improve the system's performance.

B. **Incorrect:** NTFS allows files and directories to be compressed at the file system level. This allows compressible files to consume less space on the hard disk. Although compressing files increases the free space on the hard disk, it does not improve the system's performance.

C. **Correct:** Hard disks perform best when file data is written in contiguous blocks. Over time, however, file data can become broken into discontiguous fragments. Although the hard disk is still able to access fragmented files, they take longer to load. Because the user's performance problem was most noticeable when accessing files, and no maintenance had been done in at least a year, the cause of the problem is most likely disk fragmentation. Running the Disk Defragmenter utility resolves this problem and drastically improves disk performance on affected systems.

D. **Incorrect:** The Performance Logs and Alerts service is used when logging data for performance analysis. Although it is necessary for logging performance data, simply starting the service does not improve system performance.

70-270.04.01.002

▶ **Correct Answers: A, B, and E**

A. **Correct:** CPU utilization is shown both numerically and graphically on the Performance tab of the Windows Task Manager.

B. **Correct:** Network utilization is shown both numerically and graphically on the Networking tab of the Windows Task Manager.

C. **Incorrect:** Page file utilization information is not available from the Windows Task Manager.

D. **Incorrect:** Packet loss cannot be viewed from the Windows Task Manager. However, executing the command NETSTAT -S -P TCP from the command line shows the Segments Retransmitted statistic, which is very similar to overall packet loss.

E. **Correct:** Memory usage is shown both numerically and graphically on the Performance tab of the Windows Task Manager.

F. **Incorrect:** Open files cannot be viewed from the Windows Task Manager.

70-270.04.01.003

▶ **Correct Answers: A and D**

A. **Correct:** The Performance Logs and Alerts MMC snap-in, available through the Computer Management console, is the correct graphical tool for creating performance logs.

B. **Incorrect:** The System Monitor MMC snap-in is useful for monitoring real-time performance data, but it cannot log performance data.

C. **Incorrect:** The Windows Task Manager is useful for viewing a real-time snapshot of a system's performance. However, it cannot be used to log performance data.

D. **Correct:** Using the LOGMAN utility is the correct way to start logging of performance data from the command line.

E. **Incorrect:** RELOG is useful for analyzing logged data, but it is not used for starting the logging process. RELOG is used to resample logged data at a longer interval in order to reduce the amount of data being analyzed.

70-270.04.01.004

▶ **Correct Answers: D**

A. **Incorrect:** The System Monitor is useful for viewing the processor utilization of a given process, but it cannot change a process' priority.

B. **Incorrect:** The Performance Logs and Alerts snap-in is useful for logging performance data, and allows you to record a given process' processor utilization. However, it cannot be used to change the priority of a process.

C. **Incorrect:** The Computer Manager provides access to both the System Monitor and the Performance Logs and Alerts snap-ins, but none of these tools can be used to change the priority of a process.

D. **Correct:** The Processes tab of the Task Manager is used to change the priority of a process. Right-click the name of a process, choose Set Priority, and select the desired level.

70-270.04.01.005

► **Correct Answers: B**

   A. **Incorrect:** The Adjust For Best Appearance option enables every visual feature of the Windows XP Professional operating system. This provides the best user experience on systems that have sufficient processing capability. However, it reduces system responsiveness, and must not be used on systems experiencing performance problems.

   B. **Correct:** The Adjust For Best Performance option disables all unnecessary visual effects. This reduces the amount of work Windows XP needs to do to display the user's graphical interface, thereby improving system responsiveness. Changing this setting is the best way to make the computer seem faster.

   C. **Incorrect:** Optimizing processor scheduling for background services is useful on servers because it ensures interactive applications do not reduce the performance of a server's primary tasks. However, it does reduce system responsiveness for users working interactively with the computer because background services receive higher priority than interactive applications.

   D. **Incorrect:** Optimizing memory usage for system cache improves the performance of file sharing and Web services. However, when you allocate more of the system RAM to these services, interactive applications suffer.

   E. **Incorrect:** Windows XP uses virtual memory as an extension of the system's physical RAM. It is a slow process to page data from the physical memory to the virtual memory located on the system's hard disk, but decreasing the size of the paging file does not improve system performance.

70-270.04.01.006

► **Correct Answers: A and B**

   A. **Correct:** The settings selected on the Schedule tab are correct to launch the task every Sunday at 1 A.M.

   B. **Correct:** Selecting a Domain Admin account is the best way to ensure a scheduled task copied to many different systems has local Administrator rights on all systems. If a Domain Admin account is not used, a local Administrator account must be selected for each individual system—and account names and passwords might vary.

C. **Incorrect:** The proper method for ensuring that scheduled tasks do not interfere with user sessions is to select the Only Start The Task If The Computer Has Been Idle For At Least check box from the Settings tab of the Task Properties dialog box.

D. **Incorrect:** The Wake The Computer To Run This Task check box was not selected while the task was being configured. This check box is located on the Settings tab of the Task Properties dialog box.

E. **Incorrect:** This desired result was not accomplished. To ensure the scheduled task doesn't consume the system's battery, select both the Don't Start The Task If The Computer Is Running On Batteries and Stop The Task If Battery Mode Begins check boxes from the Settings tab of the Task Properties dialog box.

70-270.04.01.007

▶ **Correct Answers: D**

A. **Incorrect:** The Task Scheduler graphical administrative utility is capable of modifying tasks created with the AT command. Further, AT is not able to display the task because tasks that have been modified by the Task Scheduler are not visible to AT.

B. **Incorrect:** The Task Scheduler graphical administrative utility can update tasks created with the AT command, but makes the tasks invisible to the AT command-line utility after they have been modified.

C. **Incorrect:** The Task Scheduler does not duplicate tasks when making a modification, but it does make them invisible to AT.

D. **Correct:** The Task Scheduler and the AT command maintain entirely separate lists of scheduled tasks. Although the Task Scheduler can display tasks created with the AT command, it cannot directly modify those tasks. To modify a task created with the AT command, Task Scheduler removes the task from the AT command's list and adds the task to its own list. Therefore, tasks created with AT become invisible to AT after being modified with the Task Scheduler.

OBJECTIVE 4.2

Manage, monitor, and optimize system performance for mobile users.

Recent improvements in portable computer hardware have pushed more users toward mobile computing. Windows XP Professional supports these improvements in hardware by offering improved power management, hardware profiles, and offline capabilities. Even users who don't travel frequently use portable computers because they enable users to take their computing environment with them wherever they might be, with almost no drawbacks. Windows XP Professional's mobile computing environment is so intuitive that mobile users do not need special training. Administrators, however, need to have a detailed understanding of how the latest hardware and software work together to enable the mobile environment.

Power schemes provide a simple way to adjust the balance between power consumption and performance. Windows XP Professional includes six default power schemes: Home/Office Desk, Portable/Laptop, Presentation, Always On, Minimal Power Management, and Max Battery. You must understand how each of these affects system performance to complete this domain. Additionally, you must understand how to add and modify power schemes.

Standby and **hibernation** features work together to maximize battery life when a portable computer is used intermittently. Both features reduce power consumption when the system is not in use, but they function very differently. Standby turns off the display, hard disk, and other system components but draws small amounts of power to maintain the system's memory. Hibernation copies the contents of the system's memory to the hard disk, and then shuts down all components. Hibernation does not use any power, but takes longer than standby to restart.

Windows XP Professional has been designed to support **PnP** standards. PnP standards provide the operating system with a tremendous amount of information about the underlying hardware, and even allow the operating system to adjust to dynamically varying configurations. For example, Windows XP can automatically detect a printer the first time it is connected to the computer. If that printer is removed from the system, Windows XP detects this change and adapts to it. Although PnP makes managing computer hardware painless, not all hardware fully supports PnP standards. To accommodate this, Windows XP Professional can be configured to use **hardware profiles**.

Hardware profiles allow the user to select a subset of **drivers** to load. If hardware profiles are enabled, the user might be prompted to select from those hardware profiles before Windows XP Professional boots. Hardware profiles define a set of drivers that are enabled or disabled, and are useful only on computer systems that lack PnP support and have changing hardware configurations. For example, if Windows XP is installed on a legacy computer that is occasionally used with a modem that Windows XP cannot detect, it might be necessary to create different hardware profiles that enable and disable the modem driver.

To create a hardware profile, open Control Panel, select Performance and Maintenance, and click System. From the System Properties dialog box, select the Hardware tab, and click the Hardware Profiles button. This launches the Hardware Profiles tool, which allows you to specify that a computer will be used with a docking station or to manually create additional profiles.

Note There is no need to create a profile if a computer is being used in a docking station. Instead, select This Is A Portable Computer from the profile's properties.

The **Device Manager** is used to specify which devices will be enabled in a given hardware profile. To change the enabled drivers for a profile, first boot the computer using the profile you want to modify. Then, launch Device Manager. Right-click the driver you want to enable or disable, select Properties, and select the desired behavior at the Device Usage drop-down list.

Objective 4.2 Questions

70-270.04.02.001

You are configuring a new, fully PnP-compatible laptop for a user who will use the laptop both in a docking station and separate from the docking station. After installing Windows XP Professional, how must you configure the hardware profiles?

A. Make no changes to the hardware profiles.

B. Insert the laptop into the docking station and boot the computer. View the current hardware profile properties, select the This Is A Portable Computer check box, and select the option labeled The Computer Is Docked.

C. Create two new hardware profiles. Name the profiles Docked and Undocked.

D. Insert the laptop into the docking station and boot the computer. Create a copy of the current profile and name it Undocked.

70-270.04.02.002

Which is the correct tool for specifying which drivers will be loaded in a given hardware profile?

A. Task Manager

B. Device Manager

C. Computer Manager

D. System Monitor

70-270.04.02.003

Which power scheme is the correct choice for a mobile user who wants to maximize the lifetime of the battery, but needs the display to remain on at all times?

A. Home/Office Desk

B. Portable/Laptop

C. Presentation

D. Always On

E. Minimal Power Management

F. Max Battery

70-270.04.02.004

Which of these are advantages of standby mode over hibernation? (Choose two.)

A. Shorter wake-up period

B. Provides compliance with airline regulations regarding the use of electronic devices during takeoff and landing

C. Lower power consumption

D. No risk of data loss

E. Does not consume hard disk space

Objective 4.2 Answers

70-270.04.02.001

▶ **Correct Answers: A**

A. **Correct:** Hardware profiles are designed for computers that are not fully PnP-compatible. Computers with full PnP compatibility do not require hardware profiles to be configured.

B. **Incorrect:** Hardware profiles do not need to be configured for laptops that are fully PnP-compatible. This is the correct procedure, however, if the computer were not PnP-compatible.

C. **Incorrect:** Hardware profiles do not need to be configured for laptops that are fully PnP-compatible.

D. **Incorrect:** Hardware profiles do not need to be configured for laptops that are fully PnP-compatible.

70-270.04.02.002

▶ **Correct Answers: B**

A. **Incorrect:** The Task Manager is used to set process priorities and monitor processor performance, among other things. It cannot be used to specify which drivers are loaded in a given hardware profile.

B. **Correct:** The Device Manager is used to disable drivers for the current profile. To disable a driver for the current profile, start Windows XP using the profile that you want to configure. Then, launch Device Manager to view the properties of a driver. From the Device Usage drop-down list, select Do Not Use This Device In The Current Hardware Profile (Disable).

C. **Incorrect:** The Computer Manager is a set of snap-ins used to manage many aspects of a Windows XP Professional computer. However, it cannot be used to specify which drivers are loaded in a given hardware profile.

D. **Incorrect:** The System Monitor is used to monitor hundreds of performance counters, but it cannot be used to specify which drivers are loaded in a given hardware profile.

70-270.04.02.003

► **Correct Answers: C**

A. **Incorrect:** This power scheme does not meet the requirements. The Home/Office Desk scheme maintains constant power when the system is plugged in, but may turn off the display while on battery power.

B. **Incorrect:** This power scheme does not meet the requirements. The Portable/Laptop scheme turns off all system components after a short period of inactivity. This causes the display to shut down.

C. **Correct:** The Presentation power scheme maximizes battery life by allowing any component except for the display to be turned off when not in use. When the system is plugged in, the Presentation power scheme maintains constant power to the hard disk and system.

D. **Incorrect:** This scheme does not meet the requirements. The Always On scheme disables all power-saving features, ensuring optimum performance at the cost of battery life.

E. **Incorrect:** This scheme does not meet the requirements. The Minimal Power Management scheme maintains constant power when the system is plugged in, but may turn off the display while on battery power.

F. **Incorrect:** This scheme does not meet the requirements. The Max Battery scheme is excellent for conserving battery power, but may turn off the display.

70-270.04.02.004

► **Correct Answers: A and E**

A. **Correct:** Standby mode has a shorter wake-up period than hibernation mode. Waking from hibernation requires reading the contents of the system's memory from the hard disk.

B. **Incorrect:** A mobile computer running Windows XP Professional may wake up from standby mode to execute a scheduled task or switch to hibernation mode. This possibility restricts this mode from being used during the takeoff or landing of a commercial airplane.

C. **Incorrect:** Standby mode minimizes battery usage by shutting down as many components as possible. However, it maintains the state of the computer in the system's RAM, which requires small amounts of power. Hibernation writes the contents of the system's RAM to the hard disk, and shuts the system down completely. Therefore, hibernation has a lower power consumption than standby mode.

D. **Incorrect:** Standby mode maintains the state of the computer in the system's RAM, which requires small amounts of power. If power is lost suddenly, for example if the battery is removed, data is lost. Hibernation does not have this limitation because no power is required to maintain that state.

E. **Correct:** Standby mode maintains the state of the computer in system's RAM—only hibernation mode writes the system's memory to the hard drive. As a result, you must have enough free disk space to store the contents of the system's memory to use hibernation mode.

OBJECTIVE 4.3

Restore and back up the operating system, system state data, and user data.

Windows XP provides many tools for preventing disaster, but no operating system can prevent hardware failures. It is still critical to create a **disaster recovery** strategy that includes backups of system files and configuration information. Fortunately, Windows XP includes administrative utilities to simplify this process.

The most fundamental of these tools is the **Backup Utility**. This tool is launched from the Start menu. Select All Programs, navigate through the Accessories and System Tools folders, and click Backup. Alternatively, you can execute the command NTBACKUP.EXE. The Backup Utility includes wizards to back up files, restore files, and prepare your system for **Automated System Recovery (ASR)**.

The **System Restore** utility is launched from the same folder on the Start menu as the Backup Utility. Like the Last Known Good Configuration, the System Restore utility automatically creates a backup of vital system information. Unlike the Last Known Good Configuration, the System Restore utility keeps a history of system configurations and provides the user with the ability to restore the system state to a specific date. The System Restore utility, for example, allows a user to remove a set of **drivers** that were installed several days prior.

Note Restore Points can also be manually created using the System Restore utility— and it's a good idea to do this before installing an application or new hardware.

Windows XP includes several features to allow troubleshooting, even if the system has become so damaged that the operating system cannot successfully boot. The **Last Known Good Configuration** is a copy of critical system information that can be used if the computer cannot boot successfully. This backup of the system configuration is made after the user successfully logs on. As a result, if you were successful at logging into Windows XP since making the problematic configuration changes, using Last Known Good Configuration does not help. Press F8 at the operating system selection screen before booting to access the Last Known Good Configuration.

For problems that result in the inability to boot normally, but can't be resolved with the Last Known Good Configuration, use **Safe Mode**. Safe Mode boots a simplified version of Windows XP, and uses a minimal set of drivers and services. This often allows Safe Mode to operate when the system has been corrupted. To start Safe Mode, press F8 at the operating system selection screen and choose the desired option from the menu.

If Safe Mode doesn't work correctly, the **Recovery Console** provides a useful set of command-line utilities that can be used to troubleshoot problems. Recovery Console is similar to a command prompt, and allows you to view text files, and replace system files, among other tasks. This tool is not installed by default, but can be accessed by booting from a Windows XP Professional CD and starting the setup routine. Alternatively, you can add Recovery Console as an option on your system's boot menu by inserting the Windows XP Professional CD and executing the command \i386\winnt32.exe /cmdcons.

Objective 4.3 Questions

70-270.04.03.001

Your Windows XP Professional system fails to boot after you add a new network card driver. Which feature of Windows XP Professional must you use to return the system to the state it was in prior to adding the driver?

A. BOOT.INI

B. System Restore

C. Last Known Good Configuration

D. Recovery Console

70-270.04.03.002

After an unexpected power outage, a user's Windows XP Professional system fails to boot successfully. The boot process allows you to select an instance of Windows XP Professional to boot from, but fails partially through the startup routine. Which tools can you use to diagnose and resolve this problem? (Choose three.)

A. System Restore

B. Last Known Good Configuration

C. Safe Mode

D. Recovery Console

E. ASR

F. Device Manager

70-270.04.03.003

Which of the following tasks can be accomplished from the Windows XP Professional recovery console? (Choose four.)

A. Format a hard disk.

B. Boot to the Last Known Good Configuration.

C. Set services to be disabled or start automatically.

D. Reinstall Windows XP.

E. Restore damaged system files from a CD.

F. Restore damaged system files from a network share.

G. Edit the BOOT.INI file.

70-270.04.03.004

Which of the following tasks must you do before installing a new application that might cause a Windows XP Professional system to become unstable? (Choose two.)

A. Create a new Restore Point using System Restore.

B. Boot to the Last Known Good Configuration.

C. Back up all files using the Backup Utility Wizard.

D. Boot into Safe Mode.

E. Boot into the Recovery Console.

70-270.04.03.005

You are designing a backup strategy for your Windows XP Professional system. You cannot afford to lose more than a single day's work, so you must back up the system every night. You want to minimize the tape backup media used to store your backups, but you do not want to use more than two backup tapes to perform a complete system restore. Which of the following backup procedures meets your needs?

A. Normal backup nightly

B. Incremental backup nightly

C. Differential backup nightly

D. Normal backup weekly, incremental backup nightly

E. Normal backup weekly, differential backup nightly

Objective 4.3 Answers

70-270.04.03.001

▶ **Correct Answers: C**

A. **Incorrect:** The BOOT.INI file specifies the set of choices that are presented to the user before the operating system is loaded. The BOOT.INI file can be configured to allow for booting between several different instances of Windows, but it cannot be used to modify the configuration of Windows XP.

B. **Incorrect:** The System Restore tool is used to roll back the configuration of a Windows XP system. However, it can be used only after the operating system has booted. In this case, the System Restore tool is inaccessible because the operating system is unbootable.

C. **Correct:** The Last Known Good Configuration is a copy of the system state stored in HKLM\System\CurrentControlSet registry key when a user last successfully logged on. You can revert to this backup configuration by rebooting the computer and pressing F8 when prompted to select the operating system from which to start. From the Windows XP Professional Advanced Options menu, select the Last Known Good Configuration option.

D. **Incorrect:** The Recovery Console can be a useful tool for recovering a system that does not boot correctly, but it is not useful for restoring the last working configuration of a system. Use the Recovery Console only when all other methods have failed.

70-270.04.03.002

▶ **Correct Answers: C, D, and E**

   A. **Incorrect:** The System Restore utility is useful for troubleshooting problems caused by system mis-configurations. However, it can be used only if the system is bootable.

   B. **Incorrect:** The Last Known Good Configuration is a quick way to resolve problems caused by mis-configurations and faulty drivers. Although the Last Known Good Configuration is available at the boot menu, and can therefore be used in this scenario, it does not resolve the problem. Failure to boot after a power failure is generally caused by corrupted files or a damaged hard disk—neither of which Last Known Good Configuration is capable of repairing.

   C. **Correct:** Safe Mode might or might not work in this scenario, but it is the first thing to try. Safe Mode loads a minimal set of drivers, and as such, has a higher chance of successfully booting than Windows XP Professional's standard boot mode. If Safe Mode does start successfully, you can use the graphical user interface to diagnose the hardware problems.

   D. **Correct:** The Recovery Console is a useful tool for recovering a system that does not boot correctly. If the system has the recovery console installed, it is an option on the boot menu. If it is not installed, insert the Windows XP Professional CD and boot from the CD—the Recovery Console is an option. Recovery Console is command-line only, so it is not as convenient for diagnosis and troubleshooting as safe mode. However, because it can be loaded from a CD, it starts even if the system's hard disk is completely destroyed. In this scenario, use the Recovery Console to diagnose the extent of the damage. If you determine that system files have been damaged, you can initiate a scan of the disk and, if necessary, restore files from the system CD.

   E. **Correct:** You use ASR only after attempts to resolve the problem with Safe Mode and the Recovery Console have failed. If the hard disk is functional but files have been damaged, ASR is able to make the Windows XP Professional installation bootable. If the hard disk itself is damaged, you need to fix those errors or replace the hard disk before using ASR.

   F. **Incorrect:** The Device Manager is a useful tool for diagnosing problems relating to hardware drivers. However, it is accessible only after the system has successfully booted. In this scenario, you are not able to get access to the Device Manager tool.

70-270.04.03.003

▶ **Correct Answers: A, C, E, and F**

A. **Correct:** The FORMAT recovery console command can be used to format a hard disk. This process erases all data on the hard disk, and must be used only when all other recovery methods fail.

B. **Incorrect:** You cannot boot the computer directly from the Recovery Console. The system must be rebooted before Windows XP can be started in any configuration.

C. **Correct:** The ENABLE and DISABLE Recovery Console can be used to set the startup value of services.

D. **Incorrect:** The Recovery Console cannot be used to launch the Windows XP setup routine.

E. **Correct:** The Recovery Console can copy files from floppy drives and CDs using the COPY command.

F. **Correct:** The Recovery Console can copy files across the network after a drive letter has been mapped using the NET USE command.

G. **Incorrect:** The Recovery Console lacks a utility to edit files. Instead, copy a valid BOOT.INI file from a floppy drive, CD, or network share.

70-270.04.03.004

▶ **Correct Answers: A and C**

A. **Correct:** Creating a Restore Point is a quick, easy way to make a snapshot of a system's current configuration. Creating a restore point prior to installing a new application enables you to restore the system's configuration if the new application causes problems.

B. **Incorrect:** Use the Last Known Good Configuration only if the system becomes unbootable. It might be a useful tool if the new application stops your system from starting successfully, but it must not be used prior to installing an application.

C. **Correct:** The Backup Utility enables you to back up all files and configuration settings to removable media. Having a valid backup allows a Windows XP Professional system to be completely rebuilt in the event of a complete failure. Always create a backup of a system before installing a potentially troublesome application.

D. **Incorrect:** Safe Mode is a valuable tool for repairing a system that is having problems booting. However, only use it after the system has failed.

E. **Incorrect:** The Recovery Console can salvage systems that are otherwise completely unbootable. Do not use it prior to installing an application, however, because it does not facilitate backing up files or configurations.

70-270.04.03.005

▶ **Correct Answers: E**

A. **Incorrect:** Performing a normal backup every night enables you to restore the entire system using only a single night's backup tape. However, it uses more tape backup media than is necessary because every file on the system is backed up every night.

B. **Incorrect:** The incremental backup makes a copy of all files marked with the archive attribute. After each file has been backed up, the file's archive attribute is cleared. Therefore, the incremental backup copies only files that were modified since the last backup. Performing only incremental backups would require restoring every single backup ever made in the event of a hard disk failure.

C. **Incorrect:** The differential backup makes a copy of all files marked with the archive attribute. Unlike the incremental backup, the differential backup does not modify the archive attribute of files after creating the backup. In this way, performing a differential backup every night ensures that every file modified since the last full backup can be restored. This is useful when combined with a Normal backup, but using only differential backups results in a backup set that grows larger every night. Therefore, the differential backup does not meet the criteria of minimizing the backup media used.

D. **Incorrect:** This is a common backup strategy, but it does not meet the requirement of only needing to restore two sets of backups for a complete system recovery. Each incremental backup copies only those files that were modified since the prior night's backup. Therefore, every single incremental backup since the last normal backup must be restored to ensure total data recovery. For example, if a Normal backup was performed on a Sunday and incremental backups thereafter, restoring the system on Thursday requires restoring Sunday's normal backup and Monday's, Tuesday's, and Wednesday's incremental backups.

E. **Correct:** This backup strategy meets all the requirements. Differential backups copy all files modified since the last normal backup, enabling a maximum of two separate restores to completely rebuild a file system. For example, if a Normal backup was performed on a Sunday and differential backups thereafter, restoring the system on Thursday requires restoring only Sunday's normal backup and Wednesday's differential backup.

Configuring and Troubleshooting the Desktop Environment

The desktop environment in Microsoft Windows XP Professional is both flexible and customizable. It can be configured to meet the needs and tastes of a wide range of users and organizations. Although flexibility is desirable in many situations, some organizations need to be able to enforce specific policies for the appearance and functionality of desktop elements because of security or supportability requirements. This objective examines how to configure a Windows XP Professional desktop and how to troubleshoot problems that might arise with the desktop environment.

The first thing many people think of when they consider customizing the desktop environment is configuring the desktop interface. In Windows XP Professional, you can customize nearly every element of the interface, for example Web content can be placed on the background. You can also select from many built-in screen savers, and other ones can be acquired and installed. Additionally, standard folders such as My Documents can be redirected to network file servers. There are also many built-in themes available that define the appearance of buttons, toolbars, window frames, title bars, and other user interface elements. All of these can be selected locally using programs located in Control Panel or they can be managed centrally via **Group Policy Objects (GPOs)**. Typically you manage Group Policies on the network by using the **Active Directory service** running on Microsoft Windows 2000 Servers and the Group Policy snap-in. With one of the server editions of Windows 2000 configured as a domain controller running Active Directory, GPOs can be applied at the **domain**, **site**, **organizational unit (OU)**, computer, and group level. You can also manage local Group Policy by using the Local Computer Policy snap-in—this can be launched from a command prompt by typing **gpedit.msc**.

Windows XP Professional provides different levels of support for multiple languages in each of its three versions. Windows XP Professional International English is intended to transact most business in English; however, it can be used to read and edit documents in many other languages. Windows XP Professional Localized Language is available for many different languages—each language-specific version is intended to be used primarily in that language, however, they all can be used to read and edit documents in many other languages. Windows XP Professional Multilingual User Interface Pack allows you to quickly switch between any of the 24 included Localized Language Versions (including English), as well as edit documents in many additional languages. Although the needs of many U.S. organizations will be met by the International English Version, the other options allow multinational firms to deploy computers with user interfaces localized to the needs of users in each country where they do business.

Software application distribution can be managed over the network by blending **Group Policy** and the **Windows Installer Service**. Managing application distribution can be centralized, distributed, or somewhere in between depending on the business needs of the organization by building an effective Active Directory infrastructure. Software applications are wrapped for installation in **Windows Installer Packages** using .msi files. Applications can also be installed and uninstalled manually by using the Add or Remove Programs application located in Control Panel.

User profiles allow each user who logs on to a particular Windows XP Professional computer to maintain unique desktop settings. User profiles can also be configured to move between computers on a network so that no matter what system users log on to, their customized desktop environment appears. A profile configured in this manner is called a **roaming user profile**. Users can be prevented from permanently changing a roaming user profile by converting it to a **mandatory user profile**. Administrators can also enforce standard desktop settings by using Group Policies.

Organizations can provide support for users with special needs by taking advantage of the **Accessibility Services** included with Windows XP Professional. High contrast display settings, translation of sounds into visual captions, customized input methods, magnified displays, and a text-to-speech tool are some of the accessibility features included with Windows XP Professional. You configure these through the Accessibility Options program located in Control Panel.

Desktop interface settings, language selection, software distribution, accessibility services, and fax services might require troubleshooting. Become familiar with all the tools used to configure and troubleshoot these features.

Tested Skills and Suggested Practices

The skills you need to successfully master the Installing Windows XP Professional Objective Domain on the *Installing, Configuring, and Administering Microsoft Windows XP Professional* exam include

- **Managing user profiles.**

  - Practice 1: Launch Control Panel, select Performance And Maintenance, and then select System. Select the Advanced tab, and then select the Settings button in the User Profiles section of the dialog box. The User Profiles dialog box appears; use it to copy and delete a user profile.

  - Practice 2: Create a new local user account and log on to the computer using that account. Type **set** at a command prompt to see a list of the configured environment variables. Make note of the value for the *%userprofile%* variable. Log off the computer and log back on with an account that has local administrator privileges. Open the User Profiles dialog box as discussed in Practice 1 and delete the user profile for this new local user. Log off the computer and back on with the new local user. Type **set** at the command prompt to see how the *%userprofile%* variable has changed. Repeat these steps at least two more times with this user account.

  - Practice 3: Launch Control Panel, select Performance And Maintenance, select System, select the Advanced tab, and then select the Environment Variables button to open the EnvironmentVariables dialog box. Note which variables appear under the User variables section and which appear under the Systems variables section. Determine what happens when you create a new variable under each section and log on using different user accounts. Identify which environment variables are present regardless of which user account is logged on.

  - Practice 4: Configure a roaming user profile on a workgroup computer, and then configure a fully functional roaming user profile using Active Directory and one of the server editions of Windows 2000. Copy a local user profile to a network location and configure a domain account to use that roaming user profile and then log on to the network using that account.

  - Practice 5: Using two Active Directory domain accounts, configure each type of mandatory user profiles (NTUSER.MAN and *profile_folder*.MAN). Log on to a computer running Windows XP Professional with each of these accounts and then disconnect the computer from the network. Attempt to log on again with each account and identify which mandatory user profile allows you to log on with the cached copy of the profile.

- **Managing multiple languages.**

  - Practice 1: Using information available in the *Microsoft Windows XP Professional Resource Kit Documentation*, create a table showing which of the three versions of Windows XP Professional support the following features: ability to read and edit documents in multiple languages, language and regional support for 24 localized language versions, localized language user interface, ability to transact business primarily in English but to have access to additional languages, ability to transact business primarily in one or more languages besides English, and single worldwide rollouts for hot fixes and service packs.

  - Practice 2: Using information available in the *Microsoft Windows XP Professional Resource Kit Documentation*, create a table showing the disk requirements for adding three of the complex script and three of the East Asian language collections to the International English Version of Windows XP Professional.

  - Practice 3: Install an additional Language Group on a computer running the International English Version of Windows XP Professional. Visit two or more Web sites written in languages supported by the newly installed Language Group and copy the text into a text editor. Print a page from each Web site to verify that printing in the newly installed languages is possible. Enable the Language Bar and use it to quickly shift the keyboard from one language to another.

  - Practice 4: Install the Windows XP Professional Multilingual User Interface Pack and use the Regional and Language Options application in Control Panel to select a non-English language. Open and use several of the applications included with Windows XP Professional such as WordPad, Solitaire, and Calculator to verify that the menus, dialog boxes, and other user interface elements appear in the language you selected.

  - Practice 5: Select a different region such as English (United Kingdom) or Italian (Italy) on the Regional Options tab of the Regional and Language Options dialog box. Open the Date and Time Properties program in Control Panel to see how the appearance of the calendar and clock changes when you specify a new region.

- **Customizing desktop settings.**

  - Practice 1: Right-click the taskbar to open the Taskbar And Start Menu Properties dialog box. Customize the behavior and appearance of the taskbar and Start menu using the various options available on the Taskbar and Start Menu tabs.

  - Practice 2: Right-click the Start menu and select Explore. Right-click the Start menu and select Explore All Users. Compare the locations displayed in each

Explorer window, and examine the subfolders and files contained within each location.

- Practice 3: Use the Display program from the Appearance And Themes group in Control Panel to display a Web page as the desktop background. Visit the Internet Explorer Desktop Gallery to add several Active Desktop objects to the desktop. To access the Active Desktop Gallery from the Display program, select the Desktop tab, click the Customize Desktop button, select the Web tab, click the New button, and then click the Visit Gallery button when the New Active Desktop Item dialog box appears.

- Practice 4: Using the Display program from the Appearance And Themes group in Control Panel, select a different Theme for the desktop on the Theme tab.

- Practice 5: Select the Appearance tab in the Display Program located in the Appearance And Themes group in Control Panel and switch to Windows Classic from the drop-down list below Windows and buttons. Select different options from the drop-down list below Color Scheme. Click the Effects button and see how different choices affect the behavior of the user interface elements. Click the Advanced button and experiment with specifying custom colors for specific user interface elements.

- Practice 6: Open the Group Policy snap-in to view the Local Computer Policy. Examine the configuration choices available under the Administrative Templates folder of the User Configuration node. Experiment with some of the settings available under these folders: Start Menu And Taskbar; Desktop; and Control Panel\Display.

- **Automating software installation using the Windows Installer Service.**

  - Practice 1: In a network running Active Directory, use the Windows 2000 Server Group Policy snap-in to assign and publish software applications to users. Be sure you understand which choice forces installation and which makes the installation optionally available. Use Group Policy to assign software to a computer, and then reboot that computer and log on to it to verify that the software was installed automatically.

  - Practice 2: Perform a Windows Installer–based routine (that is, from an .msi file) installation such as Microsoft Office XP Professional or the ADMINPAK.MSI located on the Windows 2000 Server installation CD-ROM in the \I386 folder. Use the Add or Remove Programs program in Control Panel to alter the installation, and then remove the newly installed program.

■ Practice 3: Create a transform file (.mst) in order to customize the installation of a Windows Installer–based installation routine. Configure the transform file so that the installation routine runs in silent mode. Run the customized installation by specifying the transform file in the Windows Installer command line.

■ **Configuring Accessibility Services.**

■ Practice 1: Log on to your computer with an account that has user privileges. Open the Accessibility Wizard located on the Start menu in the All Programs\Accessories\Accessibility folder and step through all the available options. Log off the computer and back on with an account that has administrator privileges. Open the Accessibility Wizard again and step through all the available options, noting any differences in the available selections.

■ Practice 2: Use the Accessibility Options program from the Accessibility Options group in Control Panel to customize the behavior of various accessibility features included with Windows XP Professional.

■ Practice 3: Open Utility Manager by holding down the Windows logo key and pressing **U** on the keyboard. Users with administrative privileges can configure start options for the Magnifier, Narrator, and On-Screen Keyboard. Users without administrator privileges can open Utility Manager to manually start and stop these three tools. Users can even open Utility Manager before logging on to Windows XP Professional so that they can more readily navigate the logon procedure despite their special needs.

■ Practice 4: Configure the Magnifier, Narrator, and On-Screen Keyboard accessibility tools.

Further Reading

This section lists supplemental readings by objective. We recommend that you study these sources thoroughly before taking exam 70-270.

Objective 5.1

Open Help and Support from the Start menu and with the Help Index and the Help Search, look for the term *User Profile*. Scroll down to and view the articles about configuring user profiles such as "Assign a logon script to a profile," "Assign a mandatory user profile," "Creating a roaming or mandatory profile," and "Understanding User Profiles." Be sure to select additional articles from the Related Topics link available at the bottom of each of the articles you review.

Microsoft Corporation. *Microsoft Windows 2000 Server Resource Kit*. Volume: *Windows 2000 Server Deployment Planning Guide*. Redmond, Washington: Microsoft

Press, 2000. Review Chapter 24, "Applying Change and Configuration Management." To read this chapter online, visit the Microsoft TechNet site at *http://www.microsoft.com/TechNet/win2000/dguide/chapt-24.asp*. This chapter covers all the technologies for user configuration management available with Windows 2000 Server and Active Directory.

Microsoft Corporation. *Microsoft Windows XP Professional Resource Kit Documentation*. Redmond, Washington: Microsoft Press, 2001. Read Chapter 5, "Managing Desktops." This chapter examines options for configuring Windows XP desktops in workgroup and Active Directory domain environments; information relating to user profiles appears throughout it.

Microsoft Corporation. *MCSE Training Kit: Microsoft Windows XP Professional*. Redmond, Washington: Microsoft Press, 2001. Read and complete Lesson 4 in Chapter 3, "Setting Up and Managing User Accounts."

Objective 5.2

Microsoft Corporation. *Microsoft Windows XP Professional Resource Kit Documentation*. Redmond, Washington: Microsoft Press, 2001. Read Chapter 3, "Multilingual Solutions for Global Business." This chapter examines the levels of support for multiple languages and locations available in the different versions of Windows XP Professional.

Microsoft Corporation. *MCSE Training Kit: Microsoft Windows XP Professional*. Redmond, Washington: Microsoft Press, 2001. Read and complete Lesson 4 in Chapter 10, "Configuring Windows XP Professional."

Objective 5.3

Microsoft Corporation. *Microsoft Windows XP Professional Resource Kit Documentation*. Redmond, Washington: Microsoft Press, 2001. Read Chapter 5, "Managing Desktops." This chapter introduces desktop management features in Windows XP Professional when running in workgroups or as part of Active Directory domains using IntelliMirror, Group Policy, and the Windows Installer Service.

Microsoft Corporation. *Microsoft Windows 2000 Server Resource Kit*. Volume: *The Distributed Systems Guide*. Redmond, Washington: Microsoft Press, 2000. Read Chapter 23, "Software Installation and Maintenance," to learn about software management and the Windows Installer Service. Visit the Microsoft TechNet site at *http://www.microsoft.com/technet/win2000/dguide/chapt-23.asp* to read this chapter online.

Microsoft Corporation. "Software Installation and Maintenance." 2000. This white paper is available at *http://www.microsoft.com/windows2000/techinfo/administration/management/siamwp.asp* or, if the white paper has moved, by searching for the title at *http://www.microsoft.com*. This title examines the various technologies included with the server editions of Windows 2000 for managing software installation in an Active Directory environment.

Objective 5.4

Microsoft Corporation. *Microsoft Windows XP Professional Resource Kit Documentation*. Redmond, Washington: Microsoft Press, 2001. Read Chapter 5, "Managing Desktops." This chapter introduces desktop management features in Windows XP Professional when running in workgroups or as part of Active Directory domains using IntelliMirror, Group Policy, and the Windows Installer Service.

Microsoft Corporation. "User Data and Settings Management." 2000. This white paper is available at *http://www.microsoft.com/windows2000/techinfo/administration/management/settings.asp* or, if the white paper has moved, by searching for the title at *http://www.microsoft.com*. Review this paper for a detailed look at managing user data and settings in Active Directory using IntelliMirror and Group Policy.

Microsoft Corporation. *MCSE Training Kit: Microsoft Windows XP Professional*. Redmond, Washington: Microsoft Press, 2001. Read and complete Lessons 1, 2, 3, and 4 in Chapter 10, "Configuring Windows XP Professional."

Objective 5.5

Microsoft Corporation. *Microsoft Windows XP Professional Resource Kit Documentation*. Redmond, Washington: Microsoft Press, 2001. Read Appendix I, "Accessibility for People with Disabilities." This appendix covers enabling, configuring, and troubleshooting all the accessibility features available in Windows XP Professional.

Select Help from the Magnifier, Narrator, On-Screen Keyboard, and Utility Manager. Read all the articles available in each of these Help files.

Microsoft Corporation. *MCSE Training Kit: Microsoft Windows XP Professional*. Redmond, Washington: Microsoft Press, 2001. Read and complete Lesson 4 in Chapter 10, "Configuring Windows XP Professional."

Configure and manage user profiles.

User profiles contain desktop configuration information such as network connections, the location of the My Documents folder, the contents of the Quick Launch toolbar, and the contents of the Start menu. User profiles can be linked to a user account and they can be stored locally as a **local user profile** or on network file share as a **roaming user profile**. The settings of the local user profile are applied whenever the user with that profile linked to his or her account logs on to that particular computer. Roaming user profiles are applied whenever the user with that profile logs on to any computer on the network. This is a useful feature when a person regularly uses multiple computers, but be aware that user profiles can grow quite large—multigigabyte profiles are becoming increasingly common. The entire profile must be copied across the network whenever somebody with a roaming user profile logs on to a computer for the first time. Although it's possible to employ roaming user profiles in a workgroup setting, it is more effective and easier to implement them in a Windows 2000 **domain** environment. With the use of IntelliMirror, Folder Redirection, and Group Policy you may achieve multigigabyte profiles that are stored on the network and do not require copying across the network because they are virtually available on a local computer.

Two local profiles are created during the installation of Windows XP Professional in the *%systemdrive%*/Documents and Settings folder. The All Users Profile is located in the All Users folder and the Default Users Profile is placed in the Default Users folder. Settings for everyone who logs on to a computer are stored in the All Users Profile. When a user with no profile logs on to a computer, a new folder is created in the *%systemdrive%*/Documents and Settings folder and the contents of the Default Users Profile is copied to it. Windows XP Professional ensures that user profiles for each user of a particular computer are kept separate by automatically naming the folder for a new profile after the user's logon name. If that name has already been used for a different profile, Windows XP Professional appends either the *.computername* for a workgroup-based account or *.domainname* for a domain-based account. If that still results in a duplicate folder name, three-digit numbers are appended to the *.computername* or *.domainname* extension.

You can manage user profiles on a computer by opening Control Panel, selecting Performance And Maintenance, and clicking System. Select the Advanced tab and then click the Settings button in the User Profile section. Both local user profiles and locally cached roaming user profiles appear in the User Profiles dialog box. You can copy and delete user profiles stored on the local computer from this dialog box. You create a roaming profile by copying a local user's profile to a network file share and then editing the user's domain account. Ensure that all users have read and write permissions to their own profiles on the network share and the folder where they are stored.

You can use mandatory profiles to keep users from making changes to their profiles. Although they can make changes while logged on, the original settings are automatically restored when the user logs on again. This is a useful approach to managing systems used by many users such as public kiosks, or when you want to minimize the administrative overhead for managing desktop systems. You can implement mandatory profiles in two distinct manners: You can rename the file called NTUSER.DAT to NTUSER.MAN (this file is stored in the root folder of each user's roaming user profile), or you can append.man to the end of the name of the Roaming User Profile folder. The first approach allows users to log on using the locally cached copy of the profile if the network is unavailable. The second approach forbids logging on unless the roaming user profile is accessible on the network. Use caution when implementing this more restrictive approach because no users will be able to log on if the file server that holds their profiles in unavailable.

Objective 5.1 Questions

70-270.05.01.001

John and Mary share the same computer running Windows XP Professional. You log on to their computer with an account that has administrative access and install a suite of internally developed applications used to access data on some of your firm's mainframe computers. You confirm that the applications were correctly installed by opening and testing each from their shortcuts on the Start menu. Later, they both report that they cannot find the icons for any of the programs. Which of the following is the quickest way to ensure that both John and Mary can easily access the suite of applications you just installed?

A. Copy the program group for the suite of applications from your user profile to the Default User profile.

B. Copy the program group for the suite of applications from your user profile to John and Mary's user profiles.

C. Have John log on to the computer and install the suite of applications, and then have him log off. Have Mary perform the same installation while logged on with her user account.

D. Copy the program group for the suite of applications from your user profile to the All Users profile.

70-270.05.01.002

How do you configure a mandatory roaming user profile that allows users to log on to their computer with the locally cached copy of their profile when the network version is unavailable?

A. This is not possible because users with mandatory user profiles can never log on to computers with locally cached copies of their profiles.

B. Append .man to the end of the name of the Roaming User Profile folder.

C. Configure their user account to use a roaming profile, and then rename the file called NTUSER.DAT to NTUSER.MAN in the root folder of their roaming profile.

D. Edit the properties of the domain user account using the Active Directory Users and Computers MMC snap-in.

70-270.05.01.003

You have been told to increase security for your organization's network by designing a more tightly controlled approach to managing user desktop settings and data. The goals for your project are to

- Store user desktop settings in roaming profiles that will be available to users regardless of which computer they log on to.

- Prevent users from logging on with cached profiles when the network is unavailable.

- Minimize the amount of time required for mobile users to log on to their computers when away from the office.

- Ensure that all confidential user data is secure, even if a mobile user's laptop computer is stolen.

- Ensure that all critical user data is backed up regularly according to your organization's backup policy.

- Allow users to manage their own desktop settings.

You propose to do the following:

- Configure each user's account to employ a roaming user profile using the Active Directory Users and Computers snap-in.

- Make user profiles mandatory by appending .man to the root folder of each of the user profiles on the network.

- Use Group Policy to redirect the My Documents to a distributed file system (DFS) share located on several file servers that are secured and backed up according to your organization's policies.

- Implement Offline Folders so that users can work with their documents even when not connected to the network.

Which of the following goals does your proposed solution accomplish? (Choose three.)

A. Store user desktop settings in roaming profiles that will be available to users regardless of which computer they log on to.

B. Prevent users from logging on with cached profiles when the network is unavailable.

C. Minimize the amount of time required for mobile users to log on to their computers when away from the office.

D. Ensure that all confidential user data is secure, even if a mobile user's laptop computer is stolen.

E. Ensure that all critical user data is backed up regularly according to your organization's backup policy.

F. Allow users to manage their own desktop settings.

Objective 5.1 Answers

70-270.05.01.001

▶ **Correct Answers: D**

- A. **Incorrect:** Although copying the program group to the Default User profile ensures that any newly created profiles on the computer get a copy, existing user profiles do not.

- B. **Incorrect:** These procedures ensure that both John and Mary have access to the new program group, but there is a quicker way to accomplish this.

- C. **Incorrect:** It is possible that neither John nor Mary will be able to complete the installation if they do not have administrative privileges on the computer. Even if these procedures do work, it is an unnecessarily time-consuming solution.

- D. **Correct:** This is the quickest way to resolve the problem. Program groups present in the All Users profiles are accessible to everyone who logs on to the computer. This type of issue is common with older applications and with internally developed programs that have not met all the requirements for the Certified for Windows logo program. Certified programs are required to recognize user profiles and to give the installer the option of making the program group accessible to all users or only the user logged on during the installation.

70-270.05.01.002

▶ **Correct Answers: C**

- A. **Incorrect:** There is a way to implement mandatory user profiles that allows users to log on with a locally cached copy of their profile.

- B. **Incorrect:** This method of implementing mandatory roaming user profiles prevents users from logging on when the network copy of their profile is unavailable.

- C. **Correct:** This is the correct method of implementing a roaming mandatory user profile that will allow users to log on to computers with locally cached copies of their profile when the network is unavailable.

- D. **Incorrect:** Although you configure roaming profiles using this snap-in, you do not use this tool to configure mandatory profiles.

70-270.05.01.003

▶ **Correct Answers: A, B, and E**

   A. **Correct:** By implementing roaming user profiles, your solution ensures that each user's profile will be available from any computer on the network.

   B. **Correct:** By using the method of appending .man to the end of all users' Roaming User Profile folder, they are unable to log on to computers using locally cached copies of their profiles.

   C. **Incorrect:** Appending .man to the end of each user's Roaming User Profile folder forces Windows XP Professional to download the entire user profile every time a user logs on. Although you are redirecting the My Documents to a location separate from each user's profile, the profiles can still grow large, leading to long logon times for remote users. It is important to note that this goal conflicts with the second goal—sometimes it is not possible to achieve all desired goals.

   D. **Incorrect:** Nothing in your proposed solution addresses this goal. Implementing Certificate Services and the Encrypted File System (EFS) in combination with the Offline Files feature allows you to better protect the data of the mobile users.

   E. **Correct:** By redirecting the My Documents folder to a DFS share that is located on file servers that are backed up regularly, you have ensured that critical user data is backed up periodically.

   F. **Incorrect:** If you implement mandatory profiles, users are no longer able to manage their desktop settings. Any changes users make to their desktops will be discarded when they log off.

Configure support for multiple languages or multiple locations.

Windows XP Professional is available in three versions that provide different levels of support for multiple languages. The **English Version** includes the **Multilingual Editing and Viewing** feature, which allows the user to view, edit, and print information in more than 60 languages. The English Version is appropriate for occasional electronic communications in non-English languages. The **Translated Version** is a localized version that provides the same type of support as the English Version but all built-in menus, dialog boxes, Help files, wizards, and file systems appear in whatever language was purchased. Implement the Translated Version when support for a few languages is needed throughout the entire organization. The **Windows XP Professional Multilingual User Interface Pack (MUI Pack)** is the most flexible because not only does it provide the same level of support as the other versions, but you can also switch from one language to another on the fly. The MUI Pack is the best choice when support for numerous languages is needed across the organization. The MUI Pack also simplifies administration by allowing a single version of Windows XP Professional to be deployed in an organization with users who speak many different native languages.

In any version of Windows XP Professional, you open the Regional and Language Options program by selecting Date, Time, Language, and Regional Options in Control Panel to configure locale specific information. The Regional Options tab allows you to select format schemes for dates, times, currency, and numbers for languages such as English (United States) or Portuguese (Brazil). The Languages tab is where you install and select additional languages for viewing, editing, and printing. Enabling some languages might require installation of the corresponding Language Group from the Windows XP Professional Installation CD-ROM. Select the Advanced tab to configure support for displaying languages for programs that do not support Unicode text.

Users can add additional Input Languages using the Regional and Language Options program. The Input Languages specifies the language being entered, the keyboard layout, speech-to-text converter, or other input device being used. When you switch Input Languages, some programs offer additional features. For example, Office XP includes fonts and spelling checkers designed for different Input Languages.

To add an Input Language:

1. Select the Language tab, and then click the Details button under Text Services And Input Languages.

2. The Text Services And Input Languages dialog box appears; click the Add button under Installed Services.

3. The Add Input Language dialog box appears. Use the drop-down list to select the desired language and click the OK button to close each of the dialog boxes.

If the MUI Pack is installed, an additional drop-down list titled Menus And Dialogs appears on the General tab in the Regional and Language Options program. You can select any installed language using this drop-down list. The language selected is assigned to either a specific users profile or to the All Users Profile. You must log off for the changes to take effect—after you log in again, the text in most menus, dialog boxes, wizards, and Help files appears in the language selected. These changes affect only files and applications included with Windows XP Professional; for example, the English Version of the Windows XP Professional Resource Kit menus still appears in English.

Objective 5.2 Questions

70-270.05.02.001

Your organization has major offices in Spain, Portugal, France, Germany, Poland, Great Britain, and the United States. Many users do not speak or write English fluently. Users in many locations must regularly create and receive documents in two or more languages. Your organization has decided to migrate to Windows XP Professional and it is up to you to recommend how to best support the multilingual needs of the users. Which of the following do you suggest?

A. Create a standard base desktop using the Windows XP Professional MUI Pack. Be sure to install all the Input Languages used throughout your organization so that users can easily exchange documents in any language with one another.

B. Create a standard base desktop using the English Version of Windows XP Professional. Be sure to install all the Input Languages used throughout your organization so that users can easily exchange documents in any language with one another. Recommend to your manager that all users be signed up for extensive English language courses as soon as possible.

C. Create a standard base desktop using the English Version of Windows XP Professional. Recommend to your manager that all users be signed up for extensive English language courses as soon as possible. Require users to create all their documents in English.

D. Create standard base desktops using the English Version and the appropriate Translated versions of Windows XP Professional. Be sure to install all the Input Languages used throughout your organization so that users can easily exchange documents in any language with one another.

70-270.05.02.002

Your company has offices spread across the United States and Canada. Although all employees speak and write English fluently, your company occasionally does business with organizations in the Canadian province of Quebec. Some of these organizations do the majority of their business in French. What must you do at the Windows XP Professional computers of employees who will be working with these organizations?

A. Open WordPad and select the French (Canada) input locale.

B. Install the French Translated Version of Windows XP Professional.

C. Install the French version of WordPad by downloading it from the Windows Update Web site.

D. Use the Regional and Languages Options program by launching Control Panel and then choosing Date, Time, Language, and Regional Options to enable support for French (Canada) as an input language. If prompted, provide the location of the Windows XP Professional installation media and restart the computer.

70-270.05.02.003

You are a consultant who was asked by a worldwide commercial property management firm to plan an upgrade program to deploy the MUI Pack throughout its organization. The firm has many offices around the globe, most of which haven't been tightly managed by their information technology group. A thorough audit of the hardware and software reveals that the firm is running a variety of previous Windows versions on a multitude of hardware platforms. You determine that many systems will have to be replaced because that will be less expensive than trying to upgrade the hardware to the point where it could reliably run Windows XP Professional. Which of the following versions of Windows can be upgraded directly to the MUI Pack? (Choose four.)

A. Windows 2000 Server

B. Microsoft Windows Me

C. Microsoft Windows NT Workstation 4

D. Microsoft Windows NT Server 4

E. Microsoft Windows NT Workstation 3.51

F. Microsoft Windows 2000 Professional

G. Microsoft Windows 98

Objective 5.2 Answers

70-270.05.02.001

▶ **Correct Answers: A**

A. **Correct:** This is the easiest approach to this challenge because the information technology group within your organization will have a single standard desktop to maintain and support.

B. **Incorrect:** Although this approach might be easier on your organization's information technology group, it does not fulfill the needs of your users. Forcing the users to learn a second language is expensive and time-consuming and will likely cause resentment among some of them.

C. **Incorrect:** This solution is inappropriate for the same reasons noted in answer B.

D. **Incorrect:** Although this solution meets the multilingual requirements of the users, it will result in at least six versions of Windows XP Professional being deployed in your organization. That will cause an unnecessary challenge for your organization's information technology group.

70-270.05.02.002

▶ **Correct Answers: D**

A. **Incorrect:** Although you can view and edit documents in WordPad using any installed Input Language, you cannot switch languages from within that program.

B. **Incorrect:** This is an inefficient and expensive solution for supporting the viewing, editing, and printing of documents in multiple languages.

C. **Incorrect:** There is no French version of WordPad available for download from the Windows Update Web site.

D. **Correct:** All versions of Windows XP Professional support viewing, editing, and printing documents in multiple languages as long as the proper language group is installed. The Western Europe and United States Language Group is installed by default in the English Version of Windows XP Professional. It includes support for several languages such as French and English. Other language groups must be installed to support additional input languages, such as Greek. You must restart the computer after installing additional language groups.

70-270.05.02.003

▶ **Correct Answers: B, C, F, and G**

A. **Incorrect:** It is not possible to upgrade Windows 2000 Server to Windows XP Professional; therefore, it is not possible to upgrade this version of the operating system to Windows XP Professional MUI Pack.

B. **Correct:** Upgrade from Windows Me to Windows XP Professional and then apply the MUI Pack files. You can simplify the process by creating an unattended answer file-based upgrade installation of Windows XP Professional. Then add MUISETUP to the [GUIRunOnce] section of the answer file. Details of the procedure are available on the Windows XP MUI Pack installation media.

C. **Correct:** Like Windows Me, upgrade Windows NT Workstation 4 to Windows XP Professional English Version and then apply the MUI Pack files.

D. **Incorrect:** It is not possible to upgrade Windows NT Server 4 to Windows XP Professional; therefore, it is not possible to upgrade this version of the operating system to Windows XP Professional MUI Pack.

E. **Incorrect:** It is not possible to upgrade Windows NT Workstation 3.51 to Windows XP Professional; therefore, it is not possible to upgrade this version of the operating system to Windows XP Professional MUI Pack.

F. **Correct:** Like Windows Me, upgrade Windows 2000 Professional to Windows XP Professional English Version and then apply the MUI Pack files.

G. **Correct:** Like Windows Me, upgrade Windows 98 to Windows XP Professional English Version and then apply the MUI Pack files.

OBJECTIVE 5.3

Manage applications by using Windows Installer packages.

Windows XP Professional includes the **Windows Installer Service** for managing **software distribution**. Windows Installer Service increases the reliability and availability of applications by providing a structure for installing and maintaining them. Some or all features can be installed during the initial installation, or some can be left off the system to be installed later only when a user tries to use a particular feature not yet installed. Some or all of an application's features can also be configured to run from the installation CD-ROM or DVD, or to never be installed with the application. These latter approaches to deploying software packages can shorten the duration of the initial installation process while conserving disk space on the user's computer. Installation packages can be installed locally from downloaded .msi packages, CD-ROMs, DVDs, FTP folders, Web sites, or over the network from a file share. The Windows Installer Service increases the availability of applications by automatically repairing damaged applications. For example, if a user running Office XP inadvertently deletes WINWORD.EXE, the Windows Installer Service automatically reinstalls the file, allowing the user to continue working without having to engage the organization's Help desk. Application removal is also handled by the Windows Installer Service through the Add/Remove Programs application in Control Panel. For an application to take advantage of the Windows Installer Service, it must be packaged in an .msi file.

Note Software manufacturers create Windows Installer packages for their products; for example, Microsoft distributes all versions of Office XP as Windows Installer packages. Organizations can package their internally developed applications by using third-party installation packaging tools.

When you install a properly packaged application, the Windows Installer Service reads all the information it needs to complete the installation from an .msi file. An .msi file includes details about the entire application, its features, and its components. An **application feature** is a part of an application; for example, Microsoft Word 2002 is a part of the Microsoft Office XP productivity suite. A **feature component** is a part of a feature, for example, WINWORD.EXE is a component of Microsoft Word 2002. All of the files necessary to install an application can be placed in the .msi file or they can be compressed into cabinet (.cab) files and stored in the same folder as the .msi file or in subfolders below the Windows Installer package. For example, the Windows 2000 Server Administration Tools suite is packaged into a single file called ADMINPAK.MSI located in the \i386 folder on the installation CD-ROM. On the other hand, Office XP Professional is packaged in several .msi and .cab files. During installation, properly configured packages provide the Windows Installer Service with all the information needed for proper operation of the application including adding or modifying Registry settings, configuring shortcuts, adding program groups, creating folders, and installing application files such as .dll, .ocx, and .exe files. Some Windows Installer packages can be customized using **setup settings (.ini) files** and **transform (.mst) files**. There might be additional command line parameters included with the package. Read the documentation included with an .msi package to learn which setup settings, transform files, and command-line options it supports. By combining these optional features, you can provide default values for some or all of the options presented to the user during the installation routine, or the entire installation can be run silently with no user interaction.

Objective 5.3 Questions

70-270.05.03.001

Being the enterprising systems administrator that you are, you realize that you can install the Windows 2000 Server Administration Tools suite from any Windows 2000 server, as well as the installation CD-ROM for Windows 2000 Server and Microsoft Windows 2000 Advanced Server. From your workstation, you connect to the hidden administrative file share C$ on one of the servers in your network. You navigate to the \WINNT\SYSTEM32 folder and double-click ADMINPAK.MSI. You finish the installation normally and are able to utilize the administrative tools for several days when you accidentally delete several of the .msc files from your SYSTEM32 folder while working from a command prompt. What do you do?

A. Connect to the network file share and reinstall the entire suite by double-clicking ADMINPAK.MSI.

B. Because the installation might now be unstable, completely remove the suite of tools using the Add or Remove Programs application in Control Panel and then reinstall it by connecting to the network file share and reinstalling the entire suite by double-clicking ADMINPAK.MSI.

C. Do nothing—the Windows Installer Service automatically reinstalls the missing files from the network file share the next time you try to use one of the missing Microsoft Management Console snap-ins.

D. The Windows 2000 Server Administration Tools suite is not compatible with Windows XP Professional so you never should have installed it on your computer in the first place. Completely remove it from your system using the Add or Remove Programs application in Control Panel.

70-270.05.03.002

You are the administrator for a network running Windows 2000 Active Directory services and Windows XP Professional desktop computers. You want to use the Windows Installer Service to deploy software applications on the desktop computers. How do you configure Group Policy so that the applications are not advertised?

A. Assign the applications to computers.

B. Publish the applications to computers.

C. Publish the applications to users.

D. Assign the applications to users.

70-270.05.03.003

You are a network administrator for a sports equipment manufacturing company. Your supervisor has told you to deploy the Office XP Professional office suite to all computers belonging to the Corporate OU. You assign the .msi file for the product in a GPO. You attach the GPO to the Corporate OU, ensuring that the office suite is available only to computers within that OU. The following day you discover that the application suite has not been deployed to the computers in the Corporate OU. What do you do to complete the distribution of this software package?

A. Confirm that the permissions on the new GPO are set so that the appropriate computers have both Read and Apply Group Policy access.

B. You create a shortcut for the package and reconfigure the GPO to point to the shortcut.

C. You apply a transform file to the installed software on the Corporate OU computers.

D. You repackage the Office XP Professional package as a .zap file and deploy it to the Corporate OU.

Objective 5.3 Answers

70-270.05.03.001

▶ **Correct Answers: C**

A. **Incorrect:** It is not necessary to reinstall the entire suite of administrative tools.

B. **Incorrect:** It is not necessary to uninstall and reinstall the entire suite of administrative tools.

C. **Correct:** The Windows Installer Service attempts to restore the missing files when they are used. Because the suite was installed from a network file share, you aren't prompted to provide the installation media as long as the network path is still available. If the network path is unavailable, or if you had installed from a DVD or CD-ROM, you are prompted to insert the disk or specify a new path to the installation file, ADMINPAK.MSI.

D. **Incorrect:** The Windows 2000 Server Administration Tools suite was specifically designed to run on Windows 2000 Professional and it runs without problems on Windows XP Professional as well because the newer operating system is sufficiently backward compatible.

70-270.05.03.002

▶ **Correct Answers: C**

A. **Incorrect:** Applications assigned to computers are automatically installed the next time the computer is booted up, usually immediately after Windows XP Professional starts up. This might cause the logon process to be delayed until after the installation routine is finished.

B. **Incorrect:** Applications cannot be published to computers; they can only be assigned to computers as explained in answer A.

C. **Correct:** Publishing makes the application's Windows Installer package available for installation. Published applications can be installed by opening the Add and Remove Programs application in Control Panel or by attempting to open a document associated with the application. This differs from advertised applications because no shortcuts appear on the Start menu and the application is not automatically installed during startup.

D. **Incorrect:** Applications assigned to users are advertised to them when they log on to computers running Windows XP Professional.

70-270.05.03.003

▶ **Correct Answers: A**

A. **Correct:** For a GPO to be applied to a group of objects, those objects must have two permissions set on that GPO: Read and Apply Group Policy. Any objects that do not have both of those permissions do not have the GPO applied to them. Using permissions to define which users, groups, and computers do and do not have specific GPOs applied to them is called filtering.

B. **Incorrect:** There is no reason to create a shortcut for the package.

C. **Incorrect:** Transform files, which have the .mst file extension, customize the installation of a Windows Installer Service package file. Multiple .mst files can be applied to a single .msi package during deployment, but they cannot be applied to an existing software installation.

D. **Incorrect:** Products that are not deployed as .msi packages and that cannot be repackaged as .msi files can be packaged and deployed as .zap files. Office XP Professional is already packaged as an .msi file so there is no reason to repackage it as a .zap file.

O B J E C T I V E   5 . 4

Configure and troubleshoot desktop settings.

You customize various user interface objects by configuring the desktop. You can modify many elements of the user interface such as the taskbar, toolbars, scroll bars, menu text, the desktop background, Active Desktop objects, the Start menu, and desktop shortcuts. There are two common methods for configuring desktop settings: locally through various programs located in Control Panel or across the network via **Group Policy**. For example, you launch Control Panel, select Appearance and Themes, and then select Taskbar and Start Menu to customize the appearance and behavior of the Taskbar and Start Menu desktop elements. You launch Control Panel, select Appearance and Themes, and then select Display to enable or disable Active Desktop, and to specify a desktop Theme, background image, screensaver, and window and button appearance. Launch Control Panel, select Appearance and Themes, and then select Folder Options to customize many aspects of how folders appear and behave in Microsoft Windows Explorer.

Note There are alternative methods for accessing each of these programs that you must be aware of. You can right-click the Start menu or taskbar to access the Taskbar and Start Menu program. You can right-click the desktop background to open the Display program. In Windows Explorer, you select Folder Options from the Tools menu to launch the Folder Options program.

Group Policy primarily is a tool for enforcing desktop settings and is most effective when used in conjunction with **Active Directory**. For computers that are not members of an Active Directory **domain**, desktop settings are enforced using the Group Policy snap-in linked to Local Computer. It is accessed by typing **GPEDIT.MSC** at a command prompt or from the Run command on the Start menu. When utilized in a network running Active Directory, Group Policies are much more powerful because they can be centrally managed and applied to groups of users and computers. The Group Policy snap-in sorts configuration settings into user-specific and computer-specific nodes, and can apply during computer startup and shutdown as well as when the user logs on and off the computer. All settings specific to computers are applied during startup before the logon prompt appears and are written to the appropriate Registry locations below the HKEY_LOCAL_MACHINE key. All user-specific settings are written to the HKEY_CURRENT_USER Registry key after the user logs on but before the desktop appears. Most of the desktop settings are located in the User Configuration node under the Administrative Templates folder. For example, you disable Active Desktop by enabling the Disable Active Desktop setting which is located in the Active Desktop folder, which is below the Desktop folder located under the Administrative Templates folder within the User Configuration node. Both computer specific and user specific Group Policies are periodically refreshed while a Windows XP Professional computer is running.

You can add Web content on the desktop; this feature used to be called Active Desktop in Windows 2000, and Group Policies still refer to it as such. Web pages, ActiveX controls, and other types of files can be embedded within the desktop. Open the Display program in Control Panel and select the Desktop tab. Click the Customize Desktop button, and then select the Web tab and click the New button to add active content to the desktop. JPEG and BMP images, URLs, and ActiveX controls can all be added to the desktop. When a local file is added, it is treated as static content but when a URL is added, it is automatically handled by the **Offline Files** feature. Offline File synchronization can be configured to update content on demand, or on a schedule. Web content is made available offline, updated, browsed, and locked down in the Display Properties dialog box on the Web tab.

In the User Configuration section of the Group Policy snap-in, you find settings for removing, hiding, or showing some of the built-in desktop and Start menu icons in the Administrative Templates\Desktop Group Policy folder. You can prevent users from modifying many important desktop settings by configuring other options in this folder. Changes to the taskbar and desktop settings can also be discarded at logoff, a useful Group Policy setting for maintaining a consistent desktop for the entire organization. This particular setting is also useful when multiple users share the same user ID.

Launch Control Panel, select Appearance and Themes, and click Taskbar and Start Menu to configure the properties of the taskbar and the Start menu. After selecting the Taskbar tab you can lock or auto-hide the Taskbar, force it to float above all other windows, and allow the grouping of similar program icons on the taskbar. You can also show or hide the clock and inactive icons in the Notification area. From the Start Menu tab, you can select either the standard Windows XP Start menu or the Classic Start menu for the appearance of the Start menu. There are extensive options available for each Start menu style—click the Customize button next to whichever style you have chosen to review them.

To view the taskbar context menu, right-click the taskbar. Several commands are available on this menu including several built-in toolbars. The Quick Launch, Address, Desktop, and Links toolbars are included with Windows XP Professional. You can create a new toolbar from the Toolbars menu—a toolbar displays the contents of either a folder or a URL. Toolbars can float or remain attached to the taskbar. The All Users profile and the profile of the currently logged on user are combined to create the Programs menu, which is viewed from Start menu. Either profile can be edited by selecting it from the context menu. The Start menu for the specified profile appears in Windows Explorer where you can copy, move, edit, or delete shortcuts.

Remote Desktop is a powerful tool for remotely configuring and troubleshooting computers. Remote Desktop is based on **Terminal Services** technology, but it only allows a single remote connection. You can also use Remote Desktop to connect to your office computer from your home and access all your applications, files, and network resources as if you were sitting at your computer in your office. When you connect to a Windows XP Professional computer using Remote Desktop, display output, keyboard input, and mouse input are transmitted over the network via an efficient and secure protocol. To open connections to remote computers from the Start menu, select Accessories, select Communications, and click Remote Desktop Connection. To enable Remote Desktop on a computer running Windows XP Professional, do the following:

1. Log on to the computer as an Administrator.

2. Launch Control Panel, select Performance And Maintenance, and then click System.

3. Choose the Remote tab from the System Properties program.

4. Select the Allow users to connect remotely to this computer check box.

5. Specify which users you want to be able to connect to the computer with Remote Desktop. By default, members of the local Administrators and Remote Users groups are able to connect.

Remote Assistance is also configured from the Remote tab in the Systems Properties program. Remote Assistance allows users to send invitations to someone they trust via e-mail, the Windows Messenger Service, or as a file. Always set a strong password and a relatively short duration when sending a Remote Assistance invitation. Never tell the recipient what the password is in the same message that you send the invitation, in fact, using a different communications medium such as the telephone decreases the likelihood that an unwanted intruder will be able to intercept and use your invitation without your knowledge.

You must know how to effectively troubleshoot desktop settings to pass this objective domain. **GPOs** are the best place to start—you need to understand what settings are being to applied to the user. The Group Policy Results (GPRESULT.EXE) tool is included with the Windows XP Professional and Windows 2000 Server resource kits. This command-line tool displays the resultant set of policies for the currently logged on user. The Group Policy Reference is also included with both resource kits, although only the Windows XP Professional resource kit includes all the new settings added to Windows XP Professional Group Policies. Users are often confused by new or unfamiliar features such as Active Desktop and the new Windows XP Start Menu style—enable or disable these features as appropriate to resolve problems related to them.

Objective 5.4 Questions

70-270.05.04.001

You are the administrator of a LAN consisting of Windows XP Professional computers and Windows 2000 Servers running Active Directory. All the systems belong to the same Active Directory domain. Some users periodically access more than one computer. You want to be sure that users retain their desktop settings no matter which computer they use to log on to the network and you want them to access their documents from a secure network file server. What do you do? (Choose two.)

A. Configure group policies to redirect personal folders to the desired network location.

B. Configure the ClipBook service to redirect the personal folders to a network server.

C. Configure each of the user accounts for roaming user profiles.

D. Use the Accessibility Options program in Control Panel to specify the network location for user profiles.

E. Use Windows Explorer to specify the network location for user profiles.

70-270.05.04.002

Your manager has asked you to find ways to lower support costs for maintaining desktop computers at your company. You want to restrict what configuration changes users are able to make to their computers. You also want to prevent users from modifying certain services local to their computers. You believe it will be easier to manage these restrictions if you can hide the administrative tools from the users so that they never even see them or their icons. Which of the following do you do?

A. Use the Add Or Remove Programs application in Control Panel to uninstall the programs you want to prevent users from accessing.

B. Manually set permissions on the appropriate .cpl and .msc files from the file systems such that only administrators and the special local account called System have access to them on of each computer you want to lock down.

C. Configure a GPO that hides the desired Control Panel programs and MMC snap-ins. Link the GPO to the appropriate OUs. Set permissions on the GPO so that it applies only to the users you want to lock down.

D. Delete the appropriate .cpl and .msc files from the file systems of each computer you want to lock down.

70-270.05.04.003

The information technology team you work with has configured several drive letters on the end user's computers that point to specific network shares for their personal data, common data, and software distribution points. You want to prevent users from removing these mapped drives or mapping additional network drives.

A. Make the shares hidden by appending the dollar sign ($) to each share name.

B. Use Windows Explorer to lock each network drive.

C. Change permissions on each network share so that they have Read access only.

D. Configure a GPO that prevents users from mapping or disconnecting network drives. Link the GPO to the appropriate OUs. Set permissions on the GPO so that it applies only to the users you want to lock down.

70-270.05.04.004

You own a computer with a 300 MHz Pentium II microprocessor, 128 MB of RAM, and a 4-MB video adapter running Windows 2000 Professional. All the hardware components appear on the Hardware Compatibility List (HCL). You upgrade the computer to Windows XP Professional without any problems but you notice that performance feels significantly slower than it used to. Short of upgrading the computer hardware, what can you do to improve the responsiveness of Windows XP Professional on your computer? (Choose three.)

A. Launch the Windows XP Professional installation routine again, however this time, reformat the hard disk drive during the setup process and perform a clean installation of the operating system.

B. Reduce the size of the paging file to 2 MB.

C. Lower the screen resolution and reduce the color depth using the Display program in Control Panel.

D. Remove the paging file completely.

E. Run the Disk Defragmenter tool to reduce fragmentation on all the installed hard disks.

F. Use the Performance Options dialog box to set the display options to Adjust For Best Performance.

G. Use Task Manager to set the priority for the EXPLORER.EXE process to Real Time.

Objective 5.4 Answers

70-270.05.04.001

▶ **Correct Answers: A and C**

A. **Correct:** Normally a roaming user profile includes the My Documents, My Pictures, and other personal folders. When you use Group Policy to redirect these folders, users work on the data contained in them as if the folders were still on their workstation. Another benefit of this approach is that when a user logs off the network, these folders are not synchronized with the roaming user profile. Because user data can become quite large, this approach might save users considerable time when logging on and off of their computers. You can further enhance this solution by configuring Offline Files for these folders, allowing mobile users to transparently synchronize the network-based folders with a locally cached copy of the files. When users are working from their computer while disconnected to the network, they can continue to work with the locally cached copies of their files. Changes are automatically resynchronized with the network copies the next time they connect their system to the network.

B. **Incorrect:** The ClipBook service is for sharing documents copied to the Clipboard with other users via the network. The ClipBook service does not play a role in managing user profiles or folder redirection.

C. **Correct:** When a user's account is set up to use a roaming user profile, that user's profile is stored on the network. When the user logs on to a computer, the user profile is cached to the local system. Any changes to the profile are written to the cached copy. When the user logs off the network, the changes in the cached copy are written back to the network copy. When a user logs on to a computer that has been disconnected from the network, the locally cached copy of the user profile is loaded transparently unless mandatory roaming profiles have been employed.

D. **Incorrect:** The Accessibility Options program is for configuring keyboard, mouse, sound, and display settings to help people with mobility, vision, or hearing disabilities. The Accessibility Options program does not play a role in managing user profiles or folder redirection.

E. **Incorrect:** Windows Explorer is not used to manage user profiles or folder redirection.

70-270.05.04.002

▶ **Correct Answers: C**

A. **Incorrect:** The Add or Remove Programs application can be used to remove some Windows components such as the Indexing Service—it cannot be used to uninstall or secure specific Control Panel programs or MMC snap-ins.

B. **Incorrect:** This approach might accomplish the desired results, however, it is time-consuming and doing it manually on many computers might result in errors on some systems. Using GPOs as described in answer C is a much more efficient and reliable approach.

C. **Correct:** GPOs are an extremely effective way to lock down the desktops of users. They are very flexible, allowing you to implement whatever degree of control that is appropriate for your particular environment.

D. **Incorrect:** This is a bad solution because the Windows File Protection feature in Windows XP Professional might automatically restore some or all of the files that you manually remove. Any files that are not automatically restored are unavailable to all users who log on to those computers, including the system administrators who might need access to those files to do their jobs.

70-270.05.04.003

▶ **Correct Answers: D**

A. **Incorrect:** Hiding the shares in this manner prevents users from seeing the share names when they browse the network but it doesn't stop them from adding or removing network drives.

B. **Incorrect:** There is no feature in Windows Explorer for locking network drives.

C. **Incorrect:** Changing the permissions on the network share in this manner prevents the users from adding, deleting, or modifying files located in the shared folder but it doesn't stop them from adding or removing network drives.

D. **Correct:** This approach is the most effective way to keep users from modifying network drive settings. The Remove "Map Network Drive" and "Disconnect Network Drive" setting is located in the User Configuration section of group policy, in the folder called Administrative Templates\Windows Components\Windows Explorer.

70-270.05.04.004

▶ **Correct Answers: C, E, and F**

   A. **Incorrect:** This is a drastic approach that requires reinstalling all your applications and restoring your data from backup. Also, it is unlikely that you would notice a significant improvement in performance.

   B. **Incorrect:** This step would probably result in even slower performance of Windows XP Professional.

   C. **Correct:** Depending on the video card and how low you adjust these settings, the increase in performance might be subtle or dramatic. Dropping the resolution from 1280 x 1024 to 640 x 480 reduces the number of pixels by more than 75 percent. Cutting the color depth from 32 bits per pixel to 8 bits per pixel lowers the number of colors per pixel by 75 percent. Either of these steps reduces the workload on the video adapter by three-quarters, but it also decreases the quality of the display for the operating system and all applications.

   D. **Incorrect:** This would probably result in even slower performance.

   E. **Correct:** Depending on the level of file fragmentation, the increase in performance might be imperceptible, moderate, or quite significant. It is a good idea to regularly defragment each of your hard disks on all your Windows XP systems. Disk Defragmenter can be launched from the Start menu by selecting All Programs, then Accessories, and then System Tools.

   F. **Correct:** Slower systems such as the one described in this scenario often demonstrate much quicker responsiveness when the simpler graphical elements are selected for the user inter-face. The Performance Options dialog box is on the Advanced tab of the System program in Control Panel. You can enable or disable all the enhanced graphical user interface options together or specify settings for individual elements.

   G. **Incorrect:** When tuning performance on busy systems running Windows XP Professional or Windows 2000 Server, it is possible to improve overall system efficiency considerably by specifying appropriate priority levels for individual processes. Be sure to have a thorough understanding of how the processes for the operating system, services, and applications interact and what effect each change will have before attempting this type of system tuning on production systems. It is extremely unusual to set any process to Real Time priority because that configuration might cause the process to consume 100 percent of the CPU's processing time, making it difficult or even impossible to do anything else on the computer.

OBJECTIVE 5.5

Configure and troubleshoot accessibility services.

Windows XP Professional provides a group of accessibility features to make the computer more useful to people with various disabilities. The Accessibility Options program located in the Accessibility Options group in Control Panel is used to configure many accessibility features. You will find three accessibility tools plus the **Utility Manager** in the Accessibility program group—to access this program group, go to the Start menu, point to All Programs, and then point to Accessories. The three tools are **Narrator**, **Magnifier**, and the **On-Screen Keyboard**. Each is described in more detail later in this section.

Use the tabs in the Accessibility Options program to configure keyboard, mouse, sound, and display settings to help people with mobility, vision, or hearing disabilities. Use the General tab in the Accessibility Options program to control how the accessibility tools react to idle time, how to notify the user when an accessibility feature is enabled or disabled, and to configure **SerialKey** devices. SerialKey devices are alternative input hardware devices that connect to a computer's serial port. The **SoundSentry** and **ShowSounds** features included with Windows XP Professional are configured on the Sound tab of the Accessibility Options program and do not appear as icons in the Accessibility program group.

Utility Manager is used to start and stop each of the three accessibility tools. When started by holding down the Windows logo key while pressing the U key, Utility Manager can also be used to configure these tools to start automatically when a user logs on or when Utility Manager is launched.

Narrator helps people with low vision set up their own computers or use other people's computers. It does not work well with some applications and it speaks only English. Most vision-impaired users need a more fully featured utility for daily use. Narrator can read aloud window and dialog box titles, dialog box options, text, and more. Open the Narrator program in the Accessibility program group to configure and use it.

On-Screen Keyboard is intended for mobility-impaired users; it provides a minimal level of functionality to facilitate setting up a new system or for using another person's system. Most mobility-impaired users need a utility with greater functionality for daily use. The keyboard can be configured to display 101, 104, or 106 keys in either enhanced or standard layouts. The keys can be arranged like a typical **QWERTY keyboard** or in a simplified block format. All these and other options are configured through the program's menus.

Magnifier makes the screen more readable for users with impaired vision. Magnifier opens a separate window that displays a magnified view of a portion of the screen. When using Magnifier you can change the magnification level, customize the size of the magnification window, change the position of the magnification window, and invert the screen colors in the magnification window. You can also customize how the magnifier tracks on screen: it can follow the mouse as it moves on screen, or follow the keyboard focus, or follow text editing. The magnifier window always moves to wherever the mouse is clicked on screen.

Objective 5.5 Questions

70-270.05.05.001

You are installing and configuring Windows XP Professional on a new computer for a vision-impaired colleague named David. You configure his domain account as a member of the local Power Users group and make all other configuration changes required by your organization's policies. David has asked you to make sure that Magnifier and Narrator start automatically when he logs on. What do you do?

A. Log on to David's computer with his account and open Utility Manager by pressing the Windows logo key+U. Select Magnifier from the list of utilities and enable the Start Automatically When Windows Starts check box. Select Narrator from the list of utilities and enable the Start Automatically When Windows Starts check box. Click OK to close Utility Manager.

B. Use the Services console in the Administrative Tools folder to configure the Accessibility Services startup type to Automatic.

C. Log on to David's computer with an account that has administrative privileges and open Utility Manager by using pressing the Windows logo key+U. Select Magnifier from the list of utilities and enable the Start Automatically When Windows Starts check box. Select Narrator from the list of utilities and enable the Start Automatically When Windows Starts check box. Click OK to close Utility Manager.

D. Launch Control Panel, select Accessibility Options, and click the Accessibility Options program in to configure the startup mode for each tool.

70-270.05.05.002

A hearing-impaired friend of yours named Mary has just purchased a new computer with Windows XP Professional already installed. Mary asks you to enable the ShowSounds and SoundSentry features included with Windows XP Professional. What do you do?

A. Log on to Mary's computer with her account, open Utility Manager by pressing the Windows logo key+U, and then enable both ShowSounds and SoundSentry. Click OK to close Utility Manager.

B. Open Control Panel, select Accessibility Options, and then click Accessibility Options and select the Sound tab to enable ShowSounds and SoundSentry.

C. Open Narrator to enable ShowSounds and SoundSentry.

D. Log on to Mary's computer with an account that has administrative privileges and open Utility Manager by pressing the Windows logo key+U and then enable both ShowSounds and SoundSentry. Click OK to close Utility Manager.

70-270.05.05.003

What are the two methods for adjusting the level of magnification in the Magnifier tool? (Choose two.)

A. Right-click anywhere in the display window for Magnifier and select Options from the context menu to open the Magnifier dialog box.

B. Open Control Panel, select Accessibility Options, click Accessibility Options, and select the Display tab.

C. Open Utility Manager.

D. Select the Magnifier icon from the Start menu to view the Magnifier dialog box.

E. Double-click the Magnifier display window to cycle through the various levels of magnification.

70-270.05.05.004

You install and configure Windows XP Professional on a computer to be shared by Bob and Allen, two vision-impaired users at your company. Before handing off the computer to Bob and Allen, you configure Magnifier and Narrator to start automatically when Windows starts up. After a few days of use Bob asks you to return to their office and configure the High Contrast display option for both of their accounts so that when Allen returns from his vacation he will be able to use the computer immediately. What do you do?

A. Ask Bob to log off the computer, and then log on to the computer with an account that has administrative privileges and launch Control Panel, select Accessibility Options, and then select Accessibility Options to configure the High Contrast display. Then select the General tab and enable the Apply All Settings To Defaults For New Users.

B. Launch Control Panel, select Accessibility Options, and then select Accessibility Options to configure the High Contrast display. Then select the General tab and make the necessary changes to have the settings applied to the defaults for new users.

C. Ask Bob to log off the computer, and then log on to the computer with an account that has administrative privileges and open Control Panel, then select Appearance and Themes, and then select Display. Select the Appearance tab and specify the High Contrast theme.

D. Open Utility Manager and make the appropriate selections.

Objective 5.5 Answers

70-270.05.05.001

▶ **Correct Answers: C**

  A. **Incorrect:** Only accounts with administrative privileges are able to designate any of the three accessibility tools configurable through Utility Manager to launch when Windows starts.

  B. **Incorrect:** Narrator, Magnifier, and On-Screen Keyboard do not appear as discrete services in the Services console.

  C. **Correct:** As noted in answer A, you must have administrative access to the machine before you can make these configuration changes in Utility Manager.

  D. **Incorrect:** The Accessibility Options program is used to configure keyboard, mouse, sound, and display settings to help people with mobility, vision, or hearing disabilities. It cannot be used to configure the startup mode for Narrator, Magnifier, or the On-Screen Keyboard.

70-270.05.05.002

▶ **Correct Answers: B**

  A. **Incorrect:** You do not use Utility Manager to enable or configure ShowSounds or SoundSentry.

  B. **Correct:** The Accessibility Options program has several tabs for enabling and configuring keyboard, mouse, sound, and display settings to help people with mobility, vision, or hearing disabilities.

  C. **Incorrect:** Narrator is designed for vision-impaired users to set up their own computer or use other people's computers. It cannot be used for enabling, disabling, or configuring either ShowSounds or SoundSentry.

  D. **Incorrect:** As noted in answer A, Utility Manager is not used for this purpose.

70-270.05.05.003

▶ **Correct Answers: A and D**

A. **Correct:** You use this dialog box to adjust the magnification level of Magnifier.

B. **Incorrect:** The Accessibility Options program is used to configure keyboard, mouse, sound, and display settings to help people with mobility, vision, or hearing disabilities. It cannot be used to configure the magnification setting for Magnifier.

C. **Incorrect:** Utility Manager is used to stop, start, and configure the startup mode for Narrator, Magnifier, and the On-Screen keyboard; it cannot be used to configure specific settings for any of these tools.

D. **Correct:** From the Start menu, select All Programs, then Accessories, then Accessibility, and then click Magnifier to open Magnifier and the Magnifier Settings dialog box. As noted in answer A, this is how you adjust the magnification level for Magnifier.

E. **Incorrect:** Double-clicking the display window does not adjust the magnification level.

70-270.05.05.004

▶ **Correct Answers: A**

A. **Correct:** These are the steps required to configure the High Contrast display for all new users. Only users with administrative privileges are able to make this configuration change because the modifications are applied to the Default User profile—by default, normal users don't have permission to edit this profile.

B. **Incorrect:** As noted in answer A, changes to the Default User profile can be implemented only by users who have administrative privileges. Nothing in this answer indicates that you performed these steps while logged on as an administrator.

C. **Incorrect:** Changes to the display properties made in this manner affect only the currently logged on user; neither Allen nor Bob benefit from this approach.

D. **Incorrect:** Utility Manager is used to stop, start, and configure the startup mode for Narrator, Magnifier, and the On-Screen keyboard—it cannot be used to configure High Contrast display properties.

Implementing, Managing, and Troubleshooting Network Protocols and Services

The first versions of Microsoft Windows were not designed to communicate on networks. Now, computers are more for communication than data processing. Indeed, it is hard to imagine using a computer that wasn't capable of exchanging information with other systems. When network connections fail, users tend to panic. Now, more than ever, having a detailed understanding of networking protocols and services is a critical part of being a systems engineer.

Microsoft Windows XP Professional includes more advanced networking features than any other client operating system. Most of these features were in earlier versions of Windows, such as full **Transmission Control Protocol/Internet Protocol (TCP/IP)** support, Microsoft Internet Explorer, **Internet Information Services (IIS)**, and **Internet Connection Sharing (ICS)**. Other features are new, including **Internet Connection Firewall (ICF)**, **remote desktop**, and **remote assistance**.

Microsoft Windows XP makes it easy to stay connected, and to keep your connection secure. Dial-up capabilities enable phone lines and Integrated Services Digital Network (ISDN) circuits to be used as long-distance network connections. Most dial-up circuits connect to the public Internet—a dangerous place for the unprepared. To keep your Windows XP system safe, ICF filters incoming traffic. If you have multiple systems, ICS enables them all to access the Internet with a single connection.

After the connection is established, a virtual private network (VPN) enables you to securely access your office network—even if your traffic must cross the public Internet to reach it. Internet Explorer provides a friendly, but secure, interface to a variety of Internet services. Networking provides two-way communications, of course, and there will be times you need to share content with other users. IIS provides a robust set of Web services sufficient for most individuals' needs.

To complete this objective, you must understand how to install, configure, and troubleshoot all these technologies.

Tested Skills and Suggested Practices

The skills you need to successfully master the Implementing, Managing, and Trouble-shooting Network Protocols and Services objective domain on the *Installing, Configuring, and Administering Microsoft Windows XP Professional* exam include

- **Installing, configuring, and maintaining the proper operation of TCP/IP and core services of this protocol suite.**

  - Practice 1: Install TCP/IP and configure the computer to use Automatic Private IP Addressing (APIPA).

  - Practice 2: Install and configure the Dynamic Host Configuration Protocol (DHCP) service on a Microsoft Windows 2000 Server. Verify that the Windows XP Professional computer obtains its TCP/IP configuration from the DHCP server. Use IPCONFIG.EXE to release and renew DHCP leases on the Windows XP Professional computer.

  - Practice 3: Familiarize yourself with the other tools available for trouble-shooting network connections such as ARP.EXE, HOSTNAME.EXE, IPCONFIG.EXE, PING.EXE, PATHPING.EXE, TRACERT.EXE, NETSTAT.EXE, and ROUTE.EXE.

  - Practice 4: Configure a static TCP/IP address for a client computer that nor-mally relies on DHCP-assigned IP addresses.

  - Practice 5: Use the NSLOOKUP.EXE utility to identify the IP address for an internal DNS host name.

  - Practice 6: Edit the HOSTS file in the %windir%\system32\drivers\etc directory so that the domain name *www.microsoft.com* resolves to the IP address 127.0.0.1. Save the HOSTS file, and use the command PING *www.microsoft.com* to verify that this domain name resolves to the IP address 127.0.0.1. Edit the HOSTS file again, remove the new entry, and save the file.

- **Installing, configuring, and maintaining dial-up and VPN connections. Share these connections with other users, and tighten network security.**

  - Practice 1: Create a dial-up connection to an internet service provider (ISP) that automatically authenticates. After this connection is working properly, config-ure ICS to allow multiple computers to access the Internet across a single link.

  - Practice 2: If you have a VPN server available, establish a VPN tunnel. Config-ure this connection with ICS to allow multiple computers to use the VPN simultaneously.

  - Practice 3: Enable ICF with all default settings so that all incoming traffic is automatically filtered. Attempt to ping this system from a remote system, and note the results. Attempt to map a connection to a shared folder, and note the results. Disable ICF and repeat these steps.

- **Using Internet Explorer to access content on the Web.**

  - Practice 1: Manually configure Internet Explorer to access the Internet through an application-layer Hypertext Transfer Protocol (HTTP) proxy server such as Microsoft Internet Security and Acceleration (ISA) Server.

  - Practice 2: Configure offline Web pages to store several Web sites offline. Open the Synchronize dialog box, and adjust the properties to automatically download these sites at a specific time. After this time has passed, disconnect from the network and attempt to access one of the offline Web sites.

  - Practice 3: Press Ctrl+H to open the history toolbar. Notice that all sites visited in the last several weeks are available for recall.

  - Practice 4: Use the image toolbar in Internet Explorer to e-mail a image to a friend. To improve transmission time, reduce the size of the image.

- **Customizing IIS for Web sites with varying security and scripting requirements.**

  - Practice 1: If IIS was not installed with Windows XP, install it from the Add/Remove Windows Components applet in Control Panel. Familiarize yourself with the different IIS components available for installation.

  - Practice 2: Edit the application configuration to remove unused script mappings. Although this doesn't change the site's existing functionality, it does dramatically reduce the risk of security vulnerabilities.

  - Practice 3: Add a virtual directory, and disable anonymous access. Access the virtual directory using Internet Explorer and notice that you are prompted for authentication. Provide your username and password, and verify that you have access.

  - Practice 4: Modify NT File System (NTFS) file permissions for Web content within the IIS home directory. Notice how removing Read file permissions for the IUSR_*computername* account affects your ability to anonymously access files.

  - Practice 5: Install an IIS security hot fix if any are available.

Further Reading

This section lists supplemental readings by objective. We recommend that you study these sources thoroughly before taking exam 70-270.

Objective 6.1

Microsoft Corporation. *Microsoft Windows XP Professional Resource Kit Documentation*. Redmond, Washington: Microsoft Press, 2001. Read Chapter 18, "Connecting Clients to Windows Networks." This chapter covers the fundamentals of installing and configuring network protocols and services in Windows XP Professional. Read Chapter 19, "Configuring TCP/IP," for a detailed look at all the configuration options available in the Windows XP Professional implementation of TCP/IP. Read Chapter 20, "Configuring IP Addressing and Name Resolution." This chapter provides detailed information about configuring IP addresses and names and how to identify and resolve problems.

Microsoft Corporation. *MCSE Training Kit: Microsoft Windows XP Professional.* Redmond, Washington: Microsoft Press, 2001. Read and complete Lessons 1, 2, 3, and 4 in Chapter 4, "Installing, Configuring, and Troubleshooting Network Protocols." This chapter explains how to implement, manage, and maintain the network protocols supported by Windows XP Professional.

Objective 6.2

Microsoft Corporation. *Microsoft Windows XP Professional Resource Kit Documentation.* Redmond, Washington: Microsoft Press, 2001. Read Chapter 21, "Connecting Remote Offices," for background information about VPNs and Internet Connection Sharing.

Objective 6.3

Launch Internet Explorer, select the Help menu, and then select Contents And Index. Read through all the available topics, paying particular attention to the proxy settings, favorites, and history features.

Objective 6.4

Microsoft Corporation. *Microsoft Windows XP Professional Resource Kit Documentation.* Redmond, Washington: Microsoft Press, 2001. Read "Internet Printing" in Chapter 11, "Enabling Printing and Faxing," for general information about how IIS facilitates sharing printers. Read "Broadcasting Digital Media Presentations over Your Intranet" in Chapter 10, "Managing Digital Media," for details about how IIS provides for streaming digital media.

Objective 6.5

Microsoft Corporation. *Microsoft Windows XP Professional Resource Kit Documentation.* Redmond, Washington: Microsoft Press, 2001. Read Chapter 8, "Configuring Remote Desktop," for detailed information about remote desktop. Also read Appendix D, "Tools for Troubleshooting," for information about remote assistance.

Objective 6.6

Microsoft Corporation. *Microsoft Windows XP Professional Resource Kit Documentation.* Redmond, Washington: Microsoft Press, 2001. Read "Internet Connection Firewalls" in Chapter 21, "Connecting Remote Offices."

OBJECTIVE 6.1

Configure and troubleshoot the TCP/IP protocol.

For two computers to communicate, they must agree to speak a common language. On the Internet, and most private networks, this common language is **TCP/IP**. TCP/IP is the foundation of modern networking, and both network and systems engineers must be able to configure and troubleshoot the protocol. This domain is designed to exercise and test your TCP/IP knowledge.

Each device on a TCP/IP network is assigned one or more unique **IP addresses**. The larger the network, the more difficult it is to configure all systems with IP addresses. Fortunately, there are two methods for simplifying IP address management. **Automatic Private IP Addressing (APIPA)** is enabled by default, and functions with absolutely no configuration. However, it is appropriate only for small networks with a single segment because each computer uses a random, non-routable IP address.

The second method for simplifying IP address management is **Dynamic Host Configuration Protocol (DHCP)**. Unlike APIPA, DHCP requires a server to be configured. However, after a DHCP server is configured and connected to the network, all Windows XP Professional clients that start while connected to the network automatically retrieve their IP configuration. This configuration includes an IP address, **default gateway**, **subnet mask**, **Domain Name System (DNS)** server addresses, and any other configuration information that the administrator has configured. A **lease** is provided along with the IP address information, and the DHCP clients automatically renew this lease before it expires.

IP addresses take the form of four numbers in the range of zero to 255, separated by dots. 192.168.2.1, 10.1.1.254, and 127.0.0.1 are all examples of valid IP addresses. Computers understand IP addresses, but people prefer names. Windows associates two different types of names with IP addresses: DNS host names and **Network Basic Input/Out System (NetBIOS)** names. Examples of DNS host names are *www.msn.com* and *www.microsoft.com*. NetBIOS names can be any combination of letters and numbers of up to 15 characters, such as FILESERVER and PRINTSERVER.

Windows XP Professional has several methods for resolving human-friendly DNS host names and NetBIOS names into computer-friendly IP addresses.

- Broadcasts can be used to locate computers on the same subnet.

- A static HOSTS file can be stored locally with a list of host names and their corresponding IP addresses.

- A query can be sent to a DNS server.

- A static LMHOSTS file is stored locally containing a list of NetBIOS names paired with the appropriate IP address.

- A query can be sent to a **Windows Internet Naming Service (WINS)** server.

Windows XP Professional also requires a client redirector to communicate with Windows or NetWare servers. **Client for Microsoft Networks** is used to access shared files and printers on Windows servers; **Client Services for NetWare (CSNW)** is used to access shared files and printers on NetWare servers.

If a computer cannot communicate with another computer on the network, you must verify that the network adapter is installed and operational in Device Manager. Next, verify that it is physically connected to the network. Then run protocol-specific utilities designed to test network connections. Configuration and testing varies between the different network protocols and services; some of the tools for testing TCP/IP connectivity included with Windows XP Professional are ARP.EXE, HOSTNAME.EXE, PING.EXE, PATHPING.EXE, TRACERT.EXE, NETSTAT.EXE, ROUTE.EXE, and IPCONFIG.EXE.

To successfully answer questions in this objective, you must know how to install, configure, manage, and troubleshoot network adapters. You also need to know how to install, configure, manage, and troubleshoot the network protocols and services that are available in Windows XP Professional.

Objective 6.1 Questions

70-270.06.01.001

Which of the following is the correct order Windows XP Professional uses for resolving a DNS host name?

A. (1) Check the local computer's host name for a match. (2) Check the NetBIOS name cache. (3) Send a WINS query if configured. (4) Send a broadcast query for a matching NetBIOS name. (5) Check the LMHOSTS file for a match. (6) Check the HOSTS file for a match. (7) Send a DNS query.

B. (1) Check the local computer's host name for a match. (2) Send a DNS query. (3) Check the HOSTS file for a match. (4) Check the NetBIOS name cache. (5) Send a WINS query if configured. (6) Send a broadcast query for a matching NetBIOS name. (7) Check the LMHOSTS file for a match.

C. (1) Check the local computer's host name for a match. (2) Check the HOSTS file for a match. (3) Send a DNS query. (4) Check the NetBIOS name cache. (5) Send a WINS query if configured. (6) Send a broadcast query for a matching NetBIOS name. (7) Check the LMHOSTS file for a match.

D. (1) Check the local computer's host name for a match. (2) Check the HOSTS file for a match. (3) Send a DNS query. (4) Check the NetBIOS name cache. (5) Check the LMHOSTS file for a match. (6) Send a WINS query if configured. (7) Send a broadcast query for a matching NetBIOS name.

70-270.06.01.002

Your computer is able to connect to some network resources with no problem, but you feel that performance is abnormally slow when connecting to some specific servers located in remote offices. You suspect that there might be a routing issue on your network. Which tools included with Windows XP Professional are best for examining these types of problems? (Choose two.)

A. PATHPING.EXE

B. ARP.EXE

C. TRACERT.EXE

D. PING.EXE

E. IPCONFIG.EXE

70-270.06.01.003

You are a consultant and have just started working at the office of a new client. The company has a DHCP server on the network, so you should be able to plug your Windows XP laptop into the network and get immediate access to the Internet. You turn on your laptop computer, connect the network cable, and log on to the desktop. You open Microsoft Internet Explorer and receive a The Page Cannot Be Displayed Error no matter which Web page you try to access. You open a command prompt and run IPCONFIG.EXE. You notice that your computer has the following IP address: 169.254.0.2 and a subnet mask of 255.255.255.0.

Why are you unable to browse the Web from your laptop computer?

A. Your computer was unable to get an IP address from the DHCP server; therefore it used APIPA to assign an address to itself.

B. The network adapter is malfunctioning.

C. The network cable is disconnected from either your computer's network adapter or the network port.

D. TCP/IP is not installed on your laptop computer.

70-270.06.01.004

Which of the following problems is resolved by clearing the ARP cache by typing the command **netsh interface ip delete arpcache**?

A. Clients cannot reach a server on the local subnet that has recently had the IP address changed.

B. Clients cannot reach a server on the local subnet that has recently had the network card replaced.

C. Clients cannot reach a server that has recently had the DNS entry changed.

D. Clients cannot reach a server that has moved to a different network segment.

Objective 6.1 Answers

70-270.06.01.001

▶ **Correct Answers: C**

A. **Incorrect:** Windows XP Professional always attempts to resolve names using the HOSTS file and DNS first. NetBIOS name resolution methods such as WINS and the LMHOSTS file are used only as a last resort.

B. **Incorrect:** Windows XP Professional checks the HOSTS file for host name resolution before sending a DNS query. However, the LMHOSTS file is not checked until after a WINS resolution request is attempted.

C. **Correct:** Windows XP Professional first checks the specified host name against the local machine name. It then begins the DNS name resolution process, first checking the HOSTS file and then sending a DNS query. Finally, the NetBIOS name resolution process is used, which is as follows: check the NetBIOS name cache, send a WINS query, send a broadcast query, and scan the LMHOSTS file.

D. **Incorrect:** A DNS query and the HOSTS file are very similar to a WINS query and the LMHOSTS file. Windows XP standard DNS name resolution scans the HOSTS file before sending a DNS query. However, by default, NetBIOS name resolution scans the LMHOSTS file *after* sending a WINS query.

70-270.06.01.002

▶ **Correct Answers: A and C**

A. **Correct:** PathPing is a command-line tool for tracing routes through TCP/IP networks. It combines features of both PING.EXE and TRACERT.EXE and provides additional information that neither offers. It is an excellent tool for troubleshooting routing problems.

B. **Incorrect:** You use the Arp tool to view, edit, and clear the Address Resolution Protocol (ARP) cache on the local computer. Arp is used to map IP addresses to Media Access Control (MAC) addresses of specific network adapters on the same network segment. It does not provide any information about routing IP traffic to other network segments and therefore isn't an appropriate tool for this scenario.

C. **Correct:** Tracert is a command-line, route-tracing tool that repeatedly sends Internet Control Message Protocol (ICMP) Echo Request messages with increasingly larger time-to-live values to map out the route from the local computer to the one specified in the command. It is an ideal tool for diagnosing routing problems.

D. **Incorrect:** Ping is a command-line tool for verifying IP connectivity. The Ping tool can be used to verify that your computer can communicate with another host on the network, but it doesn't provide information about the route taken across the network and therefore isn't an appropriate tool to use in this scenario.

E. **Incorrect:** IPConfig is a command-line tool for reviewing the current IP addressing configuration for the local computer. It is not used for troubleshooting problems on the network.

70-270.06.01.003

▶ **Correct Answers: A**

A. **Correct:** APIPA uses IP addresses from the range 169.254.0.1 through 169.254.255.254 and a subnet mask of 255.255.0.0, and your computer's address falls within that range. Your next step is to determine why your computer was unable to get an address from the DHCP server—likely reasons for that problem include the server being offline or the physical segment your computer is connected to being unable to send DHCP messages to the DHCP server.

B. **Incorrect:** If the network adapter was not working, you would see an error message when you ran IPCONFIG.EXE or no information would be displayed regarding your IP address.

C. **Incorrect:** If the cable was not connected properly, you would see an error message when you run IPCONFIG.EXE stating that the media is disconnected.

D. **Incorrect:** If TCP/IP were not installed correctly, you would not have had any IP address assigned.

70-270.06.01.004

▶ **Correct Answers: B**

A. **Incorrect:** When Arp looks up an IP address' associated MAC address, this relationship is stored in the ARP cache for future reference. If a server's IP address changes, Arp issues a new request for the MAC address. Therefore, clearing the ARP cache does not resolve this problem.

B. **Correct:** Every network card includes a unique MAC address. Therefore, when a network card is replaced on a system, that system's MAC address also changes. If clients attempt to reconnect to a system that has recently had the network card replaced, they may address network communications to the cached MAC address of the failed network card. The server does not respond to these communications because it is listening for requests addressed to the MAC address of the new network card. Clearing the ARP cache of the clients on the same subnet resolves this problem.

C. **Incorrect:** Changing a server's DNS host name causes new communications addressed to the previous host name to fail. However, DNS resolution does not directly involve Arp. As a result, clearing the ARP cache does not resolve the problem.

D. **Incorrect:** If a system moves between network segments, the IP address must also change. In this scenario, the ARP cache might still contain the IP address to MAC address mapping of the system's previous IP address. However, the new IP address of the server does not yet reside in the ARP cache. Therefore, clearing the ARP cache does not resolve the problem.

Connect to computers by using dial-up networking.

ICS provides a convenient way for small business and home users to connect multiple systems to the Internet using a single connection. ICS combines three software services: **DHCP**, **Network Address Translation (NAT)**, and **DNS proxy**. DHCP is used to assign private **IP addresses** to other computers on the local area network (LAN). NAT translates the private IP addresses used by the internal computers into the public IP address assigned by the ISP. DNS proxy enables systems residing on the LAN to resolve domain names to public IP addresses.

ICS functions across almost any Internet connection, including dial-up, cable modem, **digital subscriber line (DSL)**, and Ethernet. Keep in mind that all users are sharing a single connection, and performance suffers if too many users attempt to access the Internet simultaneously. Also, ICS must be running for users to gain access to the Internet, so it must be used only with computers that stay connected and online continuously.

ICS is not the right choice for all situations. ICS must not be used in environments where administrators must maintain tight control over Web sites that users have access to. ICS is not intended as a high-performance service, and it provides no caching of content on the Internet. Finally, ICS can support at most 254 host computers. If ICS does not meet your needs because of one of these limitations, consider using **Microsoft Internet Security and Acceleration (ISA) Server**.

Objective 6.2 Questions

70-270.06.02.001

Which of the following accurately describes Layer Two Tunneling Protocol (L2TP) tunneling? (Choose three.)

A. Supports Internet Protocol security (IPSec) authentication

B. Supports header compression

C. Automatically provides privacy using Point-to-Point Protocol (PPP) encryption

D. Can be used to tunnel Internetwork Packet Exchange/Sequenced Packet Exchange (IPX/SPX) traffic across the Internet

E. Can tunnel IP traffic across frame relay links

F. Supported by Microsoft Windows NT 4

70-270.06.02.002

Which of the following remote access authentication protocols does not support sending encrypted password information?

A. PAP

B. SPAP

C. CHAP

D. MS-CHAP

E. MS-CHAP v2

70-270.06.02.003

In which of the following scenarios does ICS enable all computers to access the Internet?

A. A LAN with 100 computers and a routed T3 connection to the Internet. All the computers have IP addresses assigned by the ISP.

B. A home network with four computers connected to the Internet with a cable modem. Each of the four computers has been assigned a public IP address by the ISP.

C. A home network with four computers connected to the Internet with a single analog dial-up connection. All the computers currently use DHCP and do not have public IP addresses.

D. A small office network with 300 computers and a single DSL connection. All the computers currently use DHCP and do not have public IP addresses.

Objective 6.2 Answers

70-270.06.02.001

► **Correct Answers: A, B, and E**

A. **Correct:** L2TP tunneling supports IPSec authentication. Point-to-Point Tunneling Protocol (PPTP) tunneling does not support this type of authentication.

B. **Correct:** L2TP supports header compression, which reduces the number of bytes consumed by the header to four. PPTP does not perform header compression, and as a result, IP headers consume six bytes.

C. **Incorrect:** Only PPTP automatically provides PPP encryption. L2TP can provide IPSec encryption.

D. **Incorrect:** L2TP is capable of tunneling only IP traffic. PPTP can be used to tunnel other network protocols, including IPX/SPX.

E. **Correct:** L2TP can function over any media that provides packet-oriented, point-to-point connectivity. PPTP can tunnel across only IP networks.

F. **Incorrect:** PPTP was the only method of tunneling included with Windows NT 4. Windows 2000 and later versions of Windows include both PPTP and L2TP capabilities.

70-270.06.02.002

▶ **Correct Answers: A**

A. **Correct:** Password Authentication Protocol (PAP) does not support encryption. As a result, PAP is more vulnerable to attack than other protocols and must be used only when the remote access client does not support any other method of authentication.

B. **Incorrect:** The Shiva Password Authentication Protocol (SPAP) does support encryption. However, SPAP is not as secure as Challenge Handshake Authentication Protocol (CHAP) or Microsoft Challenge Handshake Authentication Protocol (MS-CHAP) because it sends the password across the remote access link using reversible encryption. Use SPAP only when it is the only method of authentication that the client supports.

C. **Incorrect:** The CHAP transmits authentication information using encrypted, one-way MD5 hashes. Using a one-way hash is more secure than using reversible encryption because the user can be authenticated without actually sending the password to the server.

D. **Incorrect:** The MS-CHAP provides encrypted authentication in a very similar manner to CHAP. However, MS-CHAP can also use Microsoft Point-to-Point Encryption (MPPE) to encrypt data to the client or server.

E. **Incorrect:** The Microsoft Challenge Handshake Authentication Protocol version 2 (MS-CHAP v2) provides all the features of MS-CHAP, plus authentication of both the client and server using one-way encryption. Therefore, MS-CHAP v2 provides the highest level of security available to users of Windows XP Professional.

70-270.06.02.003

▶ **Correct Answers: C**

A. **Incorrect:** The only aspect of this scenario that is not compatible with ICS is the public IP addressing. ICS can function only when the client computers on the LAN receive dynamically assigned IP addresses from the ICS computer. In this scenario, each of the 100 systems can reach the Internet directly, without requiring the assistance of ICS.

B. **Incorrect:** ICS is intended for use with small home networks and cable modems. However, in this scenario, the ISP is providing a block of four public IP addresses. Each system has its own IP address, so ICS is not needed for the systems to provide access.

C. **Correct:** ICS is the ideal method for providing all four systems in this scenario with Internet access. The computer that is connected to the dial-up connection must have ICS enabled. As soon as ICS is enabled, that system's Internet network connection is assigned the private IP address 192.168.0.1. DHCP services are automatically initiated to assign the other systems IP addresses in the range 192.168.0.2 through 192.168.0.254. The next time the client computers reboot, they retrieve a DHCP-assigned IP address from the ICS system. When the ICS system connects to the Internet, it performs NAT services to provide all systems on the network with Internet access.

D. **Incorrect:** This scenario is perfect for ICS, except for one major detail: ICS can assign IP addresses to only 253 computers. ICS is intended to be used on small networks, and is not designed to provide Internet access for larger quantities of computers. A more robust NAT/DHCP solution is required.

OBJECTIVE 6.3

Connect to resources using Internet Explorer.

Internet Explorer provides Windows XP Professional users with a secure, robust interface for viewing content on the Web. Internet Explorer's defaults are configured to provide the flexibility without sacrificing the user's security. As a result, it frequently prompts the user to choose whether to allow certain actions. For example, the first time users submit a form to an Internet site, they are warned that others might be able to read the contents. This type of warning can be annoying to experienced Internet users, so an option is provided on the same dialog box to disable future warnings.

Users connect to the Internet from a wide variety of networks, and Internet Explorer is meant to be used in all of them—as long as they use TCP/IP. Administrators of networks that have a **proxy server** protecting the connection to the Internet, such as those with **ISA Server**, must configure Internet Explorer with the address of the proxy server. Alternatively, this configuration can be done automatically using a script.

There's too much on the Internet for any single person to memorize all his or her favorite uniform resource locators (URLs). To make the Internet easier to navigate, Internet Explorer allows a user to mark useful Web sites using the **favorites** capability. User favorites are stored in Windows XP as shortcuts located in the %userprofile%\Favorites\directory.

Internet Explorer extends the favorites capability to make content available to users while disconnected from the Internet. Naturally, this content can be updated only when the computer is connected to the Internet—and that's exactly what happens. When favorites are marked for offline use, Internet Explorer keeps a cached copy stored on the local hard disk. Internet Explorer automatically displays the cached content when the user attempts to access that resource while offline.

Internet Explorer keeps a log of sites that users visit in the %userprofile%\Local Settings\History\folder. Although this enables the user to quickly return to a site, many users want to disable this feature. You must understand the privacy issues associated with having the history feature enabled.

Objective 6.3 Questions

70-270.06.03.001

You are the administrator of a 30-user LAN that connects to the Internet through a Windows 2000 Server using ISA Server. You need to closely monitor and control the public Internet sites that your users visit, so you configure ISA Server to proxy HTTP requests for all users. However, you want to maximize performance of your local intranet servers by having Internet Explorer requests bypass the proxy server for those sites. Which of the following solutions meets your requirements?

A. Configure the ISA Server to not allow requests for sites on the local intranet.

B. In each user's Internet Explorer Internet Options dialog box, select the Security tab. Select the Local Intranet Web content zone and click the Sites button. At the Local Intranet dialog box, add the URLs and IP addresses of the local intranet sites to the Web sites list.

C. In each user's Internet Explorer Internet Options dialog box, select the Connections tab and click the LAN Settings button. Select the Use A Proxy Server check box, type the address and port number of your ISA server, and click the Advanced button. On the Proxy Settings dialog box, add the URLs and IP addresses of the local intranet sites to the Exceptions text box.

D. In each user's Internet Explorer Internet Options dialog box, select the Privacy tab and click the Edit button. At the Per Site Privacy Actions dialog box, type the URL or IP address of each local intranet site, and click the Block button.

70-270.06.03.002

Which of the following types of resources can be viewed from Internet Explorer without launching a separate application? (Choose three.)

A. Web sites

B. FTP sites

C. Gopher sites

D. Hypertext Markup Language (HTML) files on the local computer

E. Telnet sites

F. TIF images

70-270.06.03.003

Which of the following options is available from the image toolbar when hovering the cursor over an image in Internet Explorer? (Choose three.)

A. Expand the image to full screen.

B. Print the image.

C. Save the image to disk.

D. Convert the image to a thumbnail.

E. Edit the image.

F. Send the image in an e-mail.

Objective 6.3 Answers

70-270.06.03.001

▶ **Correct Answers: C**

A. **Incorrect:** This solution does not meet all the requirements because it does not configure Internet Explorer to directly access the intranet systems. Instead, users are completely unable to access local intranet sites.

B. **Incorrect:** This solution does not meet any of the requirements. Placing URLs and IP addresses into the Local Intranet Web content zone increases the level of trust granted to those sites. However, it does not configure Internet Explorer for bypassing the proxy server for local intranet sites.

C. **Correct:** This solution meets your requirements. Before a request is sent to a Web site, Internet Explorer checks the Web site's address against the list of exceptions. If that Web site's name appears on the list, requests are sent directly to the site instead of to the proxy server. To make deploying and maintaining these settings easier across a large user base, consider automating this process using an automatic configuration script.

D. **Incorrect:** This solution does not meet any of the requirements. Adding the URLs and IP addresses of the local intranet sites to this list only blocks Internet Explorer from accepting cookies from those sites.

70-270.06.03.002

▶ **Correct Answers: A, B, and D**

A. **Correct:** Internet Explorer's primary purpose is to view sites on the Internet using HTTP.

B. **Correct:** Internet Explorer can be used to navigate FTP sites, view directory contents, and transfer files.

C. **Incorrect:** Gopher is a network protocol that was common during the early years of the Internet. Gopher's functionality has been replaced by HTTP. As a result, Internet Explorer does not support the Gopher protocol.

D. **Correct:** Internet Explorer can be used to view HTML files on the local computer. The easiest way to access files on the local computer is to type the file path in the Address field. An alternative method is to choose Open from the File menu, click the Browse button, and select the file.

E. **Incorrect:** Telnet is a text-based protocol used to issue commands on a remote system. An open telnet session resembles a command prompt. Although you can use Internet Explorer to launch a telnet session, Internet Explorer must launch a separate application—the telnet window. To launch a telnet session from the Internet Explorer address bar, type the address in the form *telnet://hostname*.

F. **Incorrect:** Internet Explorer is capable of viewing many types of images, including GIF and JPEG files. However, Internet Explorer cannot natively view TIF images. TIF is a common format for storing images that will be printed, but it is not common on the Internet because of the large file size.

70-270.06.03.003

▶ **Correct Answers: B, C, and F**

A. **Incorrect:** Internet Explorer does not give the user the option to expand the image to full screen.

B. **Correct:** By default, the second button on the image toolbar assists the user with printing the image. Clicking the Print This Image button prompts the user with the Print dialog box.

C. **Correct:** By default, the first button on the image toolbar enables the user to save the image to disk.

D. **Incorrect:** Internet Explorer does not give the user the option to convert the image to a thumbnail.

E. **Incorrect:** Internet Explorer does not give the user the option to edit an image from the image toolbar.

F. **Correct:** The third button on the image toolbar enables the user to easily e-mail the image. The user is then given the option to reduce the image size to make transferring the e-mail faster.

OBJECTIVE 6.4

Configure, manage, and implement Internet Information Services (IIS).

IIS is a robust, high-performance Web server included with Windows XP Professional. It's based on the same software included with the Microsoft Windows .NET Server family, used to host some of the largest sites on the Internet. The version of IIS included with Windows XP Professional has been scaled down for home and small office use, however. Understanding the features and limitations of this variety of IIS is critical for completing this objective.

To understand IIS, you must have some understanding of the underlying protocols. **HTTP** provides rich content to browsers, and is the only protocol most Internet and intranet Web sites require. **File Transfer Protocol (FTP)** is often used for downloading files—though HTTP is more common. **Simple Mail Transfer Protocol (SMTP)** is the protocol used to transfer messages between post offices. IIS uses SMTP to send outgoing mail—for example, to forward the results of a form to the site administrator.

Getting a Web site up and running with IIS is as simple as installing the software and placing HTML files in the home directory. However, to take full advantage of IIS, it is important to understand the configuration options available. For example, the Internet Server Application Programming Interface (ISAPI) provides developers with a way to intercept incoming requests before they are processed by IIS. ISAPI can be leveraged to change almost any aspect of the way IIS responds, and is the most powerful way to control a Web-based application.

Another important feature of IIS is **application configuration**. In IIS, an application is a set of **application mappings**, **Active Server Pages (ASP)** scripting options, and debug settings that are unique to a site or **virtual directory**. From the Web site properties dialog box, select the Directory or Home Directory tab and click the Configuration button to edit an application's settings.

Security is a critical aspect of every Web site. The first way to improve the security of your site is to modify the NTFS file permissions for your Web site content. This is done using Windows Explorer—just as it is done for any other file. By default, IIS creates a user account for anonymous access to your Web content. This account is named IUSR_*computername* and automatically receives the right to view Web content for which it has Read-level NTFS file permissions.

If your Web content is to be viewed only by authenticated users, you can disable anonymous access. To do this, view the properties of the Web site or virtual directory and select the Directory Security tab. Next, click the Edit button within the Anonymous Access And Authentication Control portion of the window. This dialog box also allows you to specify which authentication protocols are acceptable. For example, some browsers are compatible only with Basic Authentication. This protocol is disabled by default because it transmits user names and passwords across the Internet in such a way that they are easily intercepted.

Tip Keep track of the latest Microsoft security bulletins by visiting this Web page: *http://www.microsoft.com/technet/treeview/default.asp?url=/technet/itsolutions/ security/current.asp*.

Another way to improve a site's security is to restrict the types of access available to users. Administrators have the option of allowing read and write access, access to script source code, and directory browsing. For best security, allow only the types of access absolutely necessary. Take advantage of the ability of IIS to specify these settings on a per-virtual directory basis. For example, if you need to allow files to be written, limit this access to a single directory.

Objective 6.4 Questions

70-270.06.04.001

By default, which TCP/IP port is IIS is configured to use for HTTP?

A. 25

B. 443

C. 80

D. 21

70-270.06.04.002

What is the maximum number of users who can connect to an IIS Web site installed on Windows XP Professional?

A. 1

B. 10

C. 100

D. No enforced limitation

70-270.06.04.003

Which of the following features are available with IIS included with Windows XP Professional? (Choose three.)

A. ISAPI filters

B. Application recycling

C. Bandwidth throttling

D. IP address and domain name restrictions

E. Content expiration

F. HTTP keep-alives

70-270.06.04.004

You configure IIS on your Windows XP Professional system to allow a coworker on the Internet to view HTML files located on your computer. There is a firewall protecting your computer, and you configure the firewall to allow only HTTP traffic. You create a user account with the name Kevin for your coworker, and make that account a member of your local Administrators group. The Administrators group already has Full Control NTFS permissions to the IIS home directory and all subdirectories. On the Home Directory tab of the Web site Properties, you enable Read access, and disable Script Source Access, Write access, and Directory Browsing. What are Kevin's effective permissions?

A. Read access only

B. Write access only

C. Read and write access

D. Full control

Objective 6.4 Answers

70-270.06.04.001

▶ **Correct Answers: C**

A. **Incorrect:** TCP/IP port 25 is the IIS default port for SMTP. SMTP is used for transferring e-mail messages.

B. **Incorrect:** TCP/IP port 443 is the IIS default port for Hypertext Transfer Protocol Secure (HTTPS). HTTPS adds SSL encryption to the standard HTTP protocol.

C. **Correct:** IIS uses port 80, the Internet standard, as the default for HTTP. Web browsers automatically connect to Web servers on port 80. Therefore, if you specify a port other than 80 for Web services, you need to specify the port number as part of the Web site's URL. For example, if you change the port number to port 8080, the URL for the Web site becomes *http://<your URL>:8080/*.

D. **Incorrect:** TCP/IP port 21 is the IIS default port for FTP services. Port 21 is used only to authenticate users and accept commands—FTP uses TCP/IP port 20 for all file transfers.

70-270.06.04.002

▶ **Correct Answers: B**

A. **Incorrect:** The version of IIS included with Windows XP Professional can support up to 10 simultaneous incoming connections.

B. **Correct:** IIS, when installed on Windows XP Professional, can support a maximum of 10 simultaneous users. There is no limit to the number of incoming connections IIS can support when installed on Windows 2000 Server or the Windows .NET Server family.

C. **Incorrect:** The version of IIS included with Windows XP Professional can support up to 10 simultaneous incoming connections. To support more than 10 connections, you must upgrade to Windows 2000 Server or the Windows .NET Server family.

D. **Incorrect:** The version of IIS included with Windows XP Professional can support up to 10 simultaneous incoming connections. To support more than 10 connections, you must upgrade to Windows 2000 Server or the Windows .NET Server family.

70-270.06.04.003

▶ **Correct Answers: A, E, and F**

A. **Correct:** The version of IIS included with Windows XP Professional does support ISAPI filters. ISAPI filters process incoming requests before IIS default processing, and are capable of dramatically changing the way IIS behaves.

B. **Incorrect:** Only the Windows .NET Server family includes application recycling as a feature of IIS. This feature automatically restarts IIS applications, and ensures that active users do not get disconnected during this process.

C. **Incorrect:** Only the Windows .NET Server and the Windows 2000 Server families include bandwidth throttling as a feature of IIS. This feature limits the amount of traffic that IIS can generate. It's useful for ensuring that Web services don't consume an Internet connection, thereby reducing performance for users and other Web sites.

D. **Incorrect:** Only the Windows .NET Server and the Windows 2000 Server families include IP address and domain name restrictions. Using this capability, it's possible to allow or disallow users based on their source IP address. Alternatively, filtering can be done based on the results of a reverse DNS lookup of the source IP address.

E. **Correct:** The version of IIS included with Windows XP Professional does support content expiration. This feature improves the performance of the Web site by instructing the client and proxy servers to cache specified content. Cached content can be retrieved from the local system, without issuing a request to the Web server. Content expiration must be enabled only on content that does not change frequently, to ensure clients always retrieve an up-to-date version of the content.

F. **Correct:** The version of IIS included with Windows XP Professional does support HTTP keep-alives. This is a function of HTTP/1.1, an update to the original Web communication protocol. This enables clients to use a single TCP session throughout the span of a visit to a Web site. By reducing the number of connections that need to be initiated, Web site performance is improved and the maximum capacity of the Web server is improved.

70-270.06.04.004

▶ **Correct Answers: A**

A. **Correct:** If Kevin logs on interactively, he has Full Control over the files in the home directory. However, because Kevin can access the Web content only using HTTP, IIS controls access and limits rights to Read access only. NTFS permissions do not override limitations enforced by IIS. Instead, effective permissions are always equal to the lesser access allowed by IIS and NTFS. As a result, the Full Control provided by the file permissions has no effect.

B. **Incorrect:** Kevin is not capable of updating files using HTTP, because IIS does not have Write access enabled.

C. **Incorrect:** Kevin is able to read files in the home directory, because IIS has read access enabled. However, write access is not enabled. NTFS permissions do not override limitations enforced by IIS. Instead, effective permissions are always equal to the lesser access allowed by IIS and NTFS. As a result, the Full Control provided by the file permissions has no effect.

D. **Incorrect:** Kevin is able to read files in the home directory, because IIS has read access enabled. However, write access is not enabled. Full control also allows for file permissions to be changed, which is never possible when access to files is through IIS. NTFS permissions do not override limitations enforced by IIS. Instead, effective permissions are always equal to the lesser access allowed by IIS and NTFS. As a result, the Full Control provided by the file permissions has no effect.

Configure, manage, and troubleshoot remote desktop and remote assistance.

Remote desktop enables users to interact with a computer across a network as if they were sitting directly in front of it. Essentially, keyboard and mouse commands are transmitted from the client computer across the network to the remote desktop server running Windows XP Professional. The remote desktop server returns video and sound to the client, recreating the experience of working directly with the remote system. The **client drive redirection** feature of remote desktop automatically maps all local drives of the remote desktop server. The **printer redirection** feature allows documents printed while using remote desktop to be printed on a printer connected to the client's computer, as long as the remote desktop server has the necessary printer drivers. Other ports, including serial ports, can also be redirected.

A variation of the remote desktop is the **remote desktop Web connection**. Installed as an option in the World Wide Web Service of **IIS**, the Remote Desktop Web Connection enables users to connect to the remote desktop without installing the remote desktop client utility. When this option is installed and IIS is running, a remote desktop connection can be established from the client by typing the URL *http://computername/TSWeb/* into a browser.

There are several situations where remote desktop is useful. First, users can have complete control over their office computer while traveling—as long as they have a network connection. Second, administrators can log on to user systems after-hours to perform maintenance, without needing to travel from office to office. Only one user may control the computer at a time: If a user is logged on to the Windows XP computer interactively, that person has to be disconnected before a user can connect with remote desktop.

Tip Both Remote Desktop and Remote Assistance can be enabled from the Remote tab of the System Properties dialog box.

Remote assistance leverages the abilities of the remote desktop to enable administrators (known as *experts*) to provide technical support to remote users (known as *novices*). A novice contacts an expert using e-mail or Windows Real-Time Client and sends an invitation for remote assistance. The expert accepts the invitation and can then view the novice's desktop. If the user has enabled remote control, the expert can even take control of the keyboard and mouse to guide the novice through the problem. To ensure privacy, all communications are encrypted.

Note Windows XP 64-Bit Edition does not support remote assistance.

Objective 6.5 Questions

70-270.06.05.001

Which of the following remote desktop performance options must be enabled to optimize performance across slow dial-up connections?

A. Desktop Background

B. Show Contents Of Window While Dragging

C. Menu And Window Animation

D. Themes

E. Bitmap Caching

70-270.06.05.002

Remote desktop Web connection requires which of the following protocols to establish a connection? (Choose two.)

A. HTTP (TCP/IP port 80)

B. RDP (TCP/IP port 3389)

C. SMTP (TCP/IP port 25)

D. LDAP (TCP/IP port 389)

E. POP (TCP/IP port 110)

70-270.06.05.003

Which of the following methods of communication can be used to send an invitation for remote assistance? (Choose two.)

A. Internet Explorer

B. Internet newsgroups

C. E-mail

D. Windows Messenger

E. FTP

70-270.06.05.004

Which user groups have permissions to connect to control the remote desktop of a Windows XP Professional computer? (Choose two.)

A. Administrators

B. Power Users

C. Users

D. Guests

E. Remote Desktop Users

Objective 6.5 Answers

70-270.06.05.001

▶ **Correct Answers: E**

A. **Incorrect:** Enabling the Desktop Background option on remote desktops decreases performance because the image must be transmitted across the network to the remote desktop client. Therefore, this option must not be enabled when a slow dial-up connection is being used.

B. **Incorrect:** The Show Contents Of Window While Dragging option must be disabled when a slow dial-up connection is being used because it causes unnecessary traffic across the network connection.

C. **Incorrect:** Menu And Window Animation must be disabled when a slow dial-up connection is being used. Although this option provides the remote desktop with a richer graphical user interface, it causes unnecessary traffic to be sent across the network.

D. **Incorrect:** Enabling the Themes performance option for a remote desktop connection causes the client to retrieve customized aspects of the user interface, such as fonts and colors. This transfer causes less traffic than the other performance options, but must still be disabled for best performance. Enabling the Themes option does not automatically cause the desktop background to be transferred, even if the background is part of the theme.

E. **Correct:** Enabling Bitmap Caching reduces the number of times a single image must be sent between the remote desktop client and server. Therefore, enabling this option reduces network traffic, and can dramatically improve performance on slow dial-up connections.

70-270.06.05.002

▶ **Correct Answers: A and B**

A. **Correct:** HTTP is the protocol used by IIS and Internet Explorer for exchanging files. Remote desktop Web connection uses HTTP to prompt the user to connect. After the connection has been established, Remote Desktop Protocol (RDP) is used exclusively.

B. **Correct:** RDP is used by the remote desktop, remote desktop Web connection, and remote assistance for exchanging video, sound, keyboard, and mouse data. Remote desktop Web connection also requires HTTP to initiate the session from a browser.

C. **Incorrect:** SMTP is the protocol used to exchange messages between post offices. Remote desktop Web connection does not require SMTP.

D. **Incorrect:** Lightweight Directory Access Protocol (LDAP) is the protocol used by Windows clients to communicate with the Active Directory service. Remote desktop Web connection does not require LDAP.

E. **Incorrect:** Post Office Protocol (POP) is a common protocol used by e-mail clients to retrieve messages from a post office. Remote desktop Web connection does not require POP.

70-270.06.05.003

▶ **Correct Answers: C and D**

A. **Incorrect:** Invitations for remote assistance can be sent using either e-mail or the Windows Messenger. Internet Explorer cannot be used to send invitations.

B. **Incorrect:** Internet newsgroups are a common message-based method for seeking assistance with technical problems. However, remote assistance cannot send an invitation to an Internet newsgroup. Invitations for remote assistance can be sent using either e-mail or the Windows Messenger.

C. **Correct:** When remote assistance is initiated, it prompts the novice to send an invitation via e-mail or the Windows Messenger. After the expert receives the e-mail, clicking the link establishes a connection to the novice's computer. At that point, the novice is prompted to accept the incoming connection.

D. **Correct:** When remote assistance is initiated, it prompts the novice to send an invitation via e-mail or the Windows Messenger. After the expert receives the real-time message, clicking the link establishes a connection to the novice's computer. At that point, the novice is prompted to accept the incoming connection.

E. **Incorrect:** FTP is commonly used to transfer files across the Internet. However, it cannot be used to send remote assistance invitations. Invitations for remote assistance can be sent using either e-mail or the Windows Messenger.

70-270.06.05.004

▶ **Correct Answers: A and E**

   A. **Correct:** Members of the Administrators group have permission to connect to the remote desktop.

   B. **Incorrect:** Members of the Power Users group do not have permissions to connect to the remote desktop unless they are also a member of the Administrators or Remote Desktop Users groups.

   C. **Incorrect:** Members of the Users group do not have permissions to connect to the remote desktop unless they are also a member of the Administrators or Remote Desktop Users groups.

   D. **Incorrect:** Users authenticating with only Guest permissions do not have permissions to connect to the remote desktop.

   E. **Correct:** Members of the Remote Desktop Users group have permission to connect to the remote desktop.

OBJECTIVE 6.6

Configure, manage, and troubleshoot an Internet connection firewall.

As more computers and networks are connected to the global Internet, security becomes increasingly important. The majority of Windows XP Professional systems will be connected to the Internet at some point, and when they are, there is the possibility for a malicious hacker to attempt to intrude on the system. One of the best ways to protect a Windows XP system from intrusion across a network is to enable the **Internet Connection Firewall (ICF)**.

Note ICF is not available with Windows XP 64-Bit Edition.

ICF provides an easy-to-use method of packet filtering. When enabled, ICF examines every packet that is sent to the system and compares it against a set of rules to determine whether it is allowed to pass. Naturally, the firewall must be configured to allow desired network traffic through. Fortunately, this configuration process is very user-friendly.

ICF is enabled from the Advanced tab of a network connection's Properties dialog box. Select the check box, and click the Settings button to customize the firewall's rules. When enabled, the firewall does not allow traffic through to any service. This means that even if you have **IIS** installed and running, users are not able to view your Web site. You must select every service that you want to make available on the computer. If you add a network service later, remember to return to this window to make the service accessible.

Tip If you have multiple network adapters in a system, be sure to configure ICF for each of them.

The Advanced Settings Services tab lists most common network services. If you need to permit access to network services that are not already available on the list, click the Add button. You need to know the port number that the service requires.

Besides filtering incoming requests for network services, ICF filters Internet Control Message Protocol (ICMP) messages. Ping is the most common application that sends ICMP messages. By default, enabling ICF causes a system to stop responding to these types of messages—essentially making the system invisible. If you want the ability to ping your system, you can enable ICMP messages from the ICMP tab of the Advanced Settings Services.

By default, ICF quietly drops incoming packets that aren't explicitly permitted. However, if you want to keep track of dropped packets, you have the option of enabling logging. This can be done from the Security Logging tab.

Tip Examining the ICF log files might reveal attempted intrusions from hackers.

Objective 6.6 Questions

70-270.06.06.001

Enabling ICF can prevent which of the following types of network intrusions?

A. A hacker that exploits a vulnerability in IIS by sending malformed HTTP requests to your company's public Web server

B. A hacker that initiates a distributed denial of service intrusion to saturate the bandwidth on your company's Internet connection

C. A user who opens a virus disguised as an e-mail attachment

D. A hacker that uploads a Trojan horse into a directory on an FTP server that was accidentally started

70-270.06.06.002

Which of the following types of information is collected in the ICF security log? (Choose two.)

A. Source IP

B. Destination port

C. Source DNS host name

D. Packet data

E. Source user name

70-270.06.06.003

ICF is appropriate for use with the network adapter of what type of dedicated server?

A. VPN endpoint

B. File and print server

C. ICS server

D. Web server

Objective 6.6 Answers

70-270.06.06.001

▶ **Correct Answers: D**

A. **Incorrect:** ICF cannot prevent this type of intrusion because the Web server must be able to receive HTTP requests to legitimate users on the public Internet. ICF is capable of stopping all HTTP requests, but cannot distinguish between legitimate and malicious requests within a single protocol.

B. **Incorrect:** ICF filters packets as they are processed by a Windows XP Professional network adapter. This particular scenario is an intrusion against network equipment. The packets sent during the denial of service intrusion saturate the Internet connection before they reach hosts on the destination network. ICF can filter the packets before they reach the Windows XP Professional system, however, it cannot stop the Internet connection from being saturated.

C. **Incorrect:** ICF is capable of filtering connections only where the Windows XP Professional system is acting as the server. When users retrieve e-mail, the connection is initiated by the Windows XP Professional system. Further, ICF is capable of filtering only an entire protocol. ICF is incapable of differentiating between legitimate and malicious requests within a single protocol.

D. **Correct:** By default, ICF filters incoming FTP requests. In this scenario, the FTP server was accidentally started. ICF is designed to prevent this type of vulnerability. When ICF is enabled, only those services explicitly enabled can receive traffic—even if they are accidentally started.

70-270.06.06.002

▶ **Correct Answers: A and B**

A. **Correct:** The source IP is one of the fields of data collected in the ICF security log.

B. **Correct:** The destination port is one of the fields of data collected in the ICF security log.

C. **Incorrect:** The ICF security log does contain the source's host name. The source IP address is included, however, so you can perform a reverse DNS lookup based on the source IPs in the log.

D. **Incorrect:** ICF security logs do not contain the data that was contained in the dropped packets. Only information contained in the header of packets is recorded.

E. **Incorrect:** Although some protocols do pass user name information, the ICF security log does not attempt to record this information. Indeed, in the case of malicious intrusions, the user name information included is never accurate.

70-270.06.06.003

▶ **Correct Answers: D**

A. **Incorrect:** Unfortunately, ICF cannot be enabled on a system that is acting as the endpoint of a VPN tunnel. Enabling ICF disables all access to the VPN.

B. **Incorrect:** ICF is not compatible with file and print services. If you share a folder or printer from a system, you must disable ICF.

C. **Incorrect:** ICF cannot be enabled on the internal interface of an ICS server. Doing so prevents other hosts on the network from accessing the Internet.

D. **Correct:** ICF can be configured to allow HTTP traffic. Therefore, it is recommended that ICF be enabled on Web servers.

Configuring, Managing, and Troubleshooting Security

Computers hold some of our most valuable and private data. The vastness and complexity of the Internet, however, makes securing computer systems connected to the Internet extremely challenging. Although absolute security is impossible, you can design a security plan that is adequate for the needs of your organization. By implementing defense in depth and proactively managing risk, you balance the business needs of your organization, the resources and tools you have at your disposal, and the vulnerabilities that your computer systems face. Higher security requires more resources to implement and usually makes using the secured systems harder to use. Keep all these factors in mind when designing security for the systems you manage. Also remember that computer security is a process, not a destination. Technology is evolving rapidly and it is up to you to keep track of the latest vulnerabilities, hotfixes, and service packs that are relevant to the computer systems you manage.

The concept of defense in depth means that you implement multiple layers of security. There is host-based security such as the permissions you set on files and folders on a Windows **NT file system (NTFS)**–formatted storage volume. There are network-based security measures such as **proxy servers** and firewalls. Some security tools such as Active Directory can be considered both host-based and network-based. This objective domain is concerned with the host-based security tools included with Microsoft Windows XP Professional. You restrict access to computers running Windows XP Professional by implementing **user authentication** with user accounts with passwords. The process of logging on to a Windows XP Professional system is done through a secure tool that reduces the likelihood of users unknowingly typing their user name and password into a **Trojan** program. The graphical interface for logging on to a Windows XP Professional system is called the **Graphical Identification and Authentication (GINA)** component that requires users to press Ctrl+Alt+Del before typing their user name and password. You can further secure the process of users logging on to computers by implementing **smart cards**.

Caution When you install Windows XP Professional in a stand-alone configuration, you are not required to provide a password when logging on—you simply click your user name on the Welcome screen. Although this arrangement might be appropriate for home users, it is unacceptable for most enterprises. To disable the Welcome screen, launch Control Panel and select User Accounts, click Change The Way Users Log On Or Off and then disable Use The Welcome Screen. Click Apply Options. To require that users press Ctrl+Alt+Del before logging on, open the Local Security Policy MMC from Administrative Tools and disable the Interactive Logon: Do Not Require Ctrl+Alt+Del option located in the Security Options folder, which you can find in the Local Policies folder.

The authentication process is further protected in Windows XP through sophisticated authentication algorithms and **encryption**. Information transmitted across network connections can be secured with network-based encryption such as virtual private networks (VPNs) and **IP Security (IPSec)**. Windows XP Professional uses the NTFS which supports **access control lists (ACLs)** to prevent unauthorized access to files and folders; this protection can be enhanced by implementing the **Encrypting File System (EFS)**. You monitor authorized and unauthorized access to sensitive systems by implementing **auditing** and periodically reviewing the Security log where audited events are recorded. Managing all these security tools is complex; to make that task easier, Windows XP Professional supports **security templates** and the **Local Group Policy Object (LGPO)**, also referred to as local security policy. The **Security Configuration and Analysis snap-in** allows you to compare your current security policy with a template, and then apply the template when you have configured it correctly. With these tools, you can deploy a consistent security configuration across multiple computers. Management of security policies becomes even more flexible and powerful in an Active Directory domain because you can implement **Group Policy Objects (GPO)** across the organization. GPOs are powerful management tools that are referred to occasionally in this book, but a thorough discussion of them is beyond the scope of this work.

Tested Skills and Suggested Practices

The skills you need to successfully master the Configuring, Managing, and Troubleshooting Security objective domain on the *Installing, Configuring, and Administering Microsoft Windows XP Professional* exam include

- **Implementing EFS and recovering encrypted data.**

  - Practice 1: Encrypt and decrypt files and folders on a storage volume formatted with NTFS using Microsoft Windows Explorer.

  - Practice 2: Use the command-line tool CIPHER.EXE to view the encryption settings on some files encrypted in Practice 1. Use CIPHER.EXE to encrypt and decrypt additional files and folders. Type **cipher /?** at a command prompt to view all the command-line switches for this tool.

- Practice 3: Use the command-line tool EFSINFO.EXE from either the Windows 2000 Professional Resource Kit or the Windows XP Professional Resource Kit to view the encryption settings on some of the files and folders used in Practices 1 and 2. Type **efsinfo /?** at a command prompt to view all the command-line switches for this tool.

- Practice 4: Recover encrypted files from a Windows XP Professional computer in a workgroup and in a domain.

- **Configuring and troubleshooting local security policy.**

  - Practice 1: Open the Local Security Settings console and expand the Local Policies folder. Select the Audit Policy folder and review each of the settings available. Select the Security Options folder and examine all the settings.

  - Practice 2: Open the Local Security Settings console and expand the Account Policies folder. Select and configure settings available under both the Password Policy and Account Lockout Policy folders.

  - Practice 3: Open the Local Security Settings console snap-in and expand the Software Restriction Policies folder. Right-click the Software Restriction Policies folder and select Create New Policies from the context menu. Configure a new policy so that NOTEPAD.EXE is restricted from execution. Verify that you are no longer able to launch Notepad from the Start menu. Carefully review all the other options available under the Software Restriction Policies folder.

  - Practice 4: Open the Event Viewer MMC snap-in. Right-click each of the event logs and select properties to configure the log size options. Clear the Security log, open the Security log, and note what event is written to the log immediately after it has been cleared.

- **Configuring and troubleshooting user accounts in a workgroup.**

  - Practice 1: Open the Computer Management MMC snap-in and expand the Local Users and Groups folder. Create several test accounts and groups, and then make some of the accounts members of some of the groups.

  - Practice 2: Open the Local Security Settings console and expand the Local Policies folder. Select the User Rights Assignment folder and review the available settings. Experiment with some of these settings using one of the accounts you created in Practice 1. What happens when you try to log on to Windows XP Professional with the test account if it does not have the Log On Locally user right?

- **Configuring and troubleshooting user authentication in a Windows 2000 domain.**

  - Practice 1: Create a local user account and log on to the Windows XP Professional computer with this account. Try to access some shared resources in the Windows 2000 domain with this account. What happens?

  - Practice 2: Create an account in the Microsoft Windows 2000 domain that has the same user name and password as the local account. Give the domain account permission to access a network share. Now try to access the network share from the Windows XP Professional computer.

  - Practice 3: Join the Windows XP Professional computer to the Windows 2000 domain. Create a user account in the Windows 2000 domain. Open the Computer Management MMC snap-in and expand the Local Users and Groups folder, and then add the domain account to the local Administrators group on the Windows XP Professional computer.

- **Configuring and applying a consistent security configuration on multiple computers.**

  - Practice 1: Open a blank MMC console and add the Security Templates and Security Configuration and Analysis snap-ins to the console. Save the console to a convenient location—you will use it for some of the other practices.

  - Practice 2: Use the Security Templates MMC snap-in to view the security templates included with Windows XP Professional. Create a new template and configure several options in it. Save the template. Launch Notepad and open the template that you just created. Notice the layout and organization of entries in the text file.

  - Practice 3: Copy the template to either a floppy disk or a shared folder on the network. Import the template into other Windows XP Professional computers.

  - Practice 4: Use the Security Configuration and Analysis snap-in to create a security database. Import a security template into the database and analyze the local security settings.

  - Practice 5: View the log created during the analysis process.

- **Configuring and troubleshooting security in Microsoft Internet Explorer.**

  - Practice 1: Launch Internet Explorer and visit some Web sites that include active content. Open the Internet Options dialog box from the Tools menu in Internet Explorer. Select the Security tab and set the Reset Custom Settings drop-down list to High and click the Reset button. Click Yes when prompted. Restart Internet Explorer and revisit the same Web sites. What happens?

Restore the security settings in Internet Explorer to their defaults. Note that you can add specific sites to the predefined site collections: Internet, Local intranet, Trusted sites, and Restricted Sites. You can also customize the security settings for each of these collections.

- Practice 2: Launch Internet Explorer. Open the Internet Options dialog box from the Tools menu and select the Privacy tab to review the options for customizing how Internet Explorer handles cookies.

- Practice 3: Launch Internet Explorer, and then open the Internet Options dialog box from the Tools menu and select the Content tab. Click the Certificates button to open the Certificates dialog box. View all the tabs available in this dialog box. With a certificate selected, click the Advanced button to examine the purpose of the certificate. Close this dialog box and click the View button to examine the certificate itself.

- Practice 4: Launch Internet Explorer, and then open the Internet Options dialog box from the Tools menu and select the Advanced tab. Scroll to the bottom of the list to examine the additional security settings that can be configured for Internet Explorer, such as enabling or disabling Secure Sockets Layer (SSL) 2 and SSL 3.

Further Reading

This section lists supplemental readings by objective. We recommend that you study these sources thoroughly before taking exam 70-270.

Objective 7.1

Microsoft Corporation. *Microsoft Windows XP Professional Resource Kit Documentation*. Redmond, Washington: Microsoft Press, 2001. Read Chapter 17, "Encrypting File System." This chapter takes a close look at how to implement and resolve common problems with EFS.

Microsoft Corporation. *MCSE Training Kit: Microsoft Windows XP Professional*. Redmond, Washington: Microsoft Press, 2001. Read and complete Lesson 3 in Chapter 14, "Managing Data Storage."

Objective 7.2

Microsoft Corporation. *Microsoft Windows XP Professional Resource Kit Documentation*. Redmond, Washington: Microsoft Press, 2001. Read Chapter 13, "File Systems," focusing on the sections that discuss NTFS. Read Chapter 15, "Logon and Authentication" for information about configuring account policies and other security settings relating to user authentication. Review Chapter 16, "Authorization and Access Control" and Appendix B, "User Rights." Chapter 16 explains how objects in Windows XP have ACLs, and how to use the permissions available with different types of objects to secure them from unauthorized access. Appendix B defines all the user rights available under Windows XP Professional.

Microsoft Corporation. *MCSE Training Kit: Microsoft Windows XP Professional.* Redmond, Washington: Microsoft Press, 2001. Read and complete all lessons in Chapter 8, "Securing Resources with NTFS Permissions." Read and complete all lessons in Chapter 9, "Administering Shared Folders." Read and complete all lessons in Chapter 13, "Configuring Security Settings and Internet Options."

Objective 7.3

Microsoft Corporation. *Microsoft Windows XP Professional Resource Kit Documentation.* Redmond, Washington: Microsoft Press, 2001. Read Chapter 15, "Logon and Authentication," for information about creating and managing user accounts and groups. Review Chapter 16, "Authorization and Access Control." This chapter explains how to configure and troubleshoot permissions on objects in Windows XP Professional.

Microsoft Corporation. *MCSE Training Kit: Microsoft Windows XP Professional.* Redmond, Washington: Microsoft Press, 2001. Read and complete all lessons in Chapter 3, "Setting Up and Managing User Accounts."

Objective 7.4

Microsoft Corporation. *Microsoft Windows XP Professional Resource Kit Documentation.* Redmond, Washington: Microsoft Press, 2001. Read the sections in Chapter 13, "File Systems," that discuss NTFS. Read Appendix E, "Security Event Messages," for a list of events that will appear in the Security Log.

Microsoft Corporation. *MCSE Training Kit: Microsoft Windows XP Professional.* Redmond, Washington: Microsoft Press, 2001. Read and complete Lesson 4 in Chapter 3, "Setting Up and Managing User Accounts."

Objective 7.5

Microsoft Corporation. *MCSE Training Kit: Microsoft Windows XP Professional.* Redmond, Washington: Microsoft Press, 2001. Read and complete Lesson 4 in Chapter 13, "Configuring Security Settings and Internet Options."

Launch Internet Explorer, select the Help menu, and then select Contents and Index. Read all the articles and related topics under the headings "Sending Information over the Internet Safely" and "Understanding Security and Privacy on the Internet."

O B J E C T I V E   7 . 1

Configure, manage, and troubleshoot Encrypting File System (EFS).

When Microsoft introduced the **NTFS** in Microsoft Windows NT 3.1, Windows NT 3.1 was the only operating system that was able to read it. NTFS secures individual files and folders by maintaining **access control lists (ACLs)** for each. Third-party software developers have released tools that can be used to mount NTFS volumes from other operating systems such as MS-DOS and Microsoft Windows Me. These tools bypass the NTFS permissions; therefore anyone who has physical access to a computer running Windows XP Professional may be able to view sensitive data on that system. The **Encrypting File System (EFS)** overcomes this vulnerability by encrypting the files before writing them to the hard disk. EFS requires NTFS version 5 or later, and therefore cannot be used on writeable CD-ROMs, writeable DVDs, and other removable media.

EFS uses public key-based **symmetric encryption algorithm** and is seamlessly integrated with Windows XP Professional's file system management tools, making it easy for users to manage while providing effective protection of sensitive information. To encrypt files and folders from Windows Explorer, select one or more items, right-click to bring up their properties dialog box, and then click the Advanced button and enable the Encrypt Contents To Secure Data check box. Normally you must encrypt both the folder and the file because encrypted files stored in unencrypted folders might become unencrypted when the file is modified and saved at a later time. You can also use the command-line tool CIPHER.EXE to manage encryption of files and folders. Type **cipher /?** at a command prompt to view all the options available with this tool.

When a user attempts to access an encrypted file, EFS checks to see whether the user's profile has a copy of the correct **private key** for decrypting the file. If the user does not, access is denied. If the user does, the person is able to access the file transparently. When an encrypted file is moved to a File Allocation Table (FAT) partition, or to a different computer running a version of NTFS older than version 5, the file is decrypted. If the user does not have the private key, the copy operation fails. When you are using EFS, it is a good idea to encrypt any folders where applications create temporary files so those transient files are as well secured as the originals.

Caution The encryption key is stored with a user's profile, so the operating system does not have access to the key during the boot-up process; therefore, you must never attempt to encrypt any core operating system files with EFS because the computer may no longer be bootable.

Although a thorough explanation of **public key encryption** is beyond the scope of this book, as the person responsible for implementing and managing EFS on Windows XP Professional computers, you must understand some basic concepts. When EFS encrypts a file, it creates fast symmetric keys designed for bulk encryption. The file is encrypted one block at a time, using a different encryption key for each. These file encryption keys are themselves encrypted and then stored in the file header. When you attempt to decrypt a file, EFS uses your certificate and private key to unlock the encrypted fields within the file header. It then uses the decrypted keys to decrypt the rest of the file. The user certificates and private keys used for EFS can be stored in the user's profile; the private keys are encrypted with a master key that is unlocked when the user logs on to a system. You can further protect these encryption keys by implementing the **startup key** with the **Syskey** tool. The startup key protects many sensitive system files by encrypting them with yet another key. You can store this key locally via a complex obfuscation algorithm that hides pieces of the key throughout the system registry or on a floppy disk that must be inserted whenever the computer is booted up. Floppy disk storage is more secure, but if the disk is lost or destroyed, you are not able to boot up the computer.

Windows XP Professional helps protect against the risk of lost private keys belonging to individual users by supporting **data recovery agents (DRAs)**. Typically this is the local administrator account created during the installation of the operating system. Windows XP Professional differs from Windows 2000 in that no default DRA is created on stand-alone computers. Windows XP Professional computers belonging to a Windows 2000 domain automatically add all DRA certificates within the scope of the EFS recovery policy to the local certificate store. Additional local and domain accounts can be specified as key recovery agents via group policy or by using the Add Recovery Agent Wizard, which you start by opening the Local Security Settings console clicking Public Key Policies, right-clicking Encrypting File System, and selecting Add Recovery Agent. The Add Recovery Agent Wizard appears—follow the prompts to specify a DRA.

Objective 7.1 Questions

70-270.07.01.001

You recently upgraded all your organization's desktop computers to Windows XP Professional. Those systems had been running a variety of Windows operating systems—each had been installed with the default file system used by their respective operating system. You used automated installation scripts to upgrade each computer, but forgot to convert all the local disk drives to Windows XP Professional's default file system, NTFS 6.

The users of which computers will be able to use EFS without having to convert their file systems to NTFS? (Choose two.)

A. Those whose computers were upgraded from Microsoft Windows NT 4 Workstation

B. Those whose computers were upgraded from Microsoft Windows 98

C. Those whose computers were upgraded from Microsoft Windows 2000 Professional

D. Those whose computers were upgraded from Microsoft Windows 95 to Windows Me and then to Windows XP

E. Those whose computers were upgraded from Windows Me

70-270.07.01.002

You are the administrator for a network of computers running Windows XP Professional. You want to write a script and schedule it to run once on each system. The script encrypts each user's My Documents folder using EFS. What tool must you call from the script to encrypt the desired folder?

A. Windows Explorer

B. Efsinfo

C. Syskey

D. Cipher

70-270.07.01.003

You are the administrator of a Windows 2000 domain with 50 Windows XP Professional desktop computers. All users have their own home folder on a file server where they save their documents. John leaves the company and his manager, April, asks you to move John's documents to her home folder. You log on to the network with your account that belongs to the Domain Admins group and move the files. When April tries to open the files, she sees an Access Denied error message. How can you give April access to the encrypted files?

A. Grant April the Full Control NTFS permission.

B. Log on as a domain administrator and recover the files.

C. Log on as a local administrator and recover the files.

D. Restore the files from the most recent backup tape.

70-270.07.01.004

Your company's network includes Windows Me desktop computers, Windows XP Professional desktop and laptop computers, and Window 2000 servers. Michelle recently encrypted a file called EMPLOYEEREVIEW.DOC with EFS on her local hard drive. She copies the file to an unencrypted folder on a Windows 2000 file server and later complains to you that other users have made changes to her document. Why are users able to access the file?

A. You cannot store encrypted files on network shares.

B. Encrypted files copied to an unencrypted folder lose their encryption.

C. The file is stored on a volume that has been formatted with NTFS.

D. The file is stored on a volume that has been formatted with FAT32.

Objective 7.1 Answers

70-270.07.01.001

▶ **Correct Answers: A and C**

   A. **Correct:** The default file system for computers running Windows NT 4 Workstation is NTFS 4. During the upgrade to Windows XP, any local drives formatted with NTFS are automatically upgraded to NTFS 6. NTFS 6 supports EFS.

   B. **Incorrect:** The default file system for computers running Windows 98 is FAT32. During the upgrade to Windows XP, local drives can be converted to NTFS but you must specify that you want to do so whether doing an automated or manual upgrade because the default option is to leave the existing file system intact.

   C. **Correct:** The default file system for computers running Windows 2000 Professional is NTFS 5. During the upgrade to Windows XP, any local drives formatted with NTFS are automatically upgraded to NTFS 6. NTFS 6 supports EFS.

   D. **Incorrect:** The default file system for computers running Windows 95 is FAT32. During the upgrade to Windows XP, local drives can be converted to NTFS but you must specify that you want to do so whether doing an automated or manual upgrade because the default option is to leave the existing file system intact.

   E. **Incorrect:** The default file system for computers running Windows Me is FAT32. During the upgrade to Windows XP, local drives can be converted to NTFS but you must specify that you want to do so whether doing an automated or manual upgrade because the default option is to leave the existing file system intact.

70-270.07.01.002

▶ **Correct Answers: D**

   A. **Incorrect:** Although you can use Windows Explorer to manually encrypt files and folders, it is a graphical tool that can't be easily incorporated into a script.

   B. **Incorrect:** Efsinfo (EFSINFO.EXE) is a command-line tool that displays information about encrypted files and folders—you can't use it to encrypt or decrypt files or folders.

   C. **Incorrect:** Syskey (SYSKEY.EXE) is the graphical Startup Key tool for encrypting sensitive operating system files—it can't be used to encrypt user's data files.

   D. **Correct:** Cipher (CIPHER.EXE) is a command-line tool for creating file encryption keys, viewing encryption settings, encrypting files and folders, and decrypting files and folders. It is the best tool to use in a script for encrypting files and folders.

70-270.07.01.003

▶ **Correct Answers: B**

    A. **Incorrect:** Encryption is separate from NTFS permissions. As a member of Domain Admins group, you are able to modify the permissions on Jim's documents but giving April Full Control will still not enable her to decrypt the files because she is not a recovery agent.

    B. **Correct:** Windows XP Professional computers that are members of a Windows 2000 domain automatically specify the domain administrator account (*domain_name*\Administrator) as EFS recovery agents because those accounts are designated as encryption recovery agents in the Default Domain Policy GPO.

    C. **Incorrect:** When a Windows XP Professional computer joins a Windows 2000 domain, the domain administrator account (*domain_name*\Administrator) becomes the default recovery agent. Whether the computer is a stand-alone system or a member of a Windows 2000 domain, the local Administrator account is never automatically made a recovery agent. Note that there is an alternative solution to this situation—if John's domain account has not been deleted yet, you can reset the password for that account and then log on with her account and decrypt the files.

    D. **Incorrect:** Files encrypted via EFS remain encrypted when backed up to tape—the restored files are still encrypted and inaccessible to April.

70-270.07.01.004

▶ **Correct Answers: D**

    A. **Incorrect:** EFS is available on volumes that have been formatted with NTFS, even when those volumes are being accessed via shared network folders.

    B. **Incorrect:** Encrypted files retain their encryption when copied to other locations as long as the destination volume is formatted with NTFS 5 or NTFS 6.

    C. **Incorrect:** NTFS 5 supports EFS. The volumes formatted as NTFS on the Windows 2000 server would be running version 5 of that file system, not version 4.

    D. **Correct:** The network share must be on a volume formatted with FAT32, a file system that does not support EFS. Michelle's document was unencrypted automatically when she copied the file to the file server. FAT32 also does not support file and folder level permissions or auditing. These are reasons you must always format volumes that will be shared on the network with NTFS.

OBJECTIVE 7.2

Configure, manage, and troubleshoot local security policy.

Group policy is often implemented with Active Directory: policies are applied based on a user's and computer's membership in sites, domains, and organizational units. Windows XP Professional computers also have a **Local Group Policy Object (LGPO)** that contains numerous security settings organized in five major categories: **Account Policies**, **Local Policies**, **Public Key Policies**, **IP Security Policies**, and **Software Restriction Policies**. To configure the LGPO, use the Group Policy console; you can launch this from the Start Menu by selecting Run and then typing **GPEDIT.MSC**. You can open the subset of the LGPO called Security Settings by opening Control Panel, clicking Performance And Maintenance, clicking Administrative Tools, and then clicking Local Security Policy to launch the **Local Security Settings** console. Account Policies include **Password Policy** and **Account Lockout Policy**—these are discussed in detail in objective 3 of this domain.

Local Policies are further subdivided into three folders. **User Rights Assignment** are specific rights to access various functions of Windows XP locally or over the network—they must be granted explicitly to users or groups and they are located in the User Rights Assignment folder. Log On Locally is one such right—for users to be able to log on interactively to a computer running Windows XP, they must have that right. **Audit Policy**, located in the Audit Policy folder, specifies which types of security events are recorded to the local security log. For example, you enable Success and Failure auditing for Audit Account Logon Events if you want to have an entry written to the security log every time anyone attempts to authenticate with the computer. The **Security Options** contained in the Security Options folder holds many other security settings that don't fit into any of the other categories. For example, you can prevent Windows XP from displaying the user name of the last user to have logged on to the computer in the logon prompt by enabling the Interactive Logon: Do Not Display Last User Name Setting.

Tip When you are auditing access to the files and folders, the file system must be **NTFS**. You configure the auditing policy for files, folders, and printers in the Audit Policy folder by double-clicking Audit Object Access and then enabling Success, Failure, or both Success and Failure Auditing. You then have to configure auditing on the file, folder, and printer objects themselves using Windows Explorer. Right-click the object to be audited, select Properties, click Advanced, click the Auditing tab, and click Add to specify the group or account to be audited and which types of access to monitor.

These settings are all contained locally, however any GPO settings configured through Active Directory take precedence. Domain-based **GPOs** always override local policies. This behavior is covered in more detail in objective four of this domain.

Objective 7.2 Questions

70-270.07.02.001

Jim and Lisa share the same desktop computer running Windows XP Professional. They log on to the system with their own local accounts that are members of the local Users group. While trying to tighten security on the computer, Jim resets permissions on many of the files and folders located on the local hard drive. Both Jim and Lisa can still log on to the system but they are unable to launch some programs that they were using previously such as Microsoft Word and Microsoft Outlook. You want to use auditing to locate the files and folders that have their permissions set too restrictively—which of the following do you do? (Choose two.)

A. Configure auditing in Event Viewer.

B. Open the Local Security Settings console and enable Failure auditing for the Audit Object Access setting.

C. Open the Local Security Settings console and configure Software Restriction policies on the programs that Jim and Lisa need to use.

D. Load the Security Configuration and Analysis snap-in, import the HISECWS.INF security template, and analyze the computer.

E. Use Windows Explorer to configure failure auditing for the desired groups or accounts on the files and folders you believe Jim might have configured incorrectly.

70-270.07.02.002

You manage a handful of Windows XP Professional computers in a workgroup environment. You want to specify how many failed logon attempts are allowed before an account is locked out and how long before the account is automatically reset. How can you do this?

A. Open the Local Security Settings console, expand the Account Settings folder, select the Account Lockout Policy folder, and configure the appropriate settings located there.

B. Open the Local Users and Groups snap-in located in the Computer Management console by launching Control Panel, selecting Performance and Maintenance, and then selecting Administrative Tools.

C. Launch Control Panel and select User Accounts.

D. Launch Control Panel, select Accessibility Options, select Accessibility Options, and click the General tab when the Accessibility Options program window appears.

70-270.07.02.003

Your company's legal department has decided that all corporate computer systems must display a brief message when users log on to the computers interactively. You are responsible for a half dozen Windows XP Professional computers that are set up as a workgroup separate from the company's Active Directory domain. A member of the legal department provides you with the text that she wants displayed on these systems—how do you configure them?

A. Open the Services and Applications group from the Computer Management console, expand the Services folder, scroll down the list, and double-click the Workstation service. Configure the startup parameters for the Workstation service to display the message text.

B. Launch Control Panel, select Appearance and Themes, select Display, and click the Settings tab.

C. Open the Local Security Settings console, expand the Local Policies folder, and then select the Security Options folder. Scroll down the list of policies and double-click Interactive Logon: Message Text For Users Attempting To Log On and type the desired text.

D. Open Notepad, copy the text message into the document, and then save the document as a file called LOGON.TXT into the *%systemroot%* folder.

70-270.07.02.004

Bob is a Web developer in your organization. He has installed Internet Information Services (IIS) on his Windows XP Professional computer for testing and development purposes. He is writing a Web application that will access files stored on other Windows 2000 servers and he wants the IIS service on his computer to be able to access those other systems across the network. He asks you to create an account in the domain called BobIIS. He adds the account to the local Power Users group and then configures the World Wide Web Publishing service to start with the new domain account but when he tries to start the service, he receives a logon failure message. When he reboots the computer, the service still fails to start. What do you do?

A. Add the domain account to the local Administrators group.

B. Open the Local Security Settings console, expand the Local Policies folder, select the User Rights Assignment folder, and scroll down the list of user rights until you see Log On As A Service. Double-click Log On As A Service and add the new domain account to the list of accounts that have this user right.

C. Configure the IIS Admin service's startup so that it runs under the BobIIS domain account as well.

D. Open the Local Security Settings console, expand the Local Policies folder, select the User Rights Assignment folder, and scroll down the list of user rights until you see Log On Locally. Double-click Log On Locally and add the new domain account to the list of accounts that have this user right

Objective 7.2 Answers

70-270.07.02.001

▶ **Correct Answers: B and E**

A. **Incorrect:** Although you use Event Viewer to view the Security log, you cannot configure auditing settings here.

B. **Correct:** This is one of the two steps you must perform to enable failure auditing for specific files and folders. In this scenario, this setting is stored in the LGPO; it can also be configured in a Windows 2000 domain environment by using Active Directory-based GPOs.

C. **Incorrect:** The problems described in this scenario were caused by improperly set NTFS permissions—configuring Software Restriction policies does not correct them.

D. **Incorrect:** You can use this snap-in to compare the current NTFS permissions with those contained in a security template but the HISECWS.INF security template does not include any NTFS permissions settings. Also, the scenario states that you want to configure auditing, which you cannot accomplish by analyzing the computer.

E. **Correct:** This is the second step you must perform to enable failure auditing for specific files and folders. When this step is combined with setting auditing policy, an event is written to the local Security log each time an account attempts an unauthorized access on an audited object.

70-270.07.02.002

▶ **Correct Answers: A**

A. **Correct:** The Local Security Settings console contains the Security Settings extension of the LGPO. You configure settings for stand-alone and workgroup computers using this console; the settings made apply to the local computer, therefore you must log on to each targeted computer to make the settings.

B. **Incorrect:** You can add and remove users and groups, set properties for users and groups, and reset passwords for users using the Local Users and Groups snap-in, but you cannot configure account lockout policies with this tool.

C. **Incorrect:** The User Accounts program located in Control Panel includes some of the features available through the Local Users and Groups snap-in, but you cannot use it to configure account lockout policies.

D. **Incorrect:** The Accessibility Options program is for configuring Windows XP for people with disabilities—it is not used for configuring account lockout policies.

70-270.07.02.003

▶ **Correct Answers: C**

A. **Incorrect:** The startup parameters field is located on the General tab in the Properties dialog box for each service. The parameters in this field are included in the command that launches the service when the service is started from this dialog box; there are no command-line parameters for configuring the logon message text.

B. **Incorrect:** The Display program is used for configuring desktop appearance, screen saver options, display resolution, color depth, and other display-related options; you cannot configure a logon message from this tool.

C. **Correct:** This is how you configure this setting on stand-alone and workgroup computers. There is a second setting usually configured with this one called Interactive Logon: Message Title For Users Attempting To Log On that is displayed in the title bar for the dialog box displaying the logon message. When you are configuring this setting on large numbers of Windows XP Professional computers, it is more efficient to apply this setting via a domain-based GPO.

D. **Incorrect:** Windows XP Professional does not use a text file to determine whether it should display a text message when users attempt to log on interactively, nor does Windows XP store a logon message in a text file.

70-270.07.02.004

▶ **Correct Answers: B**

A. **Incorrect:** Although adding the account to that group ensures that it has access to all the local files, folders, and other resources that it might need, it probably already had sufficient access since it was added to the Power Users group. This step is unlikely to resolve the problem.

B. **Correct:** Services that run on Windows XP must run in the context of accounts that have the user right called log on as a service. The account must also have access to files, folders, and other resources utilized by that service.

C. **Incorrect:** These procedures do not resolve the problem; the account used to launch the IIS Admin service will not impact the behavior of the World Wide Web Publishing service. You will see the same logon failure for this service when you try to start it as well.

D. **Incorrect:** This user right is required for any accounts that are going to log on to the system interactively. It is also needed for any users, including the built-in account for anonymous Web access, that are going to access any Web sites running on the computer. The log on locally user right is not needed for the account used to launch services though, so this procedure will not resolve the problem.

O B J E C T I V E   7 . 3

Configure, manage, and troubleshoot local user and group accounts.

When you go to your bank to withdraw cash from one of your accounts, the staff authenticates you and then authorizes your transaction. Authentication is the process of verifying that you are who you claim to be. Banks typically require a photo ID such as a driver's license and possibly a second item such as a credit card. After you convince them that you are who you claim, they then check to see whether you have an account that has sufficient funds for the transaction—this is authorization. In the world of computers, most users authenticate by typing a user name and password before accessing the secured system. Many technologies are being applied to the authentication process now to increase the level of security and sometimes to make things easier for the end user. Products that use biometrics, smart cards, and one-time password devices are all being sold today; many of these can be integrated seamlessly with the Windows XP logon interface.

This objective is primarily concerned with how to create and manage **local user accounts** and user groups. Windows XP Professional stores these objects locally in the security accounts database. In a Windows 2000 domain, these are stored in Active Directory with many other types of objects such as group policies, organizational units, and computer accounts. To pass this part of the exam, you need to know how to create and modify user accounts, modify group membership, configure account settings, and set local **account policies**. All these procedures are performed with the **Local Users and Groups snap-in**. This tool can be accessed from Control Panel by clicking Performance and Maintenance, clicking Administrative Tools, and then double-clicking Computer Management. After the Computer Management console appears, expand the Local Users and Groups folder. You add, modify, and delete user accounts in the Users folder; you add, modify, and delete user groups in the Groups folder. Windows XP

Note Note that Windows XP Professional includes another tool in Control Panel called User Accounts. The behavior of this tool is dependent upon whether the computer belongs to a domain. In a domain environment this tool allows you to modify or remove existing accounts, change the password of the currently logged on user, or add new user accounts. When you choose to add a new user a simple wizard launches prompting for the account name, domain name, and type of account. In a stand-alone environment the tool presents a different user interface that offers far fewer choices. You can only create accounts that belong to either the local Administrators or local Users group. You should be familiar with the behavior of this tool in either situation.

Professional includes the following built-in groups, to which you can add users, assign user rights, and assign permissions.

- *Administrators*   Can perform all administrative tasks on the computer.

- *Backup Operators*   Can use Windows Backup to back up and restore the computer.

- *Guests*   Have very limited access to the computer. Guests can perform only those tasks and access resources which have been specifically granted to the Guests group.

- *Network Configuration Operators*   Have limited administrative access.

- *Power Users*   Can create and modify local user accounts and share resources.

- *Remote Desktop Users*   Are able to connect to the computer via the Remote Desktop service.

- *Replicator*   Supports file replication in a domain.

- *Users*   Can perform those tasks and access resources which have been specifically granted to the Users group. All new user accounts, and the Domain Users account if the computer belongs to a domain, are automatically added to this group.

- *HelpServicesGroup*   Group for Help and Support services.

Windows XP Professional includes some additional groups that don't appear in the Local Users and Groups snap-in but are visible when setting **ACLs** on objects or when assigning user rights from the **Local Security Settings** snap-in. You cannot modify membership for these groups because the operating system automatically determines which users accessing the computer should belong in which group.

- *Anonymous Logon*   Includes any user who has not been authenticated by Windows XP Professional

- *Authenticated Users*   Includes all users who have been authenticated with a valid user name and password combination

- *Creator Owner*   Includes the user account for the account that created or took ownership of a resource

- *Dialup*   Includes any user who is accessing the computer via a dial-up connection

- *Everyone*   Includes all users who access the computer

- *Interactive*   Includes the user account that is currently logged on locally

- *Network*   Includes all users who access the computer over the network

- *Service*   Includes any accounts used to launch local services

- *System*   Includes the local system account for the computer

- *Terminal Server User*   Includes all users connected to the computer via Terminal Services, Remote Assistance, or Remote Desktop

---

Caution Be careful when assigning permissions to the Everyone group if you have enabled the built-in Guest account. Windows XP Professional allows anyone to connect to the computer without authenticating them and grants those users access to everything that has been granted to the Everyone group.

You use the Local Security Settings console to manage password and account policies. This console is accessed from Control Panel by clicking Performance and Maintenance, clicking Administrative Tools, and then clicking Local Security Policy. Expand the Account Policies folder and then click the Password Policy and Account Lockout Policy folders to access their respective settings. **Password policy** options include requiring users to use unique passwords by enforcing password history, setting maximum and minimum password age, setting minimum password length and complexity, and storing passwords with reversible encryption. The **Account Lockout Policy** specifies how many unsuccessful logon attempts are allowed before an account is locked out of the system, how long the account is kept locked, and how long before the lockout counter is reset. Locked accounts can be manually unlocked by members of the Administrators and Power Users groups. Keep in mind the fact that these settings won't have any impact if passwords are not required when logging on to computers in a stand-alone environment.

Objective 7.3 Questions

70-270.07.03.001

You are a network administrator for a manufacturing company. You have been told to remove Richard and Anthony from the Accounting1 group which has access to the Overdue shared folder. You notice that Richard and Anthony are the only members of the Accounting1 group so you remove their accounts from the group and then delete it. Several weeks later you are told Richard once again needs access to the Overdue folder—what steps do you take to restore his access? (Choose two.)

A. Recreate Richard's user account.

B. Recreate the Accounting1 group and add Richard's account to it.

C. Give Richard's user account the user right Create Permanent Shared Objects.

D. Recreate the Accounting1 group.

E. Grant the Accounting1 group the proper permissions to the Overdue shared folder.

70-270.07.03.002

You work for a small law firm. Dave, Jenny, and Joe are attorneys at the same firm who have been assigned a laptop computer to share. The laptop is delivered with Windows XP Professional and Microsoft Office XP Professional preinstalled. You install the remaining applications that your firm uses but want to make sure Dave, Jenny, and Joe have their data and user preferences stored and maintained separately from one another. What do you do?

A. Run the Sysprep tool.

B. Manually create a new local user profile for each attorney.

C. Create separate hardware profiles for each attorney.

D. Create local user accounts for each attorney.

70-270.07.03.003

You work at a small law office that upgraded its network to an Active Directory-based domain. All user accounts and computers have been migrated to the domain. An attorney named Dave recently left the company and is being replaced by a temporary attorney named Scott. What is the easiest way to give Scott the exact same access to the network that Dave had?

A. Rename Dave's account to Scott and reset the password.

B. Create a new user account called Scott and then copy the Dave user profile to Scott's account.

C. Create a new account for Scott and manually grant it access to all the resources that Dave's account had access to. Delete Dave's account.

D. Create a new account for Scott and manually grant it access to all the resources that Dave's account had access to. Disable Dave's account.

Objective 7.3 Answers

70-270.07.03.001

▶ **Correct Answers: B and E**

A. **Incorrect:** There is no need to recreate Richard's account because it has not been deleted.

B. **Correct:** Merely creating a group and calling it Accounting1 does not restore its members and permissions. You must manually add the members that need to belong to it and explicitly grant permissions to the resources it must be able to access.

C. **Incorrect:** User accounts do not require this user right to access resources shared over the network.

D. **Incorrect:** This answer is incorrect for the reasons noted in answer B.

E. **Correct:** This answer is correct for the same reasons noted in answer B.

70-270.07.03.002

▶ **Correct Answers: D**

A. **Incorrect:** The Sysprep tool is used for creating installation images of Windows XP Professional that include other applications such as Office XP; it's not used for creating user accounts or user profiles.

B. **Incorrect:** It is not necessary to manually create local user profiles for the reasons explained in answer D.

C. **Incorrect:** Hardware profiles are used when computers are regularly moved between markedly distinct hardware environments, for example, docked and undocked profiles for a laptop computer. Hardware profiles have nothing to do with individual user data or settings, so creating unique hardware profiles does not address the requirements outlined in the question.

D. **Correct:** When the users log on to the computer for the first time, a new user profile is created for them under the Documents and Settings folder located on the system volume. The profile automatically retains their user settings, and a folder called My Documents is created within their profile. Most Windows-compatible programs automatically try to store documents at this location.

70-270.07.03.003

▶ **Correct Answers: A**

A. **Correct:** Each user account has a unique security identifier (SID). The SID is granted access to resources but is typically represented by the friendlier user name for the account. Changing the account name does not change the SID, so Scott will have access to everything that Dave had access to. Changing the password ensures that Dave is no longer able to connect to the network with that account.

B. **Incorrect:** This procedure will ensure that Scott's profile settings match Dave's, but Scott's account will not have access to shared folders and printers, NTFS files and folders, and other resources that Dave's account had access to. Also, if Dave was still able to connect to the network, perhaps via a dial-up or VPN connection, he would still be able to gain access to data on the network—this is a significant security risk.

C. **Incorrect:** These procedures will accomplish the desired goals, but there is a much simpler way to give Scott the appropriate access to resources on the network.

D. **Incorrect:** These procedures will accomplish the desired goals, but there is a much simpler way to give Scott the appropriate access to resources on the network.

Configure, manage, and troubleshoot a security configuration.

After reading the first three objectives of this domain, you can see that managing security on a single computer running Windows XP Professional is challenging. Virtually every object and service can have unique permissions. Many registry settings are available for enabling or disabling various **security options**. Implementing a consistent security configuration across multiple computers is an even greater challenge. Active Directory helps simplify this work with domain **Group Policy Objects (GPOs)**; these combine all the security settings available in the **LGPO** with a host of additional options available only in an Active Directory environment. GPOs can be applied to sites, domains, and organizational units; each GPO has its own **ACL**, allowing you to filter which computers and users the policy is applied to by domain groups and accounts.

Although GPOs ease the burden of applying policies consistently across large numbers of computers and users, security templates help reduce the complexity of configuring security. Security templates always end in .inf; they are text files containing security settings. You apply a security template to a stand-alone or workgroup computer by importing them into the Security Settings node of the LGPO. To accomplish this, open Control Panel, select Performance and Maintenance, click Administrative Tools, double-click Local Security Policy, select the Security Settings node, click the Action menu, and then click Import Policy. You can also import a security template into a domain-based GPO.

Tip Keep in mind that domain-based GPOs always take precedence over any local security settings.

Windows XP Professional ships with a handful of sample templates that are ready for use; they are stored in the *%systemroot%*/Security/Templates folder. You can view and edit these templates or create brand new ones by using the **Security Templates snap-in**. You also can use the **Security Configuration and Analysis snap-in** to import security templates; this tool can merge multiple templates into a single template and then compare the settings in that template with the current system settings. The Security Templates snap-in is a powerful tool for creating templates while the Security Configuration and Analysis snap-in is a great at preparing for, applying, and trouble-shooting security settings.

Tip Neither of these snap-ins appears in the Start menu. You access them by launching an empty copy of the Microsoft Management Console and then adding the snap-ins to the console. From the Start menu, select Run and type **mmc** in the dialog box that appears. Select the File menu and click Add/Remove Snap-in. The Add/Remove Snap-in dialog box appears; click Add. The Add Standalone Snap-in dialog box appears. Scroll down the list of available snap-ins, select Security Templates, and click Add; next, select Security Configuration and Analysis and click Add. Click Close to close the Add Standalone Snap-in dialog box, and then click OK to close the Add/Remove Snap-in dialog box. You can add other snap-ins to create your own customized console; you can save your console from the File menu by clicking Save.

Objective 7.4 Questions

70-270.07.04.001

You are a consultant setting up four new desktop computers for a dental office on its local area network that is set up as a workgroup. The computers all have Windows XP Professional pre-installed. You want to design a secure configuration and apply it to all four computers; what is the most efficient and effective way to accomplish this goal?

A. Open the Local Security Settings console and configure the desired settings on each of the computers. Next, open Windows Explorer and configure the desired permissions on each folder.

B. Write a script in VBScript that makes all the desired changes; copy and run the script on each of the four computers.

C. Use the System program located in Control Panel to configure the desired settings on one computer, and then export the settings to a text file and import them into each of the other computers using the System program.

D. Open the Security Templates snap-in and create a new security template with the desired settings on one of the computers. Save the template and copy it to each of the other computers. Open the Security Configuration and Analysis snap-in, import the template, and then apply the template on each computer.

70-270.07.04.002

You are the lead network administrator for a manufacturing company. Chris is a manager in your firm's marketing department who has ordered several computers and installed them on the network herself. She explains to you that she has configured them in a workgroup called MKTG and that she wants you to adjust the domain-based GPOs to allow a less restrictive password policy because her team has trouble remembering complex passwords. Which policies must you adjust to fulfill Chris's request?

A. The Default Domain Controller Policy

B. The LGPO

C. The last domain-based GPO to be applied

D. The GPO applied to the organizational unit where the user account resides

70-270.07.04.003

You are the administrator network of desktop computers running Windows XP Professional. You want to implement IPSec with the 3DES encryption algorithm. You use the IP Security Policy Management snap-in to implement IPSec. What else must you do?

A. Download and install the High Encryption Pack from the Windows Update site on all the computers.

B. Install the Crypto API (CAPI) on all the Windows XP computers.

C. Do nothing.

D. Install a Windows 2000 Server on the network, and install and configure Microsoft Certificate Services on that server. Use that server to issue 3DES client certificates to each of the Windows XP systems.

Objective 7.4 Answers

70-270.07.04.001

▶ **Correct Answers: D**

A. **Incorrect:** Although this approach will get security configured on each of the computers, it is a time-consuming and error-prone approach. It is unlikely that all four computers will have the same settings when the process is completed.

B. **Incorrect:** This approach will result in a consistent security configuration across all four computers but writing and debugging a complex script will take a great deal of time.

C. **Incorrect:** The System program is not used for configuring security settings.

D. **Correct:** For computers that are not members of an Active Directory domain, this is the best way to apply consistent computer settings across multiple computers.

70-270.07.04.002

▶ **Correct Answers: B**

A. **Incorrect:** The computers are part of a workgroup; because they don't belong to an Active Directory domain, they will not process domain-based GPOs. The effective policies will all come from the LGPO. Computers that are members of an Active Directory domain process GPOs in a specific order. First, they process the LGPO, and then site-based GPOs, and then domain GPOs, and then organizational unit GPOs. If more than one GPO is applied at the same level within this hierarchy, they are applied in order from top to bottom.

B. **Correct:** The question states that the computers are part of a workgroup; because they are not members of an Active Directory domain, they will not process domain-based GPOs and the LGPO will be applied.

C. **Incorrect:** This answer is incorrect for the reasons stated in answer A.

D. **Incorrect:** This answer is incorrect for the reasons stated in answer A. If these computers had belonged to an Active Directory domain the account policies are machine-specific, not user-specific settings. Machine-specific settings are derived from the location of the machine account within the Active Directory hierarchy. Account Policies are an exception though; the same settings are applied throughout an entire domain. The configuration specified in the Default Domain Controller Policy applies to all the machines within the domain.

70-270.07.04.003

▶ **Correct Answers: C**

A. **Incorrect:** Windows 2000 did not ship with 128-bit encryption, or support for 3DES. Prior to Service Pack 2, you had to install the High Encryption Pack to enable advanced encryption. The United States government has relaxed its export rules for cryptographic technologies since Windows 2000 was released. Service Pack 2 for Windows 2000 includes support for 3DES and 128-bit encryption, as does Windows XP Professional.

B. **Incorrect:** The Crypto API is an application programming interface for advanced cryptographic functions; there is no need to install it to enable support for 3DES in Windows XP Professional.

C. **Correct:** Windows XP Professional is shipped with support for 3DES as well as 128-bit encryption; there is no need to take any additional steps because you can specify 3DES within the IP Security Policy Management tool.

D. **Incorrect:** In many situations, it makes sense to deploy a Windows 2000-based public key infrastructure (PKI) that is integrated with Active Directory to facilitate the use of IPSec on a network. It isn't necessary to do so though; you can use certificates from another vendor's certificate authority (CA), or you can use other methods of authentication, such as Kerberos.

Configure, manage, and troubleshoot Internet Explorer security settings.

Today's Web browsers offer far more functionality than their predecessors of five or six years ago. Early Web browsers simply downloaded text and graphics files and rendered them according to the formatting instructions embedded within the **Hypertext Markup Language (HTML)** code included within the document. Modern Web browsers can download and execute scripts, Java applets, and ActiveX controls from autonomous Web sites outside your organization's control. Some of these downloadable programs are designed to interact with the client computer's file system and other local resources. This flexibility facilitates the development of powerful business applications, but poorly implemented browser security can allow malicious Web site operators to wreak havoc on your network. For these reasons, it is important that you understand how to implement and troubleshoot security on Web browsers used in your network. Internet Explorer has many configuration options relating to security that are accessed by launching Control Panel, selecting Network and Internet Connections, and then selecting **Internet Options**. To pass this portion of the certification exam, you must be familiar with the configuration options available on each of the tabs in the Internet Options program.

Select the General tab to delete Temporary Internet Files and configure the location and size allocated to the temporary Internet files folder. These are files that have been downloaded from various Web sites and cached locally, making the next visit to that Web site much faster. You can also delete Web **cookies** that have been stored in the Cookies folder. Internet Explorer maintains a history of sites visited; you can configure how many days this list should be retained, or clear the entire list.

Select the Security tab to configure the four Web content zones: Internet, Local Intranet, Trusted sites, and Restricted sites. Each of these zones has default security settings that you can modify by selecting the zone and then clicking the Custom Level button. The Security Settings dialog box appears; you can use the drop-down list to select a predefined collection of settings, or you can scroll down the list of individual settings to specify their values. For example, you can set signed and unsigned ActiveX controls separately to be either disabled or enabled, or to prompt the user before being downloaded.

Select the Privacy tab to configure how cookies are handled in the Internet zone. You can enable, disable, or prompt the user before downloading first-party and third-party cookies. You can override the default settings for individual Web sites by clicking the Edit button in the Web Sites section.

Select the Content tab to configure **Secure Sockets Layer (SSL)** and other types of certificates. You can import, export, and remove all types of certificates. You can view and edit the properties of individual certificates. The certificates that are included with Windows XP Professional are from trusted root CAs such as VeriSign, GTE CyberTrust, and Microsoft. You can remove any of these trusted root certificates if your organization's security policy requires it. You can also import additional trusted root certificates. For example, you might want to import a code-signing certificate used by your internal application developers to sign their applications. For large enterprises, it's usually more effective to manage their **public key infrastructure (PKI)** and certificate policies through Active Directory-based **GPOs**. A complete discussion of how PKI works and how to implement a PKI using Active Directory and Microsoft Certificate Services is beyond the scope of this book.

Select the Connections tab to configure **proxy server** settings. You can configure unique proxy server settings for each network connection. Select the Advanced tab to configure other Internet Explorer settings including how SSL sessions are handled by the browser.

Objective 7.5 Questions

70-270.07.05.001

By default, which of the following Web content zones prompts the user to download an unsigned ActiveX control?

A. Internet

B. Local Intranet

C. Trusted Sites

D. Restricted Sites

70-270.07.05.002

You work for Humongous Insurance, a company that has a strong partnership with a Contoso Pharmaceuticals. Users on your network are able to access some Web servers on Contoso's intranet via a VPN connection that travels across the network. For an added level of security, the administrators of Contoso's network require HTTPS for all connections to its intranet Web servers. These servers use SSL certificates issued from Contoso's own CA. Every time users on your network visit one of the Web servers on Contoso's intranet, they receive an error message stating that the SSL certificate was not issued from a trusted root CA. What is the easiest way to allow users on your network to access Web servers on Contoso's intranet without having to view these error messages?

A. Ask an administrator from Contoso to provide you with a copy of the issuing certificate from its root CA. Use the Internet Options program located in Control Panel to import the certificate as a trusted root authority on each computer used for visiting the Contoso intranet.

B. Ask an administrator from Contoso to send the issuing certificate from its CA to Microsoft so it can be incorporated into the next service pack for Windows XP.

C. Instruct the administrators at Contoso to purchase a new certificate from an existing trusted root CA and then rebuild its internal PKI using the new certificate for the first server.

D. Use the Registry Editor tool (REGEDT32.EXE) to manually add Contoso's issuing certificate to the list of trusted root CAs on each computer that visits the Contoso intranet.

70-270.07.05.003

Your organization has a security policy that dictates the ways in which Web browsers use cookies. The policy specifically states that third-party cookies cannot be accepted. You want to ensure Internet Explorer users stay within these guidelines, but allow any other cookies. How must you configure the Internet Options?

A. Use the Default settings.

B. Use the Advanced Privacy Settings dialog box to specify that First-party Cookies will be accepted and Third-party Cookies will be blocked.

C. Use the Advanced Privacy Settings dialog box to specify that First-party Cookies will be blocked and Third-party Cookies will be blocked.

D. Use the Advanced Privacy Settings dialog box to specify that First-party Cookies will be accepted and Third-party Cookies will be prompt the user.

70-270.07.05.004

You regularly visit a hardware vendor's Web site to order computers, computer parts, and network equipment online. You have been satisfied with this arrangement for many months until the vendor introduces a revamped Web site that uses ActiveX controls to present its catalog, inventory, account information, past orders, and pending orders. When you visit the overhauled Web site, you can see many text and graphic elements but large sections appear to be blank. When you click some links, more pages with blank sections appear. What is the easiest way to allow yourself to access all the functionality on the vendor's new Web site?

A. Contact the vendor and explain that its Web site is down.

B. Ask the vendor to email the ActiveX controls to you so you can manually install them on your computer.

C. Add the vendor's URL to the list of Trusted sites using the Security tab in the Internet Options program located in Control Panel.

D. Ask the vendor to provide you with a link to its old Web site.

Objective 7.5 Answers

70-270.07.05.001

▶ **Correct Answers: C**

A. **Incorrect:** By default, sites that are placed in the Internet zone have unsigned ActiveX controls disabled. If an ActiveX control has been signed, the user is prompted to download it. This ensures the user is kept safe from potentially dangerous, unsigned ActiveX controls on the public Internet. Users can change this default by choosing Internet Options in Internet Explorer, selecting the Security tab, selecting the Internet zone, and clicking the Custom Level button.

B. **Incorrect:** By default, sites that are placed in the Local Intranet zone have unsigned ActiveX controls disabled. If an ActiveX control has been signed, the user is prompted to download it. This ensures users are kept safe from potentially dangerous, unsigned ActiveX controls on their local intranet. Users can change this default by choosing Internet Options in Internet Explorer, selecting the Security tab, selecting the Local Intranet zone, and clicking the Custom Level button.

C. **Correct:** By default, sites that have been placed in the Trusted Sites zone prompt the user to download an unsigned ActiveX control. Signed ActiveX controls are automatically downloaded. This provides users with the convenience of skipping prompts to install controls from a Web server they feel confident will never present potentially dangerous ActiveX controls for download.

D. **Incorrect:** Restricted Sites have both signed and unsigned ActiveX controls disabled. The user is not prompted to download any ActiveX controls, ever. Sites placed in the Restricted Sites zone are assumed to have potentially dangerous code. Users can change this default by choosing Internet Options in Internet Explorer, selecting the Security tab, selecting the restricted sites zone, and clicking the Custom Level button.

70-270.07.05.002

▶ **Correct Answers: A**

A. **Correct:** This is the best choice among the answers given. This process would be greatly simplified if the network were running Active Directory. The certificate from Contoso can be added to the list of trusted root CAs using domain-based GPOs instead.

B. **Incorrect:** Microsoft has tough requirements that must be met before adding new trusted root CAs to the list shipped with its operating systems. There must be compelling evidence that a wide range of users from many different organizations will benefit from the new CA being added to the list.

C. **Incorrect:** If Contoso were just starting to deploy its PKI this option might make sense, but because the PKI is already in operation it's not feasible to scrap it and start all over again.

D. **Incorrect:** It isn't possible to import SSL certificates in this manner.

70-270.07.05.003

▶ **Correct Answers: B**

A. **Incorrect:** The default setting does not block any type of cookie. Therefore, it does not comply with your organization's security policies.

B. **Correct:** These settings will block all third-party cookies while allowing other cookies to be used.

C. **Incorrect:** These settings will result in all types of cookies being blocked.

D. **Incorrect:** These settings will allow first-party cookies, but third-party cookies may still be allowed because the user will be prompted to accept or reject them.

70-270.07.05.004

▶ **Correct Answers: C**

A. **Incorrect:** Although it is possible that the Web site is having problems, it is not the most likely cause of the behavior described in the question. Because parts of the pages are rendered correctly and links to other pages function, the Web server is probably working. The issues might be caused by a failing database server or application server that is supposed to feed data to the Web server, but you don't have enough information to determine whether this is the case.

B. **Incorrect:** ActiveX, Java, and other Web-based applets are designed to be downloaded by visitors to the Web site as they go along, not to be repackaged and deployed via installation routines. Resolving the problem in this manner would add a great deal of overhead to the vendor's Web management team and force you to spend time manually installing its software.

C. **Correct:** This is an easy way around the problem. The default security settings for the ActiveX Virtual Machine in Internet Explorer 6 are set to High safety. This restrictive setting can cause problems for some downloadable ActiveX controls. The default setting for Trusted sites is Low safety, which should allow any thoroughly debugged Java applet to run correctly. Be careful adding URLs to your list of Trusted sites because malicious or poorly written programs might be downloaded and run by Internet Explorer without your knowledge. This could lead to lost or compromised data or even a damaged installation of Windows XP Professional.

D. **Incorrect:** It is unlikely that the vendor will want to maintain two different versions of its Web site simultaneously; therefore this approach is not feasible.

Glossary

A

access control entry (ACE) An entry in an object's discretionary access control list (DACL) that grants permissions to a user or group. *See also* access control list (ACL); discretionary access control list (DACL).

access control list (ACL) A list of security protections that apply to an entire object, a set of the object's properties, or an individual property of an object. *See also* access control entry (ACE); discretionary access control list (DACL).

Accessibility Services A class of software and hardware services that make a computer usable by people with one or more physical disabilities, such as restricted mobility, blindness, or deafness.

account lockout policy An account policy that defines the number of unsuccessful logon attempts allowed before a user account is locked out. *See also* account policies.

account policies A set of security-related policies that defines how Windows XP handles aspects of user account management, including password length, password complexity, and account lockout. *See also* account lockout policy.

ACE *See* access control entry (ACE).

ACL *See* access control list (ACL).

ACPI *See* Advanced Configuration and Power Interface (ACPI).

Active Directory The directory service that stores information about objects on a network and makes this information available to users and network administrators. Active Directory gives network users access to permitted resources anywhere on the network using a single logon process.

Active Server Pages (ASP) A flexible standard that provides a framework for executing scripts on Internet Information Services (IIS) Web servers. ASP contains embedded scripts in languages such as VBScript and Perl. *See also* Internet Information Services (IIS).

Active Setup A set of ActiveX components that communicate with the Windows Update Web site to efficiently retrieve and install critical software patches and upgrades.

Address Resolution Protocol (ARP) A TCP/IP protocol for determining the hardware address (or physical address) of a node on a local area network connected to the Internet, when only the IP address (or logical address) is known. An ARP request is sent to the network, and the node that has the IP address responds with its hardware address.

Advanced Configuration and Power Interface (ACPI) An open industry specification that defines power management on a wide range of mobile, desktop, and server computers and peripherals. *See also* Plug and Play (PnP).

Advanced Power Management (APM) A software interface (designed by Microsoft and Intel) between hardware-specific power management software (such as that located in a system BIOS) and an operating system power management driver.

Advanced Processor Interrupt Controller (APIC) A proprietary specification introduced by Intel for computer motherboards that support multiple processors.

Advanced Technology Attachment (ATA) A group of storage control and interface standards based on IDE technology.

Advanced Technology Attachment Packet Interface (ATAPI) A standard that allows different hardware types to connect to a single IDE bus. *See also* Intelligent Drive Electronics or Integrated Device Electronics (IDE).

answer file   A text file that you can use to provide automated input for unattended installation of Windows XP and Windows 2000. This input includes parameters to answer the questions required by Setup for specific installations. In some cases, you can use this text file to provide input to wizards, such as the Active Directory Installation Wizard, which is used to add Active Directory to Windows 2000 Server through Setup. The default answer file for Setup is known as UNATTEND.TXT. *See also* Active Directory.

API   *See* application programming interface (API).

APIC   *See* Advanced Processor Interrupt Controller (APIC).

APIPA   *See* Automatic Private IP Addressing (APIPA).

APM   *See* Advanced Power Management (APM).

application configuration   A feature of Internet Information Services (IIS) that identifies script mappings, Active Server Pages (ASP) scripting options, and debug settings for a virtual directory and its subfolders. *See also* application mapping; Internet Information Services (IIS).

application feature   An individual piece of functionality that can be installed on demand by packages designed for the native Windows Installer.

application mapping   An association within Internet Information Services (IIS) between a file extension, an executable path, and an HTTP verb. *See also* application configuration; Internet Information Services (IIS).

application programming interface (API)   A set of routines that an application uses to request and carry out lower-level services performed by a computer's operating system.

ARP   *See* Address Resolution Protocol (ARP).

ASP   *See* Active Server Pages (ASP).

ASR   *See* Automated System Recovery (ASR).

AT   A command-line utility used for scheduling tasks on Windows NT, Windows 2000, and Windows XP systems. This tool has been replaced by the Task Scheduler, however, it is still supported in Windows XP for backward-compatibility. *See also* Task Scheduler.

ATA   *See* Advanced Technology Attachment (ATA).

ATAPI   *See* Advanced Technology Attachment Packet Interface (ATAPI).

auditing   The process an operating system uses to detect and record security-related events, such as an attempt to create, to access, or to delete objects such as files and folders.

audit policy   The definition of the set of actions that cause an event to be logged in the Windows XP Event Log.

Automated System Recovery (ASR)   A feature of Windows XP that provides for backup and recovery of System State. *See also* System State.

Automatic Caching Of Documents   A setting that makes every open file in a shared folder available offline. Older copies of files are automatically deleted to make way for newer versions. *See also* Automatic Caching Of Programs; Manual Caching Of Documents.

Automatic Caching Of Programs   A setting that provides offline access to shared folders containing files that cannot be changed. This caching option reduces network traffic because offline files are opened directly without accessing the network versions. The offline files generally start and run faster than the network versions. *See also* Automatic Caching Of Documents; Manual Caching Of Documents.

Automatic Private IP Addressing (APIPA)   A feature of Windows XP TCP/IP that automatically configures a unique IP address from the range 169.254.0.1 through 169.254.255.254 and a subnet mask of 255.255.0.0 when TCP/IP is configured for dynamic addressing and a Dynamic Host Configuration Protocol (DHCP) is not available. *See also* IP address; Transmission Control Protocol/Internet Protocol (TCP/IP).

B

backup A duplicate copy of a program, a disk, or data, made either for archiving purposes or for safe-guarding valuable files from loss should the active copy be damaged or destroyed. Some application programs automatically make backup copies of data files, maintaining both the current version and the preceding version.

Backup Utility *See* Windows Backup.

basic disk A physical disk that can be accessed by MS-DOS and all Windows-based operating systems. Basic disks can contain up to four primary partitions, or three primary partitions and an extended partition with multiple logical drives. *See also* basic volume; dynamic disk; dynamic volume.

basic input/output system (BIOS) On x86-based computers, the set of essential software routines that test hardware at startup, start the operating system, and support the transfer of data among hardware devices.

basic volume A primary partition or logical drive that resides on a basic disk. *See also* basic disk.

BIOS *See* basic input/output system (BIOS).

boot sector A critical disk structure for starting your computer, located at sector 1 of each volume or floppy disk. It contains executable code and data that is required by the code, including information used by the file system to access the volume.

C

CA *See* certificate authority (CA).

cable modem A device that enables a broadband connection to the Internet by using cable television infrastructure.

caching A mechanism for storing frequently needed information in accessible storage area so it can be retrieved quickly.

Cardbus A 32-bit PC Card.

CDFS *See* CD-ROM File System (CDFS).

CD-ROM *See* Compact Disc Read-Only Memory (CD-ROM).

CD-ROM File System (CDFS) A 32-bit protected-mode file system that controls access to the contents of CD-ROM drives in Windows 9x, Windows NT, and Windows 2000.

central processing unit (CPU) The part of a computer that has the ability to retrieve, interpret, and execute instructions and to transfer information to and from other resources over the computer's main data-transfer path, the bus.

certificate A digital document that is commonly used for authentication and secure exchange of information on open networks, such as the Internet, extranets, and intranets. A certificate securely binds a public key to the entity that holds the corresponding private key. *See also* certificate authority (CA).

certificate authority (CA) An entity responsible for establishing and vouching for the authenticity of public keys belonging to users (end entities) or other CAs. *See also* certificate.

Challenge Handshake Authentication Protocol (CHAP) A challenge-response authentication protocol for Point-to-Point Protocol (PPP) connections documented in RFC 1994 that uses the industry-standard MD5, a one-way message digest encryption scheme, to hash the response to a challenge issued by the remote access server. *See also* Point-to-Point Protocol (PPP).

CHAP *See* Challenge Handshake Authentication Protocol (CHAP).

clean installation An instance of Windows XP that has not been modified after completing the setup procedure.

client Any computer or program connecting to, or requesting the services of, another computer or program. Client can also refer to the software that enables the computer or program to establish the connection. *See also* server.

client drive redirection A feature of Windows XP and the Remote Desktop that allows users to access files located on their local computers from the remote desktop. *See also* Remote Desktop.

Client for Microsoft Networks Software enabling access to Windows NT or Windows 2000 servers.

Client Services for NetWare (CSNW) A service included with Windows 2000 Professional that allows clients to make direct connections to resources on computers running NetWare 2.*x*, 3.*x*, 4.*x*, or 5.*x* server software.

Client Side Cache (CSC) The database containing information about Offline Files resides in the hidden system folder, or directory, called *%Systemroot%\CSC*.

color depth The amount of color data, per pixel, that the video adapter is configured to display. An 8-bit color depth provides for 256 different color possibilities per pixel.

Compact Disc Read-Only Memory (CD-ROM) An optical disc storage technology used to produce a low-cost platter commonly holding 650 MB that can be recorded only once.

cookies Small data files sent from a Web server to a Web browser. Cookies are stored in the Web browser's memory or hard disk, and sent back to the Web server in future requests.

counter logs A data file containing archived performance statistics. Counter logs can be viewed using Performance utility. *See also* Performance utility.

CPU   *See* central processing unit (CPU).

CSC   *See* Client Side Cache (CSC).

CSNW   *See* Client Services for NetWare (CSNW).

D

DACL   *See* discretionary access control list (DACL).

data recovery agent Recovery agents can use Encrypting File System (EFS) to recover encrypted files if users leave the organization or lose their encryption credentials.

default gateway A configuration item for TCP/IP that is the IP address of a directly reachable IP router. Configuring a default gateway creates a default route in the IP routing table.

defragmentation The process of rewriting parts of a file to contiguous sectors on a hard disk to increase the speed of access and retrieval.

Device Manager An administrative tool that can be used to manage the devices on your computer.

DHCP   *See* Dynamic Host Configuration Protocol (DHCP).

dial-up connection The connection to your network if you are using a device that uses the telephone network. This includes modems with a standard phone line, ISDN cards with high-speed ISDN lines, or X.25 networks.

differential backup A backup that copies files created or changed since the last normal or incremental backup. It does not mark files as having been backed up (in other words, the archive attribute is not cleared). *See also* daily backup; incremental backup; normal backup.

digital signature A means for originators of a message, file, or other digitally encoded information to bind their identity to the information.

digital subscriber line (DSL) A telecommunications technology for providing high-speed transmission to subscribers over the existing copper wire twisted-pair local loop between the customer premises and the telco's central office (CO).

digital versatile disc or digital video disc (DVD) A type of optical disc storage technology. A DVD looks like a CD-ROM, but it can store greater amounts of data.

direct memory access (DMA) Memory access that does not involve the microprocessor. DMA is frequently used for data transfer directly between memory and a peripheral device such as a disk drive.

DirectX Diagnostic Tool A Microsoft Windows–based DirectX tool that presents information about the components and drivers of the Microsoft DirectX application programming interface (API) installed on your system. *See also* application programming interface (API).

disaster recovery The process of restoring a system and data after a catastrophic failure. Disaster recovery must be planned for when designing a system, and the process of recovering a system after disaster must be thoroughly documented and tested.

discretionary access control list (DACL) The part of an object's security descriptor that grants or denies specific users and groups permission to access the object. *See also* access control entry (ACE).

DISKPART A command-line utility used to view, configure, and modify disk partitions.

distribution folder The folder created on the Windows 2000–based distribution server to contain the Setup files.

DMA *See* Direct Memory Access (DMA).

DNS *See* Domain Name System (DNS).

DNS Proxy A component of Internet Connection Sharing (ICS) that allows clients on the internal network to resolve DNS requests for external systems. *See also* Internet Connection Sharing (ICS).

domain In Active Directory, a collection of computers defined by the administrator. These computers share a common directory database, security policies, and security relationships with other domains. In DNS, a domain is any tree or subtree within the DNS namespace. *See also* Active Directory; Domain Name System (DNS).

Domain Name System (DNS) A hierarchical, distributed database that contains mappings of DNS domain names to various types of data, such as IP addresses. *See also* domain; IP address; Transmission Control Protocol/Internet Protocol (TCP/IP).

driver rollback The process of using Device Manager to restore the previously active device driver. Driver rollback is a common method of troubleshooting faulty drivers. *See also* Device Manager; drivers.

drivers A piece of software that interfaces between the operating system and hardware components. *See also* Device Manager, driver signing, driver rollback.

driver signing Windows XP drivers and operating system files have been digitally verified by Microsoft to ensure their quality.

DSL *See* digital subscriber line (DSL).

DVD *See* digital versatile disc or digital video disc (DVD).

dynamic disk A physical disk that can be accessed only by Windows 2000 and Windows XP. Dynamic disks provide features that basic disks do not, such as support for volumes that span multiple disks. *See also* basic disk; basic volume; dynamic volume; partition; volume.

Dynamic Host Configuration Protocol (DHCP) A TCP/IP service protocol that offers dynamic leased configuration of host IP addresses and distributes other configuration parameters to eligible network clients. *See also* IP address; Transmission Control Protocol/Internet Protocol (TCP/IP).

dynamic volume A volume that resides on a dynamic disk. Windows supports five types of dynamic volumes: simple, spanned, striped, mirrored, and RAID-5. *See also* basic disk; basic volume; dynamic disk; volume.

E

EFI   *See* Extensible Firmware Interface (EFI).

EFS   *See* Encrypting File System (EFS).

EISA   *See* Extended Industry Standard Architecture (EISA).

Encrypting File System (EFS)   A feature in Windows XP that protects sensitive data in files that are stored on disk using the NT File System. It uses symmetric key encryption in conjunction with public key technology to provide confidentiality for files.

encryption   The process of making information indecipherable to protect it from unauthorized viewing or use, especially during transmission or when the data is stored on a transportable magnetic medium. A key is required to decode the information.

English Version   A localized version of Windows XP that can be upgraded with the Multilanguage Version binaries and language groups to provide full or partial support of other languages. *See also* Translated Version; Windows XP Professional Multilingual User Interface Pack (MUI Pack).

Extended Industry Standard Architecture (EISA)   A 32-bit bus standard introduced in 1988 by a consortium of nine computer-industry companies.

Extensible Firmware Interface (EFI)   In computers with the Intel Itanium processor, the interface between a computer's firmware, hardware, and the operating system. The EFI defines a new partition style called GUID partition table (GPT). *See also* basic input/output system (BIOS); GUID partition table (GPT).

F

FAT   *See* File Allocation Table (FAT).

FAT32   *See* File Allocation Table-32 (FAT32).

favorites   Element of customization of various Windows XP applications, allowing the user to store a shortcut to a Web site, a topic, or a file.

Fax Service   Allows Windows XP users to send and receive fax transmissions on the computer rather than through a fax machine.

feature component   The granular pieces of an application within the Windows Installer Service that a user can choose to install.

File Allocation Table (FAT)   The system used by MS-DOS to organize and manage files. The FAT is a data structure that MS-DOS creates on the disk when the disk is formatted. The FAT is the only file system MS-DOS can use. *See also* File Allocation Table-32 (FAT32); NT File System (NTFS).

File Allocation Table-32 (FAT32)   A derivative of the file allocation table (FAT) file system. FAT32 supports smaller cluster sizes and larger volumes than FAT, which results in more efficient space allocation on FAT32 volumes. *See also* File Allocation Table (FAT); NT File System (NTFS).

Files and Settings Transfer Wizard (FSTW)   Utility allowing migration of user data from one computer to another.

File Signature Verification tool   The File Signature Verification utility (SIGVERIF.EXE) ensures system integrity by detecting changes to critical system files digitally signed by Microsoft.

File Transfer Protocol (FTP)   A member of the TCP/IP suite of protocols, used to copy files between two computers on the Internet. *See also* Transmission Control Protocol/Internet Protocol (TCP/IP).

firmware   Software (programs or data) that has been written onto read-only memory (ROM). Firmware is a combination of software and hardware.

fragmentation   The scattering of parts of the same disk file over different areas of the disk. Fragmentation occurs as files on a disk are deleted and new files are added. *See also* defragmentation.

FSTW   *See* Files and Settings Transfer Wizard.

FTP   *See* File Transfer Protocol (FTP).

G

GINA *See* Graphical Identification and Authentication (GINA).

globally unique identifier (GUID) A 16-byte value generated from the unique identifier on a device, the current date and time, and a sequence number. A GUID is used to identify a particular device or component.

GPO *See* Group Policy Object (GPO).

GPT *See* GUID partition table (GPT).

Graphical Identification and Authentication (GINA) A replaceable DLL component, loaded by the Winlogon process, that implements the authentication policy of the interactive logon model and performs all user interactions for user authentication.

group A collection of users, computers, contacts, and other groups. Groups can be used as security or as e-mail distribution collections. *See also* domain.

Group Policy An administrator's tool for defining and controlling how programs, network resources, and the operating system operate for users and computers in an organization.

Group Policy Object (GPO) A collection of Group Policy settings. GPOs are essentially the documents created by the Group Policy snap-in, a Windows utility. *See also* Group Policy.

GUID *See* globally unique identifier (GUID).

GUID partition table (GPT) A disk-partitioning scheme that is used by the Extensible Firmware Interface (EFI) in Itanium-based computers. *See also* Extensible Firmware Interface (EFI).

GUI-Mode Setup The portion of the Windows XP installation routine that accepts input from the user regarding user preferences. Optional services and components are added to Windows XP Professional during this phase. *See also* Setup Loader; Text-Mode Setup.

H

HAL *See* hardware abstraction layer (HAL).

hardware abstraction layer (HAL) A thin layer of software provided by the hardware manufacturer that hides, or abstracts, hardware differences from higher layers of the operating system.

Hardware Compatibility List (HCL) A hardware list that Microsoft compiles for a specific product. The Windows HCL, which is posted on the Web, lists the hardware devices and computer systems that are compatible with specific versions of Windows.

hardware ID (HID) One of the three components of the installation ID used during Windows Product Activation (WPA). *See also* product identification (PID); Windows Product Activation (WPA).

hardware profiles A set of data that describes the configuration and characteristics of a given piece of computer equipment.

HCL *See* Hardware Compatibility List (HCL).

hibernation A power management feature that saves everything in memory on disk, turns off your monitor and hard disk, and then turns off your computer. When you restart your computer, your desktop is restored exactly as you left it.

HID *See* hardware ID (HID).

hidden share A computer file with the hidden attribute enabled to hide it from view during normal file operations like a directory listing.

history Element of customization of various Windows XP applications, allowing the user to locate recently visited sites or used files.

Hosts file A local text file in the same format as the 4.3 Berkeley Software Distribution (BSD) UNIX/etc/hosts file. This file maps host names to IP addresses, and it is stored in the %Systemroot%\System32\Drivers\Etc folder.

HTML *See* Hypertext Markup Language (HTML).

HTTP   *See* Hypertext Transfer Protocol (HTTP).

Hypertext Markup Language (HTML)   An application of SGML (Standardized General Markup Language) used to create Web pages.

Hypertext Transfer Protocol (HTTP)   The protocol used to transfer information on the World Wide Web.

I

ICF   *See* Internet Connection Firewall (ICF).

ICMP   *See* Internet Control Message Protocol (ICMP).

ICS   *See* Internet Connection Sharing (ICS).

IDE   *See* Intelligent Drive Electronics or Integrated Device Electronics (IDE).

IIS   *See* Internet Information Services (IIS).

incremental backup   A backup that copies only those files created or changed since the last normal or incremental backup. It marks files as having been backed up (in other words, the archive attribute is cleared). *See also* differential backup; normal backup.

Industry Standard Architecture (ISA)   The bus architecture introduced in the PC/AT computer by IBM.

in-place upgrade   A software update that occurs directly on the computer being updated. In-place upgrades generally involve downtime, because the services being updated must be taken offline during the upgrade process.

input/output (I/O)   The complementary tasks of transferring data from one location to another so that a process or thread can work with it.

Intelligent Drive Electronics or Integrated Device Electronics (IDE)   A type of disk-drive interface in which the controller electronics reside on the drive itself, eliminating the need for a separate adapter card.

Internet   The worldwide collection of networks and gateways that use the TCP/IP suite of protocols to communicate with one another.

Internet Connection Firewall (ICF)   A feature of Network and Dial-up Connections that is used to filter the incoming traffic on a network connection.

Internet Connection Sharing (ICS)   A feature of Network and Dial-up Connections that you can use in Windows XP to connect your home network or small office network to the Internet.

Internet Control Message Protocol (ICMP)   A required maintenance protocol in the TCP/IP suite that reports errors and allows simple connectivity. ICMP is used by the Ping tool to perform TCP/IP troubleshooting. *See also* Internet Protocol (IP); protocol; Transmission Control Protocol/Internet Protocol (TCP/IP).

Internet Information Services (IIS)   Software services that support Web site creation, configuration, and management, along with other Internet functions. Besides HTTP support, Windows XP version of IIS includes File Transfer Protocol (FTP), and Simple Mail Transfer Protocol (SMTP). *See also* File Transfer Protocol (FTP); Simple Mail Transfer Protocol (SMTP).

Internet Options   Utility used to configure Internet Explorer settings and related networking functionality (for example, proxy settings configured with Internet Options are computer-wide).

Internet Protocol (IP)   A routable protocol in the TCP/IP protocol suite that is responsible for IP addressing, routing, and the fragmentation and reassembly of IP packets. *See also* Transmission Control Protocol/Internet Protocol (TCP/IP).

Internet Protocol security (IPSec)   A set of industry-standard, cryptography-based protection services and protocols. IPSec protects all protocols in the TCP/IP protocol suite and Internet communications using L2TP. *See also* Layer 2 Tunneling Protocol (L2TP); protocol; Transmission Control Protocol/Internet Protocol (TCP/IP).

Internet service provider (ISP)   A company that provides individuals or companies access to the Internet and the World Wide Web.

Internetwork Packet Exchange (IPX)   A network protocol native to NetWare that controls addressing and routing of packets within and between LANs. *See also* local area network (LAN).

interrupt request (IRQ)   A signal sent by a device to get the attention of the processor when the device is ready to accept or send information.

I/O   *See* input/output (I/O).

IP   *See* Internet Protocol (IP).

IP address   A 32-bit address used to identify a node on an IP internetwork. Each node on the IP internetwork must be assigned a unique IP address, which is made up of the network ID, plus a unique host ID. *See also* Dynamic Host Configuration Protocol (DHCP).

ipconfig   A command-line tool used in Windows NT, Windows 2000, and Windows XP operating systems for viewing IP address information on the local computer.

IPSec   *See* Internet Protocol Security (IPSec).

IP security policies   A set of policies that define which IPSec authentication and encryption protocols are required for different types of connections. *See also* Internet Protocol Security (IPSec).

IPX   *See* Internetwork Packet Exchange (IPX).

IRQ   *See* interrupt request (IRQ).

ISA   *See* Industry Standard Architecture (ISA).

ISP   *See* Internet service provider (ISP).

K

kernel   The core of layered architecture that manages the most basic operations of the operating system and the computer's processor. The kernel schedules different blocks of executing code, called threads, for the processor to keep it as busy as possible and coordinates multiple processors to optimize performance.

L

L2TP   *See* Layer 2 Tunneling Protocol (L2TP).

LAN   *See* local area network (LAN).

Last Known Good Configuration   A hardware configuration available by pressing F8 during startup. If the current hardware settings prevent the computer from starting, the Last Known Good Configuration can allow you to start the computer and examine the configuration.

Layer 2 Tunneling Protocol (L2TP)   An industry standard Internet tunneling protocol. Unlike Point-to-Point Tunneling Protocol (PPTP), L2TP does not require Internet Protocol (IP) connectivity between the client workstation and the server. L2TP requires only that the tunnel medium provide packet-oriented, point-to-point connectivity.

lease   A message sent from a Dynamic Host Configuration Protocol (DHCP) server to a DHCP client that dictates the amount of time the DHCP client may use the IP addressing information provided. *See also* Dynamic Host Configuration Protocol (DHCP).

LGPO   *See* Local Group Policy Object (LGPO).

local area network (LAN)   A communications network connecting a group of computers, printers, and other devices located within a relatively limited area (for example, a building). A LAN allows any connected device to interact with any other on the network. *See also* network basic input/output system (NetBIOS).

Local Group Policy Object (LGPO)   A set of system configurations that exist on individual systems, regardless of whether that system participates in an Active Directory. Settings defined within an LGPO can be overridden by a policy defined at the level of the Active Directory.

local policies   A set of system configurations that are defined on a system-by-system basis. Local policies can be overridden by policies defined within Active Directory. *See also* Local Group Policy Object (LGPO); local security settings console.

local security settings console A management tool used to define configuration settings on the local system. *See also* local policies.

local user accounts User accounts that exist in the local user database of a Windows XP system. These accounts reside in a different security context from accounts created within Active Directory. *See also* Active Directory.

local user profile A computer-based record about an authorized user that is created automatically on the computer the first time a user logs on to a workstation or server computer. *See also* mandatory user profile; roaming user profile.

Local Users and Groups snap-in An MMC snap-in for creating and managing user accounts in Windows XP.

LOGMAN A command-line tool used to start, stop, and schedule the gathering of performance and trace data. *See also* Performance utility.

logon credentials The information used to authenticate a user, generally consisting of a user name, password, and domain name.

M

MAC *See* Media Access Control (MAC).

Magnifier A screen enlarger that magnifies a portion of the screen in a separate window for users with low vision and for those who require occasional screen magnification for such tasks as editing art.

mandatory user profile A user profile that is not updated when the user logs off. It is downloaded to the user's desktop each time the user logs on, and is created by an administrator and assigned to one or more users to create consistent or job-specific user profiles. *See also* local user profile; roaming user profile.

Manual Caching Of Documents Provides offline access only to those files other users specifically identify. *See also* Automatic Caching Of Documents; Automatic Caching Of Programs.

master boot record (MBR) The first sector on a hard disk, which starts the process of booting the computer. *See also* Recovery Console.

MBR *See* master boot record (MBR).

Media Access Control (MAC) A layer in the network architecture that deals with network access and collision detection.

memory addresses A specific location within a computer's random access memory (RAM) used to store dynamic information.

Microsoft Challenge Handshake Authentication Protocol version 1 (MS-CHAP v1) An encrypted authentication mechanism for Point-to-Point Protocol (PPP) connections similar to CHAP. *See also* Point-to-Point Protocol (PPP).

Microsoft Challenge Handshake Authentication Protocol version 2 (MS-CHAP v2) An encrypted authentication mechanism for Point-to-Point Protocol PPP connections that provides stronger security than CHAP and MS-CHAP v1. *See also* Point-to-Point Protocol (PPP).

Microsoft Internet Security and Acceleration Server The firewall and proxy server component of the Windows .NET Enterprise Server family.

Microsoft Management Console (MMC) A framework for hosting administrative tools, called consoles. A console might contain tools, folders or other containers, World Wide Web pages, and other administrative items.

MMC *See* Microsoft Management Console (MMC).

MS-CHAP v1 *See* Microsoft Challenge Handshake Authentication Protocol version 1 (MS-CHAP v1).

MS-CHAP v2 *See* Microsoft Challenge Handshake Authentication Protocol version 2 (MS-CHAP v2).

MUI Pack *See* Windows XP Professional Multilingual User Interface Pack (MUI Pack).

Multilingual Editing and Viewing A feature in the English Version of of Windows XP that allows you to edit, view, and print information in more than 60 languages.

N

name resolution   The process of translating a name into some object or information that the name represents.

Narrator   A synthesized text-to-speech utility for users who have low vision.

NAT   *See* Network Address Translation (NAT).

NetBEUI   *See* NetBIOS Extended User Interface (NetBEUI).

NetBIOS   *See* network basic input/output system (NetBIOS).

NetBIOS Extended User Interface (NetBEUI)   A protocol supplied with all Microsoft network products. NetBEUI advantages include small stack size (important for MS-DOS–based computers), speed of data transfer on the network medium, and compatibility with all Microsoft-based networks. *See also* network basic input/output system (NetBIOS).

NetBIOS Name   A 16-character computer identifier used to find systems on a network. NetBIOS names are generally based on the computer name. *See also* NetBIOS over TCP/IP (NetBT); network basic input/output system (NetBIOS).

NetBIOS over TCP/IP (NetBT)   A feature that provides the NetBIOS programming interface over TCP/IP. It is used for monitoring routed servers that use NetBIOS name resolution.

NetBT   *See* NetBIOS over TCP/IP (NetBT).

Network Address Translation (NAT)   An advanced Windows XP service that allows LAN clients to share a single network access point, such as a connection to the Internet.

network basic input/output system (NetBIOS)   An application programming interface (API) that can be used by programs on a local area network (LAN). *See also* local area network (LAN).

normal backup   A backup that copies all selected files and marks each file as having been backed up (in other words, the archive attribute is cleared). *See also* differential backup; incremental backup.

NSLOOKUP   A command-line utility that allows you to make Domain Name System (DNS) queries for testing and troubleshooting your DNS installation.

NT File System (NTFS)   An advanced file system that provides performance, security, reliability, and advanced features that are not found in any version of FAT. *See also* File Allocation Table (FAT); File Allocation Table-32 (FAT32).

NTFS   *See* NT File System (NTFS).

NWLink   An implementation of the Internetwork Packet Exchange (IPX), Sequenced Packet Exchange (SPX), and NetBIOS protocols used in Novell networks. *See also* Internetwork Packet Exchange (IPX); network basic input/output system (NetBIOS).

O

Offline Files   A feature in Windows XP that allows a user's data to follow the user whether the user is online and connected to the network or the user is offline in a stand-alone state.

offline Web pages   Internet Explorer feature enabling the user to make Web pages or entire Web sites, including links, available for offline viewing.

On-Screen Keyboard   A tool that displays a virtual keyboard on a computer screen and allows users with mobility impairments to type using a pointing device or joystick.

organizational unit (OU)   An Active Directory container object used within domains. An OU is a logical container into which users, groups, computers, and other OUs are placed. *See also* Active Directory; Group Policy Object (GPO).

OU   *See* organizational unit (OU).

P

PAP   *See* Password Authentication Protocol (PAP).

partition   A portion of a physical disk that functions as though it were a physically separate disk. After you create a partition, you must format it and assign it a drive letter before you can store data on it. *See also* basic disk; basic volume; dynamic volume.

partition table   On a hard disk, the data structure that stores the offset (location) and size of each primary partition on the disk. *See also* GUID partition table (GPT); master boot record (MBR); partition.

Password Authentication Protocol (PAP)   A simple, plaintext authentication scheme for authenticating Point-to-Point Protocol (PPP) connections. *See also* Point-to-Point Protocol (PPP).

password policy   The definition of password length, age, and complexity requirements. These requirements are enforced by Windows XP and can be used to decrease the likelihood of a password being discovered by a malicious user.

PC Card   A removable device, approximately the size of a credit card, that can be plugged into a Personal Computer Memory Card International Association (PCMCIA) slot in a portable computer.

PCMCIA device   A removable device, approximately the size of a credit card, that can be plugged into a PCMCIA slot in a portable computer. PCMCIA devices can include modems, network adapters, and hard disk drives.

PERFMON   *See* Performance utility.

performance counter   In System Monitor, a data item that is associated with a performance object. *See also* performance object.

performance object   In System Monitor, a logical collection of counters that is associated with a resource or service that can be monitored. *See also* performance counter.

Performance Options   A Windows XP administrative utility that provides a simple way to enable or disable user interface features that impact system performance.

Performance utility   A tool for monitoring network performance that can display statistics, such as the number of packets sent and received, server-processor utilization, and the amount of data going in to and out of the server.

Personal Computer Memory Card International Association (PCMCIA)   An older name for devices that are now referred to as PC Cards. *See also* PC Card.

PID   *See* product identification (PID).

pinning   To make a network file or folder available for offline use.

PKI   *See* Public Key Infrastructure (PKI).

Plug and Play (PnP)   A set of specifications developed by Intel that allows a computer to automatically detect and configure a device and install the appropriate device drivers. *See also* Universal Serial Bus (USB).

PnP   *See* Plug and Play (PnP).

Point-to-Point Protocol (PPP)   A data-link protocol for transmitting TCP/IP packets over dial-up telephone connections, such as between a computer and the Internet.

Point-to-Point Tunneling Protocol (PPTP)   Networking technology that supports multiprotocol virtual private networks (VPNs), enabling remote users to access corporate networks securely across the Internet or other networks by dialing into an Internet service provider (ISP) or by connecting directly to the Internet. *See also* Internet Protocol (IP); Internetwork Packet Exchange (IPX); NetBIOS Extended User Interface (NetBEUI); tunnel; virtual private network (VPN).

POST   *See* power-on self tests (POST).

power-on self tests (POST)   A set of routines stored in read-only memory (ROM) that tests various system components such as RAM, the disk drives, and the keyboard, to see whether they are properly connected and operating.

power schemes   A set of options that provide different levels of power-saving features. Enabling different power schemes allows users to adjust the trade-off between power consumption and performance.

PPTP   *See* Point-to-Point Tunneling Protocol (PPTP).

printer   A device that puts text or images on paper or other print media. Examples are laser printers or dot-matrix printers.

printer redirection   A feature of Windows XP and the Remote Desktop that sends printed documents to a printer attached to the local system. This might be more convenient than printing to a device attached to the remote system. *See also* Remote Desktop.

print server   A computer that makes printing devices available to other computers on a network. The print server can be any computer or specialized printing device on the network. A computer running Windows 2000 that shares a printer is a print server.

private key   The secret half of a key pair used in a public key algorithm.

product identification (PID)   One of the three components of the installation ID used during Windows Product Activation (WPA). *See also* hardware ID (HID); Windows Product Activation (WPA).

protocol   A set of rules and conventions for sending information over a network. These rules govern the content, format, timing, sequencing, and error control of messages exchanged among network devices.

proxy server   A firewall component that manages Internet traffic to and from a LAN and can provide other features, such as document caching and access control.

public key encryption   A method of encryption that uses two encryption keys that are mathematically related. One key is called the private key and is kept confidential. The other is called the public key and is freely given to all potential correspondents.

Public Key Infrastructure (PKI)   The term generally used to describe the laws, policies, standards, and software that regulate or manipulate certificates and public and private keys. In practice, it is a system

of digital certificates, certificate authorities, and other registration authorities that verify and authenticate the validity of each party involved in an electronic transaction.

public key policies   A set of rules that dictate how and when Windows systems use certificates. *See also* certificate; certificate authority (CA).

Q

QWERTY keyboard   The most common keyboard layout. Named for the arrangement of letters in the upper-left corner of the keyboard.

R

RARP   *See* Reverse ARP (RARP).

Recovery Console   A command-line interface that provides a limited set of administrative commands that are useful for repairing a computer.

refresh rate   The speed at which a monitor completes tracing an image on the screen.

RELOG   A command-line tool used to process and summarize performance logs. RELOG filters logged performance data and produces a performance log with longer polling intervals, and therefore a smaller size. *See also* LOGMAN; Performance utility.

Remote Assistance   A feature of Windows XP that allows users to share their desktop with a technical support expert for the purpose of resolving problems. *See also* Remote Desktop; terminal services.

Remote Desktop   A feature of Windows XP that allows a user to control the desktop environment of a remote system across a network. *See also* Remote Assistance; Remote Desktop Web Connection; terminal services.

Remote Desktop Web Connection   A method of accessing a Remote Desktop that does not require that special client-side software be installed. Instead, the Remote Desktop client is invited within a Web browser. *See also* Remote Assistance; Remote Desktop.

resolution A term used to describe the sharpness of an image. It is commonly used to describe printers, video monitors, and bitmap images.

Reverse ARP (RARP) A TCP/IP protocol for determining the IP address (or logical address) of a node on a local area network connected to the Internet, when only the hardware address (or physical address) is known. *See also* Address Resolution Protocol (ARP).

roaming user profile A server-based user profile that is downloaded to the local computer when a user logs on and that is updated both locally and on the server when the user logs off. *See also* local user profile; mandatory user profile.

S

SACL *See* system access control list (SACL).

Safe Mode A method of starting Windows using basic files and drivers only, without networking. Safe mode is available by pressing the F8 key when prompted during startup.

SCSI *See* Small Computer Systems Interface (SCSI).

Secure Sockets Layer (SSL) A proposed open standard for establishing a secure communications channel to prevent the interception of critical information, such as credit card numbers.

Security Configuration and Analysis snap-in An MMC snap-in for analyzing and configuring local system security.

security options Configuration settings that allow the user to adjust Internet Explorer's behavior when responding to certificates and cookies. *See also* cookies.

security templates A set of security settings that are applied to a Group Policy Object (GPO) in Active Directory or a local computer. *See also* Security Templates snap-in.

Security Templates snap-in An MMC snap-in used for viewing, defining, or modifying security templates.

SerialKey A Windows feature that uses a communications aid interface device to allow keystrokes and mouse controls to be accepted through an alternative device connected to the computer's serial port.

server In general, a computer that provides shared resources to network users. *See also* client; shared resource.

service packs A software upgrade to an existing software distribution that contains updated files consisting of patches and hot fixes.

Setup Loader This portion of the Windows XP installation routine copies installation files from the Windows XP Professional source to the local hard disk. *See also* GUI-Mode Setup; Text-Mode Setup.

setup settings Configuration options that define how an application or operating system is installed.

shared resource A folder or printer that is made available for use across a network.

Shiva Password Authentication Protocol (SPAP) A two-way, reversible encryption mechanism for authenticating Point-to-Point Protocol (PPP) connections employed by Shiva remote access servers. *See also* Point-to-Point Protocol (PPP).

ShowSounds A feature that instructs programs that usually convey information only by sound to also provide all information visually, such as by displaying text captions or informative icons.

Simple Mail Transfer Protocol (SMTP) A member of the TCP/IP suite of protocols that governs the exchange of electronic mail between message transfer agents. *See also* protocol; Transmission Control Protocol/Internet Protocol (TCP/IP).

simple volume A dynamic volume made up of disk space from a single dynamic disk. A simple volume can consist of a single region on a disk or multiple regions of the same disk that are linked together. *See also* dynamic disk; dynamic volume; spanned volume; volume.

site One or more well-connected (highly reliable and fast) TCP/IP subnets. A site that allows administrators to configure Active Directory access and replication topology to take advantage of the physical network. *See also* Active Directory; subnet; Transmission Control Protocol/Internet Protocol (TCP/IP).

slipstreaming The process of creating a distribution share of the Windows XP operating system files and applying a service pack by typing **update /slip**.

Small Computer Systems Interface (SCSI) A standard high-speed parallel interface defined by the American National Standards Institute (ANSI). A SCSI interface is used for connecting computers to peripheral devices such as hard disks and printers, and to other computers and local area networks (LANs). *See also* local area network (LAN).

smart card A credit card-sized device that is used with an access code to enable certificate-based authentication and single sign-on to the enterprise.

SMTP *See* Simple Mail Transfer Protocol (SMTP).

software distribution The process of sending applications to multiple servers. Software distribution is a cumbersome task for large networks, and usually occurs across the network and receives some level of automation.

software restriction policies Regulations to restrict users from executing applications that are not fully trusted. Software restriction policies can be used to reduce the likelihood of a user executing viruses, Trojan horses, and unstable software. *See also* Trojan.

SoundSentry A Windows feature that produces a visual cue, such as a screen flash or a blinking title bar, whenever the computer plays a system sound.

spanned volume A dynamic volume consisting of disk space on more than one physical disk. *See also* dynamic disk; dynamic volume; simple volume; volume.

SPAP *See* Shiva Password Authentication Protocol (SPAP).

SSL *See* Secure Sockets Layer (SSL).

Standby A power state in which your monitor and hard disks turn off so that your computer uses less power.

striped volume A dynamic volume that stores data in stripes on two or more physical disks. Data in a striped volume is allocated alternately and evenly (in stripes) across the disks. *See also* dynamic disk; dynamic volume; volume.

subnet A subdivision of an IP network. Each subnet has its own unique subnetted network ID.

subnet mask A 32-bit value that enables the recipient of IP packets to distinguish the network ID and host ID portions of the IP address.

symmetric encryption algorithm Encryption algorithm where the same key is used for both encryption and decryption. *See also* encryption.

Synchronization Manager Assists in maintaining data between the local computer and a copy of the data that is replicated on the server.

synchronize A user data management feature that compares data in two locations and updates the data in these two locations so that it is identical.

Syskey An administrative tool used to enable additional encryption on the accounts database.

system access control list (SACL) An ACL that controls the generation of audit messages for attempts to access a securable object. *See also* access control list (ACL); discretionary access control list (DACL).

System Information tool (WINMSD.EXE) System Information collects and displays configuration information to help support personnel diagnose and correct problems.

System Restore A tool included with Windows XP that captures system configuration information, and can reapply a working configuration if the system later becomes unreliable.

System State A Microsoft Windows Backup type that contains a collection of system-specific data. *See also* Windows Backup.

T

Task Manager A Windows XP utility that offers an immediate overview of operating system activity and performance.

Task Scheduler A utility used to instruct Windows to execute an application at a specific time and day.

TCP/IP *See* Transmission Control Protocol/Internet Protocol (TCP/IP).

terminal services The underlying technology on that enables Remote Desktop, Remote Assistance, and Terminal Server. *See also* Remote Assistance; Remote Desktop.

Text-Mode Setup This portion of the Windows XP installation performs detailed detection and configuration of hardware drivers and is the most likely place for the installation to fail. *See also* GUI-Mode Setup; Setup Loader.

trace analysis report The result of executing the TRACERPT command on a trace event log. *See also* trace event log; TRACERPT.

trace event log A file created by the Performance utility or TRACERPT that contains a record of system events. *See also* Performance utility; TRACERPT.

trace log The trace log feature in Windows 2000 makes it possible to closely associate network input/output operations to the workload on a computer.

TRACERPT A command-line utility that processes trace event logs and outputs a trace analysis report that is human-readable. *See also* trace analysis report; trace event log.

tracert A trace route command-line utility that shows every router interface through which a TCP/IP packet passes on its way to a destination.

transform (.mst) files A type of file used to customize the installation of a Windows Installer Service package file.

Translated Version A fully localized version of Windows XP. The entire interface appears in the specified language. This version of Windows XP is more language-specific than the Multilanguage Version of Windows XP. *See also* English Version; Windows XP Professional Multilingual User Interface Pack (MUI Pack).

Transmission Control Protocol/Internet Protocol (TCP/IP) A set of networking protocols widely used on the Internet that provides communications across interconnected networks of computers with diverse hardware architectures and various operating systems. *See also* Internet Protocol (IP); protocol.

Trojan A program that maliciously deceives a user about its functionality to gain the user's privileges on the system.

tunnel A logical connection over which data is encapsulated. Typically, both encapsulation and encryption are performed and the tunnel is a private, secure link between a remote user or host and a private network.

TYPEPERF A command-line utility that displays raw performance data in real-time.

U

UDF *See* Universal Disk Format (UDF).

unattended installation An automated, hands-free method of installing Windows. During installation, unattended Setup uses an answer file to supply data to Setup instead of requiring that an administrator interactively provide the answers.

Uniform Resource Locator (URL) An address that uniquely identifies a location on the Internet.

Uniqueness Database File A test file containing computer-specific information used when automatically deploying Windows XP to multiple computers. *See also* answer file.

Universal Disk Format (UDF) A file system defined by the Optical Storage Technology Association (OSTA) that is the successor to the CD-ROM File System (CDFS). UDF is targeted for removable disk media like DVD, CD-ROM, and Magneto-Optical (MO) discs.

Universal Serial Bus (USB) An external bus that supports Plug and Play installation. Using USB, you can connect and disconnect devices without shutting down or restarting your computer. *See also* Plug and Play (PnP).

URL *See* Uniform Resource Locator (URL).

USB *See* Universal Serial Bus (USB).

user authentication In network access, the process by which the system validates the user's logon information. A user's name and password are compared against an authorized list. If the system detects a match, access is granted to the extent specified in the permissions list for that user.

user profile A set of files and folders that define customized desktop environments, including individual display settings, network and printer connections, and other specified settings.

user rights assignments A category of local policy settings that defines the permissions of user groups.

user state migration tool (USMT) An administrative tool designed for IT administrators in performing large deployments of Windows XP Professional in a corporate environment. USMT provides the same functionality as the wizard, but on a large scale targeted at migrating multiple users.

USMT *See* user state migration tool (USMT).

Utility Manager A function of Windows XP that allows administrators to review the status of applications and tools and to customize features and add tools more easily.

V

virtual directory A mapping that occurs within Internet Information Services (IIS) to retrieve information from a location on the hard drive other than a subfolder of the Web root. *See also* Internet Information Services (IIS).

virtual private network (VPN) The extension of a private network that encompasses encapsulated,

encrypted, and authenticated links across shared or public networks. VPN connections can provide remote access and routed connections to private networks over the Internet. *See also* tunnel.

volume An area of storage on a hard disk. A volume is formatted by using a file system, such as FAT or NTFS, and has a drive letter assigned to it. *See also* file allocation table (FAT); NT File System; simple volume; spanned volume.

VPN *See* virtual private network (VPN).

W

WAN *See* wide area network (WAN).

Web content zones A classification within Internet Explorer that categorizes Web sites based on the level of trust they are granted. Sites placed in the Trusted Sites Web content zone allow risky types of content to be downloaded. Sites placed in the Internet Web content zone prompt the user to allow risky types of content.

Web shares A folder or printer that is available over the network using the World Wide Web Publishing Service.

WHQL *See* Windows Hardware Quality Lab (WHQL).

wide area network (WAN) A communications network connecting geographically separated computers, printers, and other devices. A WAN allows any connected device to interact with any other on the network. *See also* local area network (LAN).

Windows Backup The backup and restore utility built-in to Windows XP. This utility provides all the common backup types, the System State backup type, and the ability to update emergency repair information. *See also* System State.

Windows Hardware Quality Lab (WHQL) An organization that tests, certifies, and signs drivers. After the WHQL has certified a driver for a particular operating system, a driver signature is created. *See also* driver signature.

Windows Installer Packages A method for encapsulating an application for standardized installation on Windows platforms. Windows Installer Packages use .msi files. *See also* Windows Installer Service.

Windows Installer Service An operating system service that allows the operating system to manage the installation process. Windows Installer technologies are divided into two parts that work in combination: a client-side installer service (MSIEXEC.EXE) and a package file (.msi file). Windows Installer uses the information contained within a package file to install the application.

Windows Internet Naming Service (WINS) A software service that dynamically maps IP addresses to computer names (NetBIOS names). This allows users to access resources by name instead of requiring them to use IP addresses that are difficult to recognize and remember. WINS servers support clients running Windows NT 4 and earlier versions of Microsoft operating systems. *See also* Domain Name System (DNS); IP address; network basic input/output system (NetBIOS).

Windows Logo Program A Microsoft service that validates applications and updates against a set of strict requirements to ensure compatibility with the Windows operating systems. Applications and updates that are certified by the Windows Logo Program receive a digital signature that Windows systems can use to verify compliance.

Windows Product Activation (WPA) A feature of Windows XP Professional that automatically contacts Microsoft and validates the provided license key provided by the user.

Windows Update A Microsoft-owned Web site from which Windows users can install or update device drivers. By using an ActiveX control, Windows Update compares the available drivers with those on the user's system and offers to install new or updated versions.

Windows XP Professional Multilingual User Interface Pack (MUI Pack) A version of Windows XP that extends the native language support in Windows XP by allowing user interface languages to be changed on a per-user basis. This version also minimizes the number of language versions you need to deploy across the network. *See also* English Version; Translated Version.

WINMSD.EXE *See* System Information tool (WINMSD.EXE).

WINS *See* Windows Internet Naming Service (WINS).

workgroup A simple grouping of computers, intended only to help users find such things as printers and shared folders within that group. Workgroups in Windows do not offer the centralized user accounts and authentication offered by domains. *See also* domain.

World Wide Web A system for exploring the Internet by using hyperlinks. When you use a Web browser, the Web appears as a collection of text, pictures, sounds, and digital movies. *See also* Internet.

World Wide Web Publishing service The Web server component of Internet Information Services (IIS) that provides Hypertext Transfer Protocol (HTTP) services. *See also* Hypertext Transfer Protocol (HTTP); Internet Information Services (IIS).

WPA *See* Windows Product Activation (WPA).

Z

ZIP archive A set of files that are compressed into a single file to minimize disk space consumption. Windows Explorer is capable of automatically expanding ZIP archives so that they function very similarly to folders.

Index

Symbols

%systemdrive%, 165
%systemroot% directory, log files in, 38, 39–40
%userprofile%, 159

A

Accelerated Graphics Port (AGP), 84
access control entries (ACEs)
  share permissions and, 57
  user rights and, 50
access control lists (ACLs)
  DACL (discretionary access control list), 50
  GPOs and, 257
  NTFS and, 239
  security protection from, 234
  share permissions and, 57
Accessibility Options program, Control Panel, 191
accessibility services
  configuring and troubleshooting, 191–92
  Q & A, 193–96
  skills and practices, 162
  special needs of users and, 158
Accessibility Wizard, 162
Account Lockout Policy, 245, 253
Account Policies, LGPO, 245
account policies, local, 251
ACEs (access control entries)
  share permissions and, 57
  user rights and, 50
ACLs. *See* access control lists (ACLs)
ACPI. *See* Advanced Configuration Power Interface (ACPI)
Active Desktop, adding Web content to desktop, 183, 184
Active Directory service
  managing group policies, 157
  security protection from, 234
  using in conjunction with Group Policy for desktop settings, 183
Active Server Pages (ASP), scripting options, 215
Add New Printer Driver wizard, 118
Add Printer Wizard, 63
Add/Remove Hardware Wizard, 92, 109
Administrators group
  built-in group accounts, 252
  creating shares, 59, 60
  installing, updating, and rolling back drivers, 120
  permissions to control remote desktop, 226
Advanced Configuration Power Interface (ACPI), 103–4
  HAL versions and, 123
  Power Options and, 107
  Q & A, 105–8
  skills and practices, 84
Advanced Power Management (APM)
  AMPSTAT.EXE and, 108
  Power Options and, 105, 107
  support for, 103

Advanced Privacy Settings, 266, 268
Advanced Processor Interrupt Controller (APIC), 123
Advanced Technology Attachment (ATA), 89
Advanced Technology Attachment Packet Interface (ATAPI), 89
AGP (Accelerated Graphics Port), 84
All Users profile, 167, 169
AMPSTAT.EXE, 103, 106, 108
Anonymous Logon group, built-in group accounts, 252
answer files
  creating, 18, 20–21
  key values and, 19, 22
  for unattended installation, 15
antivirus utilities, 23
APIC (Advanced Processor Interrupt Controller), 123
APM. *See* Advanced Power Management (APM)
Appearance and Themes group, Control Panel, 161, 183
Appearance tab, Display program, 161
application compatibility
  uninstalling service packs and, 40, 41
  upgrading to Windows XP Professional and, 26, 29
application configuration, IIS, 215
application features, 177
application mappings, IIS, 215
applications, distributing. *See also* software distribution
applications, publishing vs. advertising, 179, 181
ARP cache, 206
ARP.EXE, 202
ASP. *See* Active Server Pages (ASP), scripting options
ATA (Advanced Technology Attachment), 89
ATAPI (Advanced Technology Attachment Packet Interface), 89
AT command
  scheduling tasks with, 131, 134
  vs. Task Scheduler, 141
attended installation, 7–14
  dealing with existing operating system, 8
  hardware requirements, 7–8
  partitions and, 8
  Q & A, 9–14
  set up phases, 8
  skills and practices, 2
auditing
  configuring failure auditing, 247, 249
  security protection from, 234
Audit Policy, 245
Authenticated Users group, built-in group accounts, 252
authentication
  protocols, 208, 210
  skills and practices, 236
  for users, 233, 236
Automated System Recovery (ASR) Wizard
  included in NTBACKUP.EXE, 90
  skills and practices, 130
  startup problems and, 151, 154
Automatic Caching Of Documents, 73
Automatic Caching Of Programs, 73
automatic installation. *See* unattended installation
Automatic Private IP Addressing (APIPA)
  address range used by, 206
  IP address management, 201
  skills and practices, 198

MICROSOFT LICENSE AGREEMENT

Book Companion CD

IMPORTANT—READ CAREFULLY: This Microsoft End-User License Agreement ("EULA") is a legal agreement between you (either an individual or an entity) and Microsoft Corporation for the Microsoft product identified above, which includes computer software and may include associated media, printed materials, and "online" or electronic documentation ("SOFTWARE PRODUCT"). Any component included within the SOFTWARE PRODUCT that is accompanied by a separate End-User License Agreement shall be governed by such agreement and not the terms set forth below. By installing, copying, or otherwise using the SOFTWARE PRODUCT, you agree to be bound by the terms of this EULA. If you do not agree to the terms of this EULA, you are not authorized to install, copy, or otherwise use the SOFTWARE PRODUCT; you may, however, return the SOFTWARE PRODUCT, along with all printed materials and other items that form a part of the Microsoft product that includes the SOFTWARE PRODUCT, to the place you obtained them for a full refund.

SOFTWARE PRODUCT LICENSE

The SOFTWARE PRODUCT is protected by United States copyright laws and international copyright treaties, as well as other intellectual property laws and treaties. The SOFTWARE PRODUCT is licensed, not sold.

1. **GRANT OF LICENSE.** This EULA grants you the following rights:

   a. **Software Product.** You may install and use one copy of the SOFTWARE PRODUCT on a single computer. The primary user of the computer on which the SOFTWARE PRODUCT is installed may make a second copy for his or her exclusive use on a portable computer.

   b. **Storage/Network Use.** You may also store or install a copy of the SOFTWARE PRODUCT on a storage device, such as a network server, used only to install or run the SOFTWARE PRODUCT on your other computers over an internal network; however, you must acquire and dedicate a license for each separate computer on which the SOFTWARE PRODUCT is installed or run from the storage device. A license for the SOFTWARE PRODUCT may not be shared or used concurrently on different computers.

   c. **License Pak.** If you have acquired this EULA in a Microsoft License Pak, you may make the number of additional copies of the computer software portion of the SOFTWARE PRODUCT authorized on the printed copy of this EULA, and you may use each copy in the manner specified above. You are also entitled to make a corresponding number of secondary copies for portable computer use as specified above.

   d. **Sample Code.** Solely with respect to portions, if any, of the SOFTWARE PRODUCT that are identified within the SOFTWARE PRODUCT as sample code (the "SAMPLE CODE"):

      i. **Use and Modification.** Microsoft grants you the right to use and modify the source code version of the SAMPLE CODE, *provided* you comply with subsection (d)(iii) below. You may not distribute the SAMPLE CODE, or any modified version of the SAMPLE CODE, in source code form.

      ii. **Redistributable Files.** Provided you comply with subsection (d)(iii) below, Microsoft grants you a nonexclusive, royalty-free right to reproduce and distribute the object code version of the SAMPLE CODE and of any modified SAMPLE CODE, other than SAMPLE CODE, or any modified version thereof, designated as not redistributable in the Readme file that forms a part of the SOFTWARE PRODUCT (the "Non-Redistributable Sample Code"). All SAMPLE CODE other than the Non-Redistributable Sample Code is collectively referred to as the "REDISTRIBUTABLES."

      iii. **Redistribution Requirements.** If you redistribute the REDISTRIBUTABLES, you agree to: (i) distribute the REDISTRIBUTABLES in object code form only in conjunction with and as a part of your software application product; (ii) not use Microsoft's name, logo, or trademarks to market your software application product; (iii) include a valid copyright notice on your software application product; (iv) indemnify, hold harmless, and defend Microsoft from and against any claims or lawsuits, including attorney's fees, that arise or result from the use or distribution of your software application product; and (v) not permit further distribution of the REDISTRIBUTABLES by your end user. Contact Microsoft for the applicable royalties due and other licensing terms for all other uses and/or distribution of the REDISTRIBUTABLES.

2. **DESCRIPTION OF OTHER RIGHTS AND LIMITATIONS.**

   - **Limitations on Reverse Engineering, Decompilation, and Disassembly.** You may not reverse engineer, decompile, or disassemble the SOFTWARE PRODUCT, except and only to the extent that such activity is expressly permitted by applicable law notwithstanding this limitation.

   - **Separation of Components.** The SOFTWARE PRODUCT is licensed as a single product. Its component parts may not be separated for use on more than one computer.

   - **Rental.** You may not rent, lease, or lend the SOFTWARE PRODUCT.

- **Support Services.** Microsoft may, but is not obligated to, provide you with support services related to the SOFTWARE PRODUCT ("Support Services"). Use of Support Services is governed by the Microsoft policies and programs described in the user manual, in "online" documentation, and/or in other Microsoft-provided materials. Any supplemental software code provided to you as part of the Support Services shall be considered part of the SOFTWARE PRODUCT and subject to the terms and conditions of this EULA. With respect to technical information you provide to Microsoft as part of the Support Services, Microsoft may use such information for its business purposes, including for product support and development. Microsoft will not utilize such technical information in a form that personally identifies you.

- **Software Transfer.** You may permanently transfer all of your rights under this EULA, provided you retain no copies, you transfer all of the SOFTWARE PRODUCT (including all component parts, the media and printed materials, any upgrades, this EULA, and, if applicable, the Certificate of Authenticity), **and** the recipient agrees to the terms of this EULA.

- **Termination.** Without prejudice to any other rights, Microsoft may terminate this EULA if you fail to comply with the terms and conditions of this EULA. In such event, you must destroy all copies of the SOFTWARE PRODUCT and all of its component parts.

3. **COPYRIGHT.** All title and copyrights in and to the SOFTWARE PRODUCT (including but not limited to any images, photographs, animations, video, audio, music, text, SAMPLE CODE, REDISTRIBUTABLES, and "applets" incorporated into the SOFTWARE PRODUCT) and any copies of the SOFTWARE PRODUCT are owned by Microsoft or its suppliers. The SOFT-WARE PRODUCT is protected by copyright laws and international treaty provisions. Therefore, you must treat the SOFTWARE PRODUCT like any other copyrighted material **except** that you may install the SOFTWARE PRODUCT on a single computer provided you keep the original solely for backup or archival purposes. You may not copy the printed materials accompanying the SOFTWARE PRODUCT.

4. **U.S. GOVERNMENT RESTRICTED RIGHTS.** The SOFTWARE PRODUCT and documentation are provided with RESTRICTED RIGHTS. Use, duplication, or disclosure by the Government is subject to restrictions as set forth in subparagraph (c)(1)(ii) of the Rights in Technical Data and Computer Software clause at DFARS 252.227-7013 or subparagraphs (c)(1) and (2) of the Commercial Computer Software—Restricted Rights at 48 CFR 52.227-19, as applicable. Manufacturer is Microsoft Corporation/One Microsoft Way/Redmond, WA 98052-6399.

5. **EXPORT RESTRICTIONS.** You agree that you will not export or re-export the SOFTWARE PRODUCT, any part thereof, or any process or service that is the direct product of the SOFTWARE PRODUCT (the foregoing collectively referred to as the "Restricted Components"), to any country, person, entity, or end user subject to U.S. export restrictions. You specifically agree not to export or re-export any of the Restricted Components (i) to any country to which the U.S. has embargoed or restricted the export of goods or services, which currently include, but are not necessarily limited to, Cuba, Iran, Iraq, Libya, North Korea, Sudan, and Syria, or to any national of any such country, wherever located, who intends to transmit or transport the Restricted Components back to such country; (ii) to any end user who you know or have reason to know will utilize the Restricted Components in the design, development, or production of nuclear, chemical, or biological weapons; or (iii) to any end user who has been prohibited from participating in U.S. export transactions by any federal agency of the U.S. government. You warrant and represent that neither the BXA nor any other U.S. federal agency has suspended, revoked, or denied your export privileges.

DISCLAIMER OF WARRANTY

NO WARRANTIES OR CONDITIONS. MICROSOFT EXPRESSLY DISCLAIMS ANY WARRANTY OR CONDITION FOR THE SOFTWARE PRODUCT. THE SOFTWARE PRODUCT AND ANY RELATED DOCUMENTATION ARE PROVIDED "AS IS" WITHOUT WARRANTY OR CONDITION OF ANY KIND, EITHER EXPRESS OR IMPLIED, INCLUDING, WITHOUT LIMITA-TION, THE IMPLIED WARRANTIES OF MERCHANTABILITY, FITNESS FOR A PARTICULAR PURPOSE, OR NONINFRINGEMENT. THE ENTIRE RISK ARISING OUT OF USE OR PERFORMANCE OF THE SOFTWARE PRODUCT REMAINS WITH YOU.

LIMITATION OF LIABILITY. TO THE MAXIMUM EXTENT PERMITTED BY APPLICABLE LAW, IN NO EVENT SHALL MICROSOFT OR ITS SUPPLIERS BE LIABLE FOR ANY SPECIAL, INCIDENTAL, INDIRECT, OR CONSEQUENTIAL DAM-AGES WHATSOEVER (INCLUDING, WITHOUT LIMITATION, DAMAGES FOR LOSS OF BUSINESS PROFITS, BUSINESS INTERRUPTION, LOSS OF BUSINESS INFORMATION, OR ANY OTHER PECUNIARY LOSS) ARISING OUT OF THE USE OF OR INABILITY TO USE THE SOFTWARE PRODUCT OR THE PROVISION OF OR FAILURE TO PROVIDE SUPPORT SERVICES, EVEN IF MICROSOFT HAS BEEN ADVISED OF THE POSSIBILITY OF SUCH DAMAGES. IN ANY CASE, MICROSOFT'S ENTIRE LIABILITY UNDER ANY PROVISION OF THIS EULA SHALL BE LIMITED TO THE GREATER OF THE AMOUNT ACTUALLY PAID BY YOU FOR THE SOFTWARE PRODUCT OR US$5.00; PROVIDED, HOWEVER, IF YOU HAVE ENTERED INTO A MICROSOFT SUPPORT SERVICES AGREEMENT, MICROSOFT'S ENTIRE LIABILITY REGARDING SUPPORT SERVICES SHALL BE GOVERNED BY THE TERMS OF THAT AGREEMENT. BECAUSE SOME STATES AND JURISDICTIONS DO NOT ALLOW THE EXCLUSION OR LIMITATION OF LIABILITY, THE ABOVE LIMITATION MAY NOT APPLY TO YOU.

MISCELLANEOUS

This EULA is governed by the laws of the State of Washington USA, except and only to the extent that applicable law mandates govern-ing law of a different jurisdiction.

Should you have any questions concerning this EULA, or if you desire to contact Microsoft for any reason, please contact the Microsoft subsidiary serving your country, or write: Microsoft Sales Information Center/One Microsoft Way/Redmond, WA 98052-6399.

Get a **Free**
e-mail newsletter, updates,
special offers, links to related books,
and more when you

register on line!

Register your Microsoft Press® title on our Web site and you'll get a FREE subscription to our e-mail newsletter, *Microsoft Press Book Connections.* You'll find out about newly released and upcoming books and learning tools, online events, software downloads, special offers and coupons for Microsoft Press customers, and information about major Microsoft® product releases. You can also read useful additional information about all the titles we publish, such as detailed book descriptions, tables of contents and indexes, sample chapters, links to related books and book series, author biographies, and reviews by other customers.

Registration is easy. Just visit this Web page and fill in your information:

http://www.microsoft.com/mspress/register

Microsoft®

Proof of Purchase

Use this page as proof of purchase if participating in a promotion or rebate offer on this title. Proof of purchase must be used in conjunction with other proof(s) of payment such as your dated sales receipt—see offer details.

MCSE Microsoft® Windows® XP Professional Readiness Review; Exam 70-270
0-7356-1460-1

CUSTOMER NAME

Microsoft Press, PO Box 97017, Redmond, WA 98073-9830

System Requirements

To use the Readiness Review companion CD, you need a computer equipped with the following minimum configuration:

- Microsoft Windows 95 or Microsoft Windows NT 4 with Service Pack 3 or later, or Microsoft Windows 98, Microsoft Windows Me, Microsoft Windows 2000, or Microsoft Windows XP

- Multimedia PC with a 75-MHz Pentium or higher processor

- 16 MB of RAM for Windows 95 or Windows 98, or

- 32 MB of RAM for Windows Me or Windows NT, or

- 64 MB of RAM for Windows 2000 or Windows XP

- Microsoft Internet Explorer 5.01 or higher

- 17 MB of available hard drive space for installation

- A double-speed CD-ROM drive or better

- Super VGA display with at least 256 colors

- Microsoft Mouse or compatible pointing device